To Jack,

Love & Best wish

Alan & Val.

£2

CAMERAMEN
AT WAR

CAMERAMEN AT WAR

Ian Grant

 Patrick Stephens, Cambridge

First published 1980

British Library Cataloguing in Publication Data

Grant, Ian
    Cameramen at war.
    1. World War, 1939-1945—Cinematography
    2. World War, 1939-1945—Campaigns—Western
    I. Title
    940.54'21'0924   D810.C68/

ISBN 0 85059 489 8

Text photoset in 11 on 12pt Baskerville
by Manuset Limited, Baldock, Herts.
Printed in Great Britain on 100 gsm Huntsman Velvet,
and bound, by The Garden City Press, Letchworth,
for the publishers Patrick Stephens Limited,
Bar Hill, Cambridge, CB3 8EL, England.

Frontispiece
See page 70.

Illustration credits
Imperial War Museum
Author's own collection

What it was all about. The shoulder-flash of the Army Film and Photo Unit. Worn with pride by the bearers, but often a source of many arguments.

Chapter 1

The day Sandy McLaren walked into the NAAFI at the frontier post between the Lebanon and Syria, all he wanted was a cup of tea and no sweat from the Military Police. A few hours earlier he had received a going-over by a group of MPs back near the Dog River which, he promptly recalled, had been a real bitch. Now he was faced by a pompous RSM of the MPs who was barring his way and eyeing Sandy's shoulder-flash with some suspicion. 'A-F-P-U', he recited. Sandy nodded. 'Never heard of it', the RSM decided and, after a quick down and up look at Sandy's appearance, he asked, 'You a Polack or something?'

The dead McLarens creaked in their graves in far-off Perthshire, but all Sandy wanted was a cup of tea and no arguments. Tersely, he suggested to the RSM that surely a man of his obvious intelligence must know what the letters AFPU stood for, and, brushing him to one side, strode into the NAAFI. Indignation deepened the heavy tan on the RSM's face, but he was determined to have the last word and followed Sandy inside. 'Just you stay right there. I've got a full list of units in my office and I'll be right back'. With that, he tucked his cane under his arm, made a smart about-turn and marched out of the hut. Sandy just sighed, then applied his attentions to the delights of traditional NAAFI fare.

Ten minutes later the RSM returned and, with his face wreathed in satisfaction, advanced on Sandy's table. Standing there with meticulous parade-ground attention he ventured to speak. 'Sir', he acknowledged for the first time, 'now that I know what the letters stand for, I wonder if you could give me a few tips regarding the—ahem—psychological aspects towards the practice of discipline?' Sandy's expression obviously displayed his mystification and the RSM stabbed a finger once more at the shoulder-tab. 'A-F-P-U', he droned, 'Army Field Punishment Unit; a terrific idea'. With a sad shake of his head, Sandy stood up to leave; congratulated the RSM on his perception and excused himself by saying he had an appointment with some nursing sisters at a nearby hospital, and left. What conclusion the RSM arrived at from that statement did not trouble Sandy at all. He was after all, a rather off-beat character in an almost unknown unit of the British Army—The Army Film and Photographic Unit.

*   *   *

For reasons completely unknown to this writer, the structure of the AFPU has been tucked away behind a series of pseudonyms such as Official War Office

Photos, Imperial War Museum Material, or just plain Newsreel Sources. This tends to give the general impression that both stills and cine material were entirely the end product of the Official War Correspondents and, without knocking that esteemed body of men (who did contribute some excellent material with superior equipment), there is no way they could have covered every theatre of war during World War 2 as thoroughly, or as well as, the Army Film and Photo Unit.

Much too often, the AFPU would be confused with the AKS (Army Kinematograph Service), who did a very good job of producing training films for home consumption, and an even better one of bringing up heavy vehicles and generators to the front lines and erecting full sized cinema screens in order to entertain battle-weary troops with, more often than not, the latest Betty Grable spectacular, until an equally pyrotechnic display by the enemy would slice through the screen, giving the Hayworth or Grable cleavage a lot of mileage. But for the lonely AFPU cameraman who had probably withstood a night of heavy bombardment as far forward as he could get, so that he could use the first whisper of daylight to get an exposure, to be asked casually by some equally nerve-wrecked infantryman, 'What are you showing tonight, mate?', it was sometimes more than a mere straw breaking the old camel's back. It was also a moment of truth in which he might ask the same question again, 'What the hell am I doing here?'. Usually, there was no reply.

The answer to that question was complex, inasmuch as on the one hand there was a War Office which considered the BEF's role to be 'the trenches and dug-outs—barbed-wire and the lobbing of hand-grenades—and may be home by Christmas, old boy', and a Ministry of Information to administer the propaganda with cosy little documentary films showing 'our lads', in true Kitchener style, stabbing ferociously at straw effigies of a funny little man with a ridiculous moustache. It was fortunate that, in both departments, there were men of vision with the foresight to create something a little more objective and substantial. If they had not—there wouldn't be any little man holding a primitive box of mechanics. But they did—and by a little trial and error—with the assistance of versatile specialists and the patience of Job—produced the answer in no uncertain fashion.

He was a fully trained battle cameraman and, with the noise of a fire-fight crackling in the woods ahead, and growing louder by the moment, he knew exactly what to do. But to consider his progress from an ordinary soldier to no ordinary sergeant, one has to look back to those dark and uncertain days that followed the outbreak of war.

Fleet Street soon got their priorities right, and immediate consideration regarding picture coverage was soon organised by the photo editor of *The Times* newspaper. Van den Bogarde—father of the film actor Dirk Bogarde—hastily convened a committee to represent the Street. Under his instructions went four of the best from the leading newspapers: Len Puttnam, Leslie Davies, John Taylor and Lieutenant Barker who, I believe, represented *The Times*. The newsreels were just as quick off the mark, and each sent a film cameraman, one of whom was the very dapper Harry Rignold. It was, therefore, an unfortunate catastrophe that allowed the Ministry of Information to delegate a section of the Royal Corps of Signals to process the exposed negatives. Make no mistake, the RCS are great with the morse buzzer and shoving up 'phone cables in places that the GPO would think twice about, but when it came to developing and printing under primitive conditions, the results were—and no pun—negative.

But after a few panic buttons were pushed, a second PR unit was sent to France consisting of George Reeves, Bill Jones, Johnny Johnson, plus a stack of excess baggage which made up into a portable—or rather, transportable darkroom. This mélange eventually arrived in Arras on December 7 and for a few nights slept in a stable, until the arrival of Bill Horton of *The Times* and—as we know '*The Times* Cares'—he soon took over a large house and also control of the unit. They were open for business. But, apart from establishing good relations with the Army, it was all a bit of a 'snafu'. Christmas came and Britons saw newsreels and pictures of their loved ones eating turkey with the satisfied expressions of men who wouldn't have to clean the dishes afterwards. Apart from being a very cold winter, with troops dug into snow-covered shelters, the 'phoney war' had all the ingredients of a Bairnsfather cartoon of World War 1. It seems a pity that Army Intelligence decided on a long winter's hibernation at the same time.

Spring gradually made its appearance, and quite suddenly the world discovered a new word. It was pure German. Blitzkrieg. Its fury paralysed Belgium and Holland, and the French Maginot Line became an expensive monument to its executors. The film and photo section of the Public Relations Service—it was not to become AFPU until the Western Desert—suddenly had to deal with a flood of material from outlying cameramen. Between May 10 and 14, Bill Horton's unit did a remarkable job, processing, handling and shipping the stuff to London. But on the night of the 14th Jerry bombers hit Arras and soon part of the town was well alight. The section decided to withdraw and at dawn the next morning they slipped away to Amiens where they took over the Grand Hotel. But a blitzkrieg doesn't stop off for sleep, so, with the enemy just two miles away, they were hastily ordered to head out for Calais, leaving all the photo equipment behind.

Chaos reigned in the port as the bombers kept up their attack, but newcomer Lieutenant Danny Flood (later Major) gathered his section together and made for the quayside, where they were soon helping to unload an ammo ship to make room for the ambulances. Eventually they sailed, still half full of ammo and with the Luftwaffe doing its best to send them to another world. They made it to Dover, not realising that little Harry Rignold was heading for Dunkirk.

The blitzkrieg had achieved everything it set out to do. The distance covered in such short time had been phenomenal and the British Army had been crucified. Thousands went into the bag, but individuals made better progress, with Harry Rignold making good use of a fast-changing situation. He was a natural loner. With a single Eyemo camera and a rapidly diminishing stock of film, he finally entrenched himself in the sand-dunes overlooking the beaches. His exposure meter was long gone, left somewhere back there with most of his personal gear. He was tired. He was dirty. He was hungry. As the stunned and bitter lines of the

Where it all began. The cold and icy wastes of Norway, during the winter of 1939-40. A testing-ground for Commandos, and a tiny band of men, who would use the lessons gained, in sub-zero temperatures, to formulate a professional team in the burning sands of the Western Desert.

BEF trailed sand to the edge of the sea and the German dive-bombers took their toll, Harry began using the last of his film. Watching through his view-finder he wondered whether it was shock or discipline that kept the men in line as the little ships of England ferried them to safety. Charles Martin of Pathé must have thought much the same as he filmed from the rails of one of the rescue ships. He had bypassed the official channels to get where he was, and to do so, had finally arrived with his Newman Sinclair and two spare film magazines. Thus, between them, Rignold and Martin produced the only film record of what was hailed as the miracle of Dunkirk. It was a far cry from later achievements, and it wasn't good enough for Harry Rignold.

Whilst Ted Bacon and David MacDonald were working out a formula for No 1 AFPU in Cairo, Harry was doing it his way with the Commandos on the frozen coastline of Norway. The first foray was at Lofoten, a quick, lightning affair to test the mettle of the newly formed Commando force. It also gave Harry the opportunity to test his own theories on battle photography, ie, stay loose and think ahead and, more important, be guided by your own instincts. The raid itself was of short duration and there wasn't too much daylight, but he brought back 700 feet of usable material.

His next opportunity came on Christmas Day 1941 with another Commando raid at Vaagso. A much larger force of Commandos was used on this, but also, to Harry's dismay, a stronger section of Press would be present. This task force included Harry Watt of the Crown Film Unit—he tried very hard to make it to Dunkirk—then Roy Boulting, who later became an integral part of AFPU, Jack Ramsden from Movietone on a pool basis, Bill Malindine of PR and Ralph Walling of Reuters. Despite Harry's apprehensions— he took along two Eyemo cameras and a haversack of film—the venture was very successful. Except for a brief hesitation on landing—a very wet one into about three feet of ice cold water, and Harry Watt pausing to consider his inability to swim, leaving the diminutive figure of Harry Rignold with arms holding aloft his cameras and film, to leap ahead into the icy sea and splutter to dry land—the operation was a great success. The action ashore was sharp and bloody, with dark Commando figures etched out against burning buildings, the result of the pre-landing naval barrage. As the arctic dawn struggled with the smoke, the small unit took every advantage of exposing film and only gave up when the Commandos retired towards their landing-craft. The net result of the experiment was 6,000 feet of cine film and nearly 2,000 stills, plus the stench of fried fish engrained into their soggy uniforms. As a pointer towards the future it was a small enough step, but a resolute one which was soon to be pushed to its limit by the actual formation of the first Army Film and Photo Section under very different conditions.

Chapter 2

Major David MacDonald, a producer of documentaries for the GPO Film Unit, was given a free hand to organise No 1 AFPS from his Cairo HQ. Ably assisted by the broad-shouldered Ted Bacon, he went about it with rare enthusiasm despite the fact that, at the outset, he was faced with a shortage of good camera equipment although he had a complete muster of 32 cameramen, many of whom had had studio experience or, in the case of the stills, were from Fleet Street or well-known regional newspapers. But they were cheered by the news that a shipment of 20 cameras was on its way from the US—until a later report told them that, although they had survived the Battle of the Atlantic, they had succumbed to whatever charms lay on the bottom of the Mediterranean! But the United States were very sharp in getting off another shipment of De Vrys and Eyemos (all early models) thus, no doubt, preventing a mutiny amongst their own Signal Corps cameramen. When they arrived, it was, as Bill Jordan describes it, 'Rather like a jumble-sale, grabbing the first articles to appear, and I finished up with an Eyemo, a 12 inch lens, and a studio tripod!' He went on to say what he did with the tripod, but I'm not repeating it here! The still photographers managed to get an issue of Super Ikontas, which wasn't a bad camera for 'happy snaps'.

One of MacDonald's more successful officers was Lieutenant Derek V. Knight who arrived in Cairo in May 1942, to discover that everyone was out 'swanning' the front line. There was a message, however, that he thus deliver himself to a PR Camp at Bagush—where the hell was Bagush?—and make himself available as section officer to Captain Keating. Would Lieutenant Knight also care to avail himself of the unit transport provided? This proved to be an ancient motorcycle—Army Serial Number 941098—which Derek gingerly mounted and panted off to—where was that again?—oh, Bagush.

That Derek Knight's career with the Army Film Unit was quite remarkable must be attributed to many reasons. First, he was a professional, having worked with David MacDonald in the GPO Film Unit. This, and because he later became very popular with the Sergeant-Cameramen operating in front line areas, due entirely to his inherent sense of humour and an immediate grasp of in-field problems, must have gone a long way to his survival under the Deputy Assistant Director Public Relations attached to AFPU, Geoffrey Keating. Equally remarkable is the fact that he also went through the European campaign and,

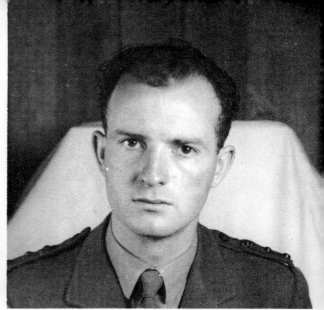

Left *Captain E. Bacon, known to all as Ted, and an experienced documentary film-maker, shouldered the heavy load of creating a film unit, with David MacDonald, the Commanding Officer of No 1 AFPS (Army Film and Photo Section).* **Right** *Captain Geoffrey Keating, Deputy Assistant Director Public Relations, whose job it was to promote the Army Film and Photo Unit in the field.*

although blasted out of his bed one night near Caen during an enemy bombardment and suffering from extreme shock and some wounds, he recovered and went on through the campaign, at all times working closely with his men, sometimes using a camera from which he was rarely parted: then going out to the Far East to take over command of a section, where he remained until VJ Day. If ever anyone believed in the maxim of doing the whole thing, that man was Lieutenant Derek Knight.

As Commanding Officer of No 1 AFPS David MacDonald tackled the job of formulating a unit that would operate as a front-line documentary production group. First, he had to maintain a constant flow of news material for cinemas, newspapers and a world's press, but he also had in mind a number of documentary films of varying lengths. Before the advent of Montgomery, he had already produced a two-reel film, *Wavell's 30,000* which, although it never attained national cinema release, was served up as a stock example of desert warfare and viewed by captive audiences in a variety of Army lecture rooms— possibly with bored apathy. For how could they understand the problems that faced those founder members of AFPU who operated with the crudest of camera equipment? Their handicaps were many and formidable, and every bit as hostile as the Germans.

This strange and ever-shifting desert, upon which the battles were fought, was an antagonist which caused unlimited problems. The penetrating sand choked their nostrils, blinded their vision and infiltrated the working parts of their cameras. The latter was their harshest problem. No matter what precautions they took, they would never know what mischief it had caused until their film was processed. A very efficient darkroom and laboratory was set up in Cairo by Bill Malindine for the stills department, but cine film had to be flown back to Kays

Left *Captain Bill Malandine, a Fleet Street professional, who set up a very efficient darkroom in Cairo, thus allowing the stills photographers to gain an enormous lead over the cine cameraman, whose work had to be flown to Kays Laboratories in London.*

Right *The fall of Tobruk. Lieutenant Arthur Graham admits, 'this was one of my toughest jobs'. The garrison was later relieved by the British 70th Division.*

Below right *The Long Range Desert Group. Lieutenant Graham was fascinated by their exploits and gained a great satisfaction from photographing this unique unit when they reconnoitred miles behind the enemy lines.*

Laboratories in London, before results could be examined in the serenity of Pinewood Film Studios.

David MacDonald's spirit and energy was unflagging and his team grew to a size that enabled him to allow small groups and individuals to rove in other domains. The afore-mentioned Sandy McLaren rambled through Syria, Palestine and the Lebanon. Eddie Smales went to the Transjordan and pictured those swarthy, bearded and fierce-looking soldiers who still lived in a long-past era. The eminent and prestigious Captain Geoffrey Keating (whose position as DADPR—Deputy Assistant Director of Public Relations—was not as a regular member of AFPU) made short safaris with the famed Long Range Desert Group. But Keating, or Bugsi as he was known to most of the unit, only scratched the surface of the LRDG and the man who was to be closely associated with them was getting blood on his nose at Tobruk.

Lieutenant Arthur Graham arrived in the desert to relieve Brian Langley for duties in the Far East. July of 1941 was a rough period for Tobruk, but the tough Australians had thumbed their noses at Rommel in his advance on Alamein and, as one story has it, a small group of Aussies left the garrison one night and about a mile from the town hid in a series of slit trenches, over which Rommel's armour was moving; as each tank rolled across, they hastily attached sticky-bomb mines to its belly, then quietly dissolved into the darkness of Tobruk. The garrison was later relieved by the British 70th Division, and became a focal point for AFPU coverage. Graham soon became a veteran during the daily dive-bombing by Stukas and long-range shelling of the town. One gun in particular, firing from some miles along the coast, was referred to as 'Bardia Bill' and was rumoured to have been brought from the Maginot Line.

Graham's stint at Tobruk ended when a break-out by Scottish troops—led by bagpipes—and several tanks, failed heroically. Through binoculars and long-focus camera lens, he watched Captain 'Pip' Gardener, a tank commander, moving about under heavy fire, rescuing wounded and placing them on his own tank, then drive out of the battle. For this action, Gardener received the VC. Together with material filmed by Keating, Lieutenant Graham's film was later

released as a two-reel documentary. Graham then spent a welcome Christmas break at the PR HQ in Benghazi, where he met many Correspondents celebrating. He was particularly impressed by Richard Dimbleby, whose lively good-humour helped to ease the strain of the past few months. At the traditional Christmas party, Dimbleby excelled himself with a passable imitation of an opera singer!

After the festivities, Graham very soon became involved with the LRDG, and it was with them he found a very rewarding association. This highly trained force would patrol as much as 200 or 300 miles inland, taking about a week to do so, where they could log and chart German convoys. Graham often spent weeks away from his own base, living an almost nomadic life, but recording a great deal of quite unusual film and often at immense risk to himself. When he returned to base, heavily bearded and suntanned, his film and dope-sheets were given VIP treatment, and he only ever spoke of these assignments in general terms, for the film he exposed was never shown to the public, and was maintained on a Top Secret level until the end of the war.

Rest periods in the desert were short at this time, for Rommel was still pressing hard on Alamein, and Graham was soon back in the front-line where he met a number of fresh faces. He teamed up with Lieutenant Stewart to film some very spectacular armoured engagements in the 'Cauldron', an area south of Tobruk which, due to the terrain, became a natural battleground for tank warfare. But during Rommel's attack on the Gazala line they ran into trouble. Unable to get hold of a Jeep, they were pursuing this attack in a car with a sunshine roof. Graham was driving, whilst Stewart navigated with head and shoulders stuck through the roof. The endless sandy wastes were tricky routes for vehicles more suited to macadam roads, and navigating was difficult with the strewn wreckage from recent battles; then there was an almighty bang as they triggered off a mine. Graham was shaken but unhurt, but saw that Stewart was severely wounded as blood pulsated from his throat in ominous spurts. Graham frantically flagged down a Red Cross vehicle, but before the orderlies could do a thing, Stewart was dead. He had literally bled to death and there was little to be done but bury him where he lay. Graham took possession of his personal effects, and made a map reference of the grave.

But Tobruk itself was the magnet that kept drawing him back and he continued the assignment there, during blistering hot days and freezing nights, until he was exhausted. It was also becoming obvious that the Germans intended to occupy the town at all costs, so Graham decided to return to Cairo. Captain Dennison Deyencourt and two other AFPU Sergeants decided to hang on, but Graham knew he was in no physical shape to take much more, so he wished them well and went back to Cairo. After a short period of local leave he returned, and was not the least surprised to be told he was about to have one more crack at Tobruk, now occupied by the Germans. But he was surprised when he was told it was to be a Commando raid from the sea. It was to be an ill-fated venture, mainly due to a leak in our own security.

Lieutenant Graham and Sergeant Crapper of AFPU boarded HMS *Sikh* with the small Commando unit and, together with the *Zulu*, sailed for the harbour of Tobruk. Disaster overtook them when the German shore batteries—alerted for such an attempt—opened up and hit the *Sikh*, killing many on board and knocking out the steering. The *Zulu* plunged into this chaos and tried to give them a tow, but without steerage, the *Sikh* could not maintain course. Another salvo hit them in the cordite chamber and Sergeant Crapper received very severe burns. The *Zulu* now cleared off, and the Captain of *Sikh* gave orders to abandon ship. When he was sure that everyone was clear, he proceeded to scuttle the ship, and they went down with colours flying.

When Graham hit the water, his camera went down like a stone, but he managed to grab hold of the stricken Film Unit Sergeant and, using a Carley Float, were able to remain afloat for nearly four hours. They were eventually picked up by an Italian lighter, but Crapper later died in Graham's arms, and he now found himself a POW. It was the end of the war for Graham, but he endured terrible hardship as he travelled the length of Italy in ghastly conditions. As the enemies' fronts gradually shrunk, Graham and his fellow prisoners were moved

Bombardment and attack at El Alamein. Montgomery's 8th Army, and MacDonald's Army Film Unit's greatest victory in the desert. The eventual film Desert Victory, *was applauded in London's West End cinemas.*

on and on, until they found themselves in Czechoslovakia, where they existed in daily fear of Allied bombing raids. From there he moved to Hanover in Germany, and finally to Brunswick where he was released by the US 8th Army in 1945.

But it was at El Alamein that the Army Film Unit threw their entire weight into a Montgomery maelstrom of crushing and total annihilation of Rommel's troops, and it was here that David MacDonald planned his film coverage as effectively as Montgomery prepared his attack. He deployed his Sergeants, such as Morris, Jordan, Taylor, Curry, Hopkinson and many others, with different units allotted for the initial attack. They waited patiently as the sands darkened into night, each of them praying that no specks of sand would mar this historic moment. Those cameramen who would cover the artillery barrage, checked and re-checked that their cameras would run at four frames a second, as opposed to the normal 24. Only by this means could they be assured of an exposure and, of course, greatly speed up the action.

Stillness and silence were painfully prolonged as they peered into the darkness, until that climatic moment when the sudden shout of 'Fire!' was dramatically carried from one mouth to the other, and 1,000 pieces of artillery unleashed the most fearsome creeping barrage of all time. As the infantry began to move, so did the men of AFPU, and all during that October day, tank battles raged and bayonet charges were made with such ferocious intensity, that Rommel's troops retreated in rapid disarray. But the attack and pursuit took a heavy toll on AFPU with four killed, seven wounded and many taken prisoner. Proportionately no other unit suffered so heavily.

Audience reactions to *Desert Victory* were, generally, very good, especially amongst women who, apart from the many actually seeing their men-folk, were made more aware of the realities of warfare. But there were always the critics; those with enough technical knowledge to point out the fact that the night sequences could only have been filmed in a studio. Perfectly true—they were. This took place at Pinewood Studios whilst I and 35 other trainees were being put through our paces for what was to be No 5 AFPS. But this artistic licence was necessary to create the full impact of Montgomery's enormous attack. What some people may not realise is that many later film sequences and stills pictures were studiously faked and passed off as the real thing. Naturally, this did not have the full approval of a large number of other members for, as was pointed out, the many troops of the 8th Army involved in this practice might get the idea that it was standard Army Film Unit method. However, it was an order that was handed down by a higher authority than David MacDonald, and I will merely quote as example from the official records of the Imperial War Museum.

'10th December 1942   W.O. Assignment No. 907

"CHET'S CIRCUS"
A UNIT OF THE A.F.P.U. IN THE WESTERN DESERT

One of the units of the A.F.P.U. is a group of four men with a driver, with a roving commission to go wherever there is action, wherever they think they can get pictures. Their leader is Sgt. Chetwyn, a former Fleet Street photographer—hence this little group has become known as "Chet's Circus". They have produced some of the finest pictures of the recent campaign and some of the most striking shots in recent newsreels have come from their cameras. Two of the men take still pictures, the other two use ciné cameras. The group consists of Sgt. Len Chetwyn, formerly with Keystone; Sgt. John Herbert, formerly with Kodak; Sgt. Jim Mapham, formerly with *Leicester Mercury*; Sgt. Chris Windows, formerly with Paramount; Driver Sampey, formerly a Manchester bus driver. They live the life of the ordinary soldier in the front line, with the same rations—often only bully and biscuits— limited water and petrol, and suffer all the hardship and difficulties that go with fighting in the Western Desert. Their weapons are cameras instead of guns, and they bring back the pictures that illustrate the deeds of the Eighth Army. These pictures show the ordinary life of the men of the "Circus" when on active service.'

But it was a short-lived experiment for, although it produced a number of well composed still photographs, the cine material lacked authenticity. The bangs and smoke produced by thunder-flashes and the occasional hand grenade, together with the lack of acting ability of the base troops used for this material, were never on a scale large enough to look real, and the idea was chopped.

*   *   *

Above *Chet's Circus. An idea born in the War Office, and handed over by David MacDonald to this group of men, a mixed bunch of cine and stills photographers headed by Sergeant Chetwyn.* **Below** *Chet's Circus, during its short life, had the time and care to take nicely composed pictures, such as this. It shows a platoon attacking over a ridge.*

As Geoffrey Keating's rank rose to Major, so his personality began to change. As 'Bugsi' Keating, just after the Alamein battle, he promoted the image of an officer who was out to prove that an AFPU Sergeant-Cameraman was as brave as any fighting soldier in the 8th Army, and the average War Correspondent was a necessary evil. Bill Jordan related the following story which bears this out. 'I was at Army HQ one day getting film stock and rations, with the accent on the rations, as my stills man was 'Tubby' Palmer, an ex-*Daily Mirror* photographer and, as his nickname indicates, food was of a high priority to my jovial companion.

'Major Keating happened to be there, and when he spied me, hustled up with the information that a big tank battle was taking place south of El Alamein. Keating—a first-class stills photographer—suggested leaving Palmer behind, and ''let's have a look at it''. Just as he jumped into the Jeep beside me, a War Correspondent turned up and suggested that he follow in his own Jeep. Geoffrey merely shrugged his shoulders and we raced off across the desert. Arriving at the location, instead of running the Jeep into some kind of cover, Keating drove the vehicle straight on to a ridge behind a Sherman tank firing at the enemy who was no great distance away. It was quite a battle—tanks were ''brewing up'', and their crews were running for cover. For a short time, it was difficult to distinguish friend from foe, but we made the most of it with our cameras getting a good view from our vantage point on the ridge. But when the armour-piercing shells began to whistle over our heads, we decided that was enough and it was time to get out. I turned to where we had left the Warco, fully intending to tell him to do likewise. Keating had done the same, but all we saw was a fast disappearing dot in the sand. We both laughed, and Keating's face bore a very satisfied look of pleasure. He had proved a point that a War Correspondent was no match for AFPU!'

Far left *Sergeants Herbert and Jimmy Mapham, members of Chet's Circus, enjoy a quiet smoke. Jimmy is the one offering the light, and, on Normandy's D-Day, would take one of the most outstanding pictures of the campaign.*

Left *Chetwyn appears to have his priorities right: De Vry cine camera, courtesy of the United States—Chianti courtesy of the Italians, vanishing over the horizon.*

Right *Sergeant Bill Jordan MM, one of MacDonald's most successful cameramen in the desert campaign. He went from the desert to Italy, and later to NW Europe.*

Thus it is very difficult to pin-point the exact stage, where this man changed from being pro-AFPU as a group, to being a 'loner' and soon found himself the accredited photographer to many of the VIP tours of the desert; with General Cakmak, Turkish leader of the Air and Military Mission in the Western Desert; exchanging pleasantries with the Duke of Gloucester and Lieutenant General Willoughby and taking exclusive pictures of Field Marshal Smuts with Lieutenant General Ritchie. From there, it was only a few brief months to flying with Montgomery in the private aircraft which the latter often displayed, recounting how he had won it in a bet.

But there is enough evidence to prove that Major David MacDonald's thoughts were far from Geoffrey Keating, as his policy after the Alamein breakthrough was one of attack and pursuit, for he had within his grasp, a great victory—a Desert Victory. For the pursuit, David MacDonald allowed his men a very loose leash; they had proved their adaptability and, apart from pairing a still and cine to Divisions who would work a Montgomery pattern, he was satisfied to allow the others to 'swan' at will. Each now had an impressive AFPU pass, containing his photo and signature, and countersigned by several Corps Commanders.

With the relief of Tobruk and Benghazi, the name of AFPU became so well known with the men of the 8th Army, that it was an accepted phenomenon that they often made their appearance *ahead* of the advancing troops. On one occasion a senior officer, questioned whether a certain town had fallen, said, 'Yes, the Army Film Unit photographed it this morning!' There was no trick or mystique about this type of situation—merely damned hard work and fast moving action on their part. For example: Bill Jordan was working with the 9th Battalion Rifle Brigade, equipped with small Honey tanks and 25 pounders and, using much the same type of tactics adopted by the Long Range Desert Group, would travel way down south into the desert, then once behind the enemy lines, head north to attack their supply lines.

These surprise attacks usually brought them back to the main desert road running along the coast and so, after filming the attack and resulting confusion arising from this rear assault, Bill Jordan often found that if he put his toe down and blasted along the coast road, he would run into the forward elements of other British troops advancing down the road. Sometimes this was not possible, so he and 'Tubby' Palmer would be faced with the long trip south and back up to their own positions, just to get their exposed film back to Army HQ. A distance of up to two hundred miles, it was often a lonely trip, two men in one truck and not another living thing in sight; not a tree or a building; just mile upon mile of hot burning sand.

Except for one day when they met another loner—a single Heinkel III returning from a bombing raid. The pilot spotted them and made his first run over them to make his identification then, reassured he had a British target, turned and began his second run. Jordan and Palmer knew what that meant, so jamming the accelerator pedal with the nearest heavy object, they took a header into the sand and crawled behind a dune. The Heinkel made straight for the 5 cwt truck they had been using, and ripped off what was possibly the last of his ammunition. Another run, this time the last one, and the German pilot waved the two recumbent figures a cheerful goodbye and was gone. It took Jordan and Palmer almost an hour to reach their riddled truck which had kept going for about another five miles. Apart from bullet holes, it was still a good runner, but Bill swore chunks of invective that he hadn't got a film shot of the plane. His camera was still in the truck!

A great deal of the best work came from these loners. Arthur Graham went off with the Long Range Desert Group, driving deep into the desert and often behind enemy lines. Rough it was, and Arthur lived as one of the Group with minimal rations and little protection from the white heat of equal portions of sand and blistering sun. Sandy McLaren was also a loner—just he and a driver named Frank Scott aboard a 15 cwt truck called 'The Fair Maid of Perth'. News of the possibility of a colourful story with the French Foreign Legion drew Sandy far from his base. Other than the fact that they proved to be a bunch of scruffy multi-nationals dressed in a curious mixture of uniforms and getting plonked on red wine as they lounged around a water-hole near Bir Hacheim, there was no story. Sandy dropped his shutter a few times to show willing, then made his departure to the accompaniment of multi-lingual curses and a solitary 'up yours' from a disillusioned Yank.

Very shortly he was joined by a fast scout-car with a young Scots Grey officer doing a Rommel from the turret. Sandy was then told that the Greys (which Sandy had been using as a base), had moved off in the vanguard of the pursuit. Sandy elicited some vague map references, and the scout car soon became a diminishing flurry of sand. Sandy altered course and told driver Scott to shove that pedal through the floor-boads. Very soon he spied a cloud of sand that gave indication of a small convoy. With caution he approached, and was relieved to see they were British trucks. He was about to complete his approach, when he realised the occupants were German and the trucks had obviously been captured.

Very quietly he spoke to Scotty, telling him to keep on going but remain a respectable distance on their flank. He was about to attempt a small bluff. The uniform he wore was as unorthodox as Sandy himself—an old Italian officer's tunic which had been slightly altered to suit his taste; non-British issue sand-goggles swept his hair back from a deeply tanned face. The only flaw was that Scotty was wearing British issue shirt and shorts, fortunately caked in sand, but Sandy determined to create himself as the centre of interest and began waving wildly and even taking pictures. When the Germans began to return the waves and all seemed well, Sandy directed Scotty to gently break away from the column, and it was not long before they managed to disappear behind some dunes. He was just leaning forward to congratulate Scotty, when he heard two dull thuds against his wheels and as the axles buried themselves into the nearest dune, Sandy realised this was no ordinary blow-out.

He looked to his rear and, sure enough, three German armoured cars with giant swastikas came to a halt on three sides, their crews half-heartedly waving a whole arsenal of automatic weapons in his direction. Sandy and Scotty were well and truly in the bag. They were soon taken to a small HQ where the CO demanded that Sandy surrender both the Film Unit Super Ikonta and a German Leica he had acquired some time back from a dead German. And it was the latter that was nearly proving his undoing. Sandy was well aware of his rights under the Geneva Convention, but he decided to invent one or two to his own satisfaction.

They argued at length about possession of two cameras (one of them German), and Sandy reasoned that as the Ikonta was British Government property, he would hand it over, provided he received a receipt. But the Leica was his own and there was no way he would give it up. The fact that no violence had been used, and no attempt made to take the cameras, gave Sandy the impression that here was a German officer, speaking faultless English, whose sympathies did not wholly rest between the pages of *Mein Kampf.* For hours the argument continued, over countless cups of vile German coffee, until quite late that night the German produced a bottle of cognac. Sandy now knew he had him and, although he is fond of his own wee dram, he managed to control his intake with liberal doses of water.

The argument ended in compromise; Sandy agreed to hand over both cameras on the production of two separate receipts. From there it was all downhill. Every glass that was consumed, the German would give a cynical 'Heil Hitler'—to which Sandy would reply with a rousing 'Heil Churchill'. By morning, the German was also convinced that Sandy was purely and simply a photographer and not a fighting soldier, so after a breakfast of black bread and foul coffee, Sandy and driver were released with vague references as to where the 8th Army might be.

There is one curious epilogue to this event. When the Afrika Korps surrendered and prisoners were pouring in by thousands, Sandy was there with his new issue Super Ikonta, photographing this scene. Sandy had opted for a line of German officers, when one detached himself (despite the shouts from the guards) and approached Sandy. They recognised each other at once, and Sandy even shook his hand—not missing the opportunity to slip in a query about the Leica. The officer sadly shook his head and said he had handed it over to his own authorities—but would he accept this ebony stick as a parting gift. Sandy took it and the German turned and rejoined the ranks marching to POW obscurity. When Sandy examined the stick he observed the top was carved into four heads, Churchill, Stalin, Roosevelt and Chiang Kai Shek. He managed to keep it until the end of the war when, early in 1964 he read that Frau Rommel had opened a museum to the Afrika Korps in Stuttgart. Partly from sympathy, but also holding a good ration of hope in recovering his precious Leica, Sandy decided to send the stick to the museum. He later received a letter from Manfred Rommel which stated in brief:

'Dear Sir,

My mother has asked me to send you her sincere thanks for your kind letter of 9th October, 1964, and for the stick you have received in 1942/43 from a German officer. We shall display this interesting stick here and try to trace this officer; if we succeed we shall give him your address. We also hope that you shall get the camera back that you lost in Afrika.

Again many thanks, very sincerely yours,

Manfred Rommel'

To date, any idea of recovering the missing Leica must remain a memory with Sandy McLaren, as he glumly sits on the banks of Loch Ness, surrounded with a battery of cameras, looking for monsters.

Chapter 3

The Tunisian section of AFPU, under command of Major Hugh Stewart, arrived on the mainland in random fashion. They were to pioneer the way into a combined unit that was to be totally unlike that of Major MacDonald. Stewart, rather proudly, named them his 'buccaneer unit'. Operation Torch was launched in November 1942 and AFPU cameramen were slipped ashore from the various convoys which had arrived under Top Secret wraps. Sergeants West and Bowman landed at Algiers and produced the first ever shots of British and American troops in action together in World War 2.

Sergeant Martin Wilson went in with the Commandos at Cape Serrat, not very far from Bizerta. It was here that he was to earn his Military Medal. After a night march of nearly 12 miles they hit the enemy head-on, and Wilson was unfortunate in losing his camera as German shells fell all around. But that was not going to stop his usefulness and he grabbed up a Bren gun from a fallen Commando, shouted a few Gaelic oaths at the bastards who had destroyed his camera, and started spraying them with the Bren. Thus Wilson was to become the first of Stewart's buccaneers.

Sergeant Martin Wilson, MM, did not resemble any popular image one might have of the description used by Hugh Stewart, but he did possess a quality that made others look to him for leadership. No doubt this encouraged Stewart to give him a commission later on but, probably due to his unorthodox tactics, Wilson never got beyond the rank of Lieutenant. Other than the fact that he was always 'short of a few bob or two', as he invariably put it, this did not bother Wilson at all, for he enjoyed immense popularity with any cameramen who worked with him. One of his main attributes was that he never displayed fear during a battle, and this apparent calm and cool-headedness would communicate itself to whoever he was with. He was also a first-class pianist and wherever a piano could be found, he would sit there of an evening and entertain his immediate circle of 'AFPUglians'. Those rare moments of complete togetherness would be remembered for a long time afterwards, and Martin Wilson's magic touch would endure through the Tunisian campaign and on into Europe.

That little bomb of concentrated energy and skill, Harry Rignold, was also with the Hugh Stewart unit. His tiny, energetic figure became a familiar sight with front line troops and, because he very often switched partners, the name of AFPU gained in prestige. His liaison officer in the field was Captain Hone

Left *Hugh St Clair Stewart, Commanding Officer of the Tunisian section of the AFPU, which, under his command, operated in a much looser fashion than the No 1 Section. The success of this method paid handsome dividends when he later commanded No 5 Section in the European campaign.* **Right** *Lieutenant Martin Wilson MM, was only a Sergeant when he landed in Tunisia at Cape Serrat during the night. Running head-on into the enemy, his camera was destroyed, but he gained an MM, and much satisfaction, when he replied with a Bren.*

Glendinning, a documentary film specialist who had previously worked with Hugh Stewart back in England on *Special Despatch*. 'Glenny' very shrewdly kept switching Rignold's partners—he knew a professional when he saw one—and at the end of November he would assign Harry to operate with Sergeants Meyer or Wackett around the Bone sector; then come December he threw another switch and Sergeants French and Gunn would have Rignold as company during the 6th Armoured Division's probe at Medjy el Bab.

Hugh Stewart was not a CO to sit back at HQ and let his buccaneers do all the slogging, for even in the simple every day administration of the units' needs and requirements it was a hectic round-the-clock flogging duty. There was never any let-up. Specific orders would come down from Major Mackintosh, DADPR of 1st Army or Lieutenant Colonel MacCormack, PR for Allied HQ, which Stewart would study and then outline his own requests to his section officers. Transportation was always a headache and sometimes a cameraman would move on foot with infantry, or ride the back of a tank if he was with armour. Often it was the only way and the one that made sense, despite being laden with perhaps a De Vry or Eyemo and several 100-foot rolls of film. But somehow, Stewart scrounged a couple of Simca-Fiats and half-a-dozen motorcycles, and he also set up a few well-known drop-areas at BHQ's, where cameramen could leave exposed film. They were very simple empty sandbags painted a distinctive colour with lettering 'AFPU—Exposed Film—Urgent'.

But Hugh Stewart's personal delight was to go along with his cameraman during an attack and, such was his personality, that this never inhibited the men involved, although the word would soon pass around that 'the old man is here'. Such an occasion was during an unexpected German counter-attack on British defences in the area of Bon Arada. Sergeants Rignold and Courtney were well up in the area with Hone Glendinning when they were attacked by Stuka dive-bombers. It was a surprise attack but did not prevent Courtney getting a shot of one Stuka, whilst in its steep bombing dive, receiving a direct hit and blowing up. Rignold was equally fast and doing the same, but he was too close. He got the Stukas in his view-finder, saw the cluster of bombs leave and panned down with them into a spectacular explosion. Harry must have realised just how close he was and, with the explosion captured on film, turned his back on the blast. A small piece of shrapnel hit him there and hurtled him on to his face. Glendinning pulled him into the relative safety of a low wall, found the wound was not serious but Rignold in deep shock, when they were joined by Hugh Stewart. Still the dive-bombers came on and AFPU had a field day with Courtney, Glenny and Stewart now all taking pictures, but the latter was still concerned about Rignold. Stewart returned to where he lay to find him now out of shock but in some pain and decided to move him, especially now that he was aware of the presence of boxes of ammunition not five yards away. As the Stukas began another wailing bomb-dive Stewart hefted Rignold on to his shoulders and did the fastest piggy-back hundred yards to safety when the dump went up with a roar. Harry was OK afterwards and soon returned to action with the unit, his eagerness in no way impaired by his near miss.

Rignold was the acknowledged veteran, but the rest of the unit were coming up fast and developing their own techniques of battle photography. For tank battles they now had their own Crusader tank, which was a great compliment to the recognition now gained by Stewart's unit, and this was further implemented by the use of a scout car. The latter nearly cost the life of one cameraman. Sergeant Huggett elected to go along on what should have been just a probe, but they stuck their noses in too far and smacked into an ambush. German anti-tank guns opened up from a nearby farmhouse and the British lightweight carriers dispersed at a rate of knots, but not before Huggett's scout car received a direct hit, killing the driver outright. The cameraman made a fast evacuation and dived for cover and found he was clutching a 35 mm lens but no camera. It was brewing up 20 yards away in the now blazing scout car. A reverse situation involved Sergeant Joe West when he was filming an attack on Long Stop Hill. Killing stuff was flying in both directions when Joe West felt a tug on the camera as though someone was trying to pluck it from his hands. He stopped filming and looked at the front of the camera—he had been exposing film through a ragged gash, his two-inch lens had been neatly sliced off by shrapnel.

Through February and March the unit matched the progress of the 1st Army who were working closely with the Americans. This was a unique chance to observe US troops in action, most of whom had never fired a gun before other than at a moving target back on State-side. This observation made the following entry in Major Hugh Stewart's war diary—'My opinions of the American troops

begin to crystallise. They seem to have guts enough but are green enough still not to realise what are the essentials, ie, that sometimes one has to stay put whatever is happening. They appear to be poorly led and several have declared an open admiration for the qualities of British officers, which is surprising for Americans. Some people still regard them as being somewhat yellow'.

Unlike the endless sand-dunes of the Western Desert, the terrain of Tunisia had an English garden quality to it and the spring flowers around Beja and Medjez had the same delicate quality and colouring of any that bloomed at Kew. Corn, too, was plentiful and amongst it grew miles of scarlet poppies splashed across the valley. For the film man it was a fascinating spectacle amidst this carnage of war and they often wished that colour film was in general use. It also made them homesick.

With all these apparent blossomings of spring the campaign itself was showing every sign of fulfilling all its objectives. Rommel was about to be crushed by two armies in a catastrophe which would later be called 'Tunisgrad' and the final assault on Tunis and Bizerta was a spectacular affair which was enjoyed to its full by most members of AFPU. With a clear blue sky empty of a crushed Luftwaffe, there came a majestic surge forward of tanks, half-tracks, scout cars and troop-carrying vehicles of all kinds, nose to tail and four abreast pouring across the countryside. It was just unfortunate that the amount of dust raised by this solid, unbelievable movement restricted the cameramen with many of the long-shots. Of course, Hollywood would have had wind-machines blowing the stuff away from camera, but the advance notice had been too short!

During this fantastic drive into Tunis by the two desert units of AFPU, Bill

Left *Joe West began as a Sergeant in Tunisia, and found it rather difficult to take pictures through a camera which had the lens ripped off by shrapnel. He later joined No 5 unit in Europe as an officer, and is seen using a Vinten Normandy.*

Right *Captain Alan Whicker was first introduced to members of AFPU at a party in Tunis, after the final victory in the desert, and CO Hugh Stewart observed in his diaries that he, 'was impressed, and was sure he would go far'. Today's TV audiences would be inclined to agree.*

Jordan of No 1 Unit was sitting on top of an armoured car of the leading echelon, filming the highlights of this victory, when two German officers drove up in a car. Jordan's camera immediately swung in their direction and, to his horror watched as they stood up and threw a hand grenade directly at him. Jordan was wounded, but he continued to use his camera. The British armoured cars, in recognition of the Nazis' gesture of welcome, proceeded to blow them and their car into small pieces. Bill Jordan still continued to film this scene, realising probably, that this was the first occasion in movie history that a cameraman ever saw his subjects shot in both senses! For this, and other exploits, he was awarded the MM.

AFPU recorded the great joy of the liberation of Tunis and the massive rounding up of thousands upon thousands of prisoners. It was a temendous finale and enjoyed in regal manner when as many of AFPU met together for a general binge-up. It was an odd occasion too, for many of them met for the first time and introductions piled one upon the other. The two Military Medals, Martin Wilson and Bill Jordan exchanged tall stories until Wilson sat down at the piano and sadly played *Lili Marlene*. Harry Rignold, now happily recovered, remained long enough to chat with friends and observed Keating in conversation with Alan Moorhead, the War Correspondent. Keating paused long enough to give a big 'hello' to the now eminent Sidney Bernstein. Someone called for a small hush in one corner to introduce an energetic young officer: 'This is Alan–Alan Whicker'. Most went back to their serious drinking, but Hugh Stewart gave a welcoming smile, for he regarded Whicker as 'a very good lad, full of pep and ideas'. 'Take my word—he will go far!' Stewart then returned to his earnest conversation with Alf Black regarding the future of AFPU and his now confirmed resolution to return to Pinewood and take charge of the fully operational 'school of battle photography' where it now had its home.

After the conquest of Tunisia and the final surrender at Cap Bon, the unit moved to Sidi-Bon-Said awaiting orders. Many were returned to Pinewood where their experiences would be valuable in the training of No 5 Section. Others went on for the Salerno landings and the long weary drag up the boot of Italy. A few—very few—were left behind in Tunisia to do recovery and reconstruction stories. One of those was Sergeant R.P.G. Meyer. He was returning from Tunis airport one day, after shipping film back to London, when he noticed two Staff Officers walking across a field towards a large villa by the sea near Carthage. He pulled up and followed these officers rather warily. But he went a shade too far and eventually found himself in a kitchen faced with an irate Commander Thompson asking what the hell he was doing. Meyer showed him his AFPU identity card and the officer cooled, and even asked for his 'phone number.

Two days later—it was a Christmas Day—the 'phone rang, and it proved to be Commander Thompson inviting him and his cine colleague over to the villa. What sort of Christmas present was this going to be, wondered Meyer? They arrived very promptly at the villa, where they were met by General Eisenhower's lady driver—Kay Summersby, whom Meyer had met in London before the war. She ushered the bewildered pair into a larger room, one entire wall made of glass giving a wonderful panoramic sea-view. But it wasn't the sea-view that stopped Meyer in his tracks—it was the distinguished group made up of General Eisenhower, General Alexander, General Wilson, Air Commodore Tedder and Winston Churchill! The latter was recuperating from pneumonia, but was up and about in a dressing-gown.

Meyer and his colleague were invited to take pictures of this group and he was congratulating himself on this wonderful scoop, and could almost read the congratulatory reports that would come winging their way from England. Nothing. No report every reached Meyer and he never did see a copy of the photo until 1972 when he was looking at some stalls in a Brighton market. To his complete astonishment, there was an enlarged copy of the very photograph, all tutti-fruited in passe-partout and priced 6d. Naturally, he bought it, and it remains the sole reminder of that Christmas Day in Tunisia when he mixed company with the Supremos of an era.

Chapter 4

Now came the time for the formation of No 5 Section at Pinewood Studios, where the training had reached a high in sophistication. Men were now travelling from units all over the country—some as far as 600 miles. I was fortunate that I was stationed at Upminster and had no more to do than travel by London Underground to Baker Street, and hump my worldly possessions down Marylebone Road to the transit centre. During this short journey, I had been giving this Army Film Unit undertaking a great deal of thought, and I had a shrewd suspicion what might be involved. The AKS set-up was purely and simply engaged in making training films, so, obviously this system just had to be a training school for front-line action. In other words, battle photography—and the thought gave me a twinge of apprehension. With a teeny-weeny doubt in my mind, I entered the gloomy and austere setting of the Marylebone Centre; little knowing that in just over two days time I would walk through the more glamorous gates of Pinewood Film Studios.

Pinewood lies in the heart of Buckinghamshire at Iver Heath, just a few miles from Uxbridge on one side and Slough on the other. Its name was derived from the many pine trees that stand in the magnificent landscaped gardens with its lush lawns, sculpted shrubbery and a small lake with hump-backed bridge. The entrance is made through a twin-arch lodge house from Pinewood Road immediately opposite the top-bracket houses of Iver Heath itself, but a grander entrance can be made through the giant oak fireplace from Allum Hall, said to have been carved by three generations of craftsmen. Its 85 acres house sound stages, viewing theatres, dressing rooms, cutting rooms, restaurant and cafeterias and a variety of departments for painters, plasters, carpenters, make-up and wardrobe. This is all inter-connected by a bewildering series of tunnels designed to baffle the uninitiated.

During the war years it functioned mainly for the Army Film Unit, the RAF Film Unit and the Crown Film Unit who carried out a programme of propaganda films for the Ministry of Information. Upon our arrival we were first directed to our sleeping quarters in what had been dressing-rooms for extras so there was no problem in lodging all 36 of us. These rooms had been designed to accommodate much larger numbers, with complete four wall mirrors and a wash-basin—with hot and cold—for each member! Bearing in mind that all of us had come from two years of basic Army accommodation such as barracks, tent-towns and even converted stables, the shocks were about to pile up thick and fast. Courtesies were extended by all the officers we met on this first day—most of whom had merely exchanged their civilian clothes for a uniform, but rightly so as they were all professional technicians, and were to be our instructors, our mentors and our liaison officers in the field.

After a quick tour of the studios to orientate ourselves—although it would take most of us a week to do this—we had a meal in the cafeteria served by a mixture of chattering, laughing ATS and WAAF girls. Most of us made a mental note that this was to be another additional perk to the job. Then it was into a large comfortable lecture room where the first basics of the three-month course were outlined, and we were introduced to the two sergeants, Len Harris and Les Carpenter, and Lieutenant Barker, a stills officer from Fleet Street, who would each take half of our numbers through the techniques of camera usage. Briefly, it was pointed out how the units had operated in the desert and how the general plan for the future would consist of two cameramen, a still and a cine, who would work together as a team. At this point we were asked about past experience and whether we wished to remain as stills—and most of the Fleet Street boys opted for this—or try for the cine course. As I had done neither—I had crashed my way through the interview and written examination at Marylebone by unashamed cribbing from the paper of my neighbour, Bob Turner, who was to become a very close friend, I elected to go for the cine course.

A particularly close friend of mine, Len Sutton, had completed a four-year training course with the well-known company of Zeiss and had specialised in the manufacture of cameras and lenses. He was gratefully plucked from REME at Derby, where he had been overhauling telescopic sights and binoculars, to the AFPU at Pinewood, and was having his own problems. Lieutenant Barker had listened to Len Sutton's technical credentials with a sympathetic acknowledgement, then issued the AFPU credo, 'that you are now going to re-learn photography the Army way'. With that, he turned him over to a Sergeant Payne, in charge of camera and optical repairs.

The lectures for this were held in a tent, and for the initial one on the Super Ikonta 531/2, which was to be the standard issue for all stills photographers, the lecture was attended by all the officers and technical NCOs. Private Len Sutton listened with respectful interest as Sergeant Payne pursued the technical facts of a cross-section of a Tessar lens sketched on a blackboard until, as he says, 'I must have had a brainstorm'. Somehow, he found himself on his feet, giving a sharp 'one-two' in his hob-nailed boots, and before Sergeant Payne could open his mouth, blurted out, 'Please, Sergeant, you've got it wrong. The lenses are back to front!' You could have heard a pin drop whilst Payne eyed him with a grim look. 'So, Private Sutton', with the direct emphasis on 'Private', 'You know more about it than I do?' Len gulped. 'Yes, Sergeant', Payne's eyes didn't flicker. 'You could give the lecture then, and point out what is wrong with my sketch?' By this time every eye was on Len Sutton, and his adrenalin began to surge. Very controlled now, he replied, 'Yes, Sergeant'. Sergeant Payne gestured that he take the rostrum, and handed him the pointer.

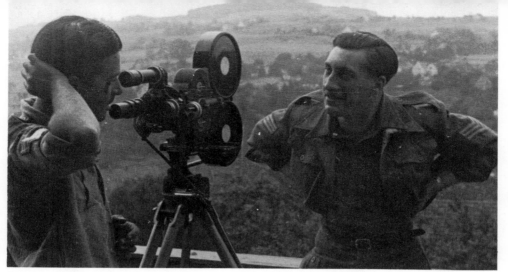

Sergeant Carl Sutton (facing camera), in conversation with Sergeant Bob Baker, recent producer of The Saint *TV series, was only a private with No 5 Section at Pinewood when he received the Carl nickname, due to his superior knowledge of lens manufacture—he was trained at the Carl Zeiss factory! At the end of the war in Europe, he got his biggest scoop—the death of Himmler!*

Very firmly, Len Sutton recited the brief details concerning the formation of lenses, then whacked the blackboard with the tip of the pointer. 'This sketch', he concluded 'is wrong because it shows the crown glass where the flint glass should be'. Defensively, Payne retorted, 'Who says you're right and I'm wrong?' Len looked at him with a slow smile, 'Four years apprenticeship with the Zeiss company and tutored by Germans!' Payne was an honest man, and gave him 'best'. They became firm friends, and Payne often referred to 'old Carl Zeiss himself'. In time, the Zeiss vanished, but 'Carl' Sutton stuck.

There was only one snag on the horizon—he was small and very noisy and his name was Sergeant-Major Lewis. Discipline, after all, was not to be left out of the course. One hour per day, plus early morning PT was to be his allowance and he was to make every minute count. The square-bashing sessions took place on the fairly large car-park which was overlooked by the row of cutting-rooms elevated on a long verandah. Amongst the staff who worked there were several attractive ATSs and WAAFs, and they never hesitated to make their presence known whenever our paragon of parade-ground perfection made us march and counter-march. Chairs were pulled out on to the balcony as they made ready to view the spectacle. No doubt it made a change from chopping 35 mm frames from endless rolls of film and slinging them in the bin. But it also proved to be a two-way spectacle as they sat with legs crossed, legs apart, or legs stretched upwards to hook their heels over the rail. This hourly charade proved two things: these girls never wore service issue, and Sergeant-Major Lewis was flogging a dead horse.

The most interesting period of the training—apart from the girls—was a daily showing of the film which had come in from the cameramen over the past 18 months, and a great deal from those in Jordan, Jerusalem, Sicily and the Italian front. By this means we were able to identify with individual cameramen and also learn a great deal of the techniques they used. Sometimes captured German film would be shown and in this way we learned how much better equipped they were, and how their PK Units were used in much larger numbers. These daily showings, apart from creating a slight uneasiness towards the day that we would have to face the same dangers, did create a certain camaraderie with those hitherto unknown cameramen. Thus we heard of Jordan, MacLaren, Wilson, Rignold, Lambert, Chetwyn, Keating and a host of others. Their personal backgrounds were still unclear, but the stories and rumours were rife. The courage of Rignold and Wilson was carried without a doubt. Chetwyn's spoof circus seemed possible. But the sound of Major Hugh Stewart's 'Tunisian Buccaneers' gave the thing a bounce, and we looked forward to serving under him with renewed interest.

As the training course progressed at Pinewood, we were able to assess and appreciate the hard work and careful thought behind this smoothly operating school. The practical expertise displayed by Lieutenant Barker and Sergeants Harris and Carpenter produced a very neat and concise state of order that made easy the problems of optics, depths of focus and the ability to judge an exposure aperture by eye alone. We were given the opportunity to go outside the studio and 'shoot' a picture story entirely from imagination. As most of us chose to use the town of Uxbridge as a background, and the story-lines ran along familiar themes as 'cops and robbers' or 'goodies and baddies' with the surprised assistance of local banks, stores and post office, it is amazing that none of us was ever arrested!

Hugh Stewart had now taken over command and his officers were Hone Glendinning, Bob Verrall, Alan Goatman, Del Strothers, Peter Handford, Leslie Evans and Tony Keyes. The latter was the younger brother of Basil Keyes and John Paddy Carstairs and was filled with irrepressible humour, enjoying nothing more than having a pint with the boys at the nearby Crooked Billet. We had also formed personal attachments with each other and my closest friend was Norman Clague who had come from the Liverpool Irish and wore what I called a comic hat with a feather. As we were both Lance-Corporals and our homes far away from the south, we invariably took weekend about in charge of fire-picket whilst the other went on 48-hour pass. There was one other Lance-Corporal, Freddie Woods, five foot something and a half and a bundle of mischief, but he was crafty inasmuch his home was in the London area and come 4.30 every Friday afternoon he was off!

Perhaps it was the pleasant atmosphere of Pinewood that induced an all-round spirit of equable friendliness amongst the 36 who were taking the course, for there was none of the average barrack-room bickering. There were no tantrums, no snide remarks and no one had cause to be envious of another, and all developed a character which was for ever to be his own.

Bill Leeson will always be remembered for his everlasting pretence of constipation and the hours he spent in the toilet reading a book. How this came about was very simple. At some time prior to his AFPU days an advertising company had chosen him as a 'model' for the Eno's Fruit Salts campaign. Eno's was supposed to relieve constipation, and Bill Leeson's healthy, smiling features were pictured as one who had found relief from the salts. The caption on the photo read—'To Relieve Stress and Strain'. Whilst at Pinewood someone found a magazine with this photo, and Bill was immediately dubbed 'Old Stress and Strain'. Bill just went along with the joke, hence the time he spent on the toilet.

Little Billy Greenhalgh, the tiniest man of the unit—even shorter than Freddie 'Midge' Woods—did a hilarious send-up of Sergeant-Major Lewis. Bill Gross and Vic Watkins, an inseparable pair, became the star performers at a local dance-hall where, by some mysterious means, they would invite a number of different girls to the same Saturday night hop, then make a very short appearance and disappear with the girls of their choice. They named the place Scrubbers Hall. Bob Turner was probably the youngest, but he was a big lad nevertheless and his high-spirited capers were often dampened by 'dunking' him in the wash-basins. This was carried out with cries of 'Weight on' from Norman, myself and often George Laws, for it took the three of us to wrestle the big ape. When sex was discussed—and when is it never between groups of men—Georgie Laws always claimed that, to achieve absolute penetration, he always launched himself from the top of his wardrobe! For some odd reason I don't believe him! Mike Lewis, another of our larger built characters, was nicknamed Rag-Bag—he never could get a battledress that fitted properly and invariably appeared on parade with his cuffs shot half-way up his arms and the collar of his tunic turned up to his ears.

An unlikely collection, you might feel, who were destined to put on film the greatest involvement of the war—the invasion of Europe and the crushing of the mighty Swastika. True, we had had a pretty soft number up to now and no doubt our CO, Hugh Stewart, was of the same opinion, for we began a programme designed to toughen us and maybe give us a more soldier-like bearing. For the latter section we were sent to Chelsea Barracks for a few weeks and became the complete and utter despair of all Parade and Regimental Sergeant-Majors with the Scots Guards. Maybe it did smarten us up a bit, but Mike Lewis's collar still stuck up on parade.

We returned to Pinewood and found an enormous ditch had been dug out on the back lot, where some 'real soldiers' were being used as extras for night sequences to finish *Desert Victory*. Special permission from War Office and other authorities was granted to use lights at nights—the ARP were alerted all the way to the coast to track any air activity in the direction of Buckinghamshire. The ditch was supposed to be a wadi in the Western Desert, but some tortured mind soon realised its potential as a kind of obstacle course for our toughening process. We charged up and down its sides wearing small pack and pouches loaded with film tins packed with nitrate film and endeavoured to take pictures of the others taking pictures of us. Then another idea was born by some warped mind who now probably works on special-effects for Hammer Productions; a rope was slung across and we had to negotiate this on our stomachs, one leg dangling to give balance, and still wearing the same equipment. After a few days of rain, the bottom of the wadi was pretty soggy and gooey, but we still pressed on and I guess about one in three finished the day encased in mud. I know—I know, people spend pounds on having mud-pack baths—it creates a healthy body and gives you a wonderful complexion, but we were not trying for a Mr Universe contest!

The famous wadi dug within the grounds of Pinewood. Sergeant Jerry Rennison of No 5 Section, reflects on the 'horrors' of the training period, when it was used as part of our assault course. Originally dug for the Desert Victory *night sequences.*

But we were later rewarded by receiving our Sergeant's stripes and so we were all now entitled to crowd into the tiny Sergeant's Mess, much to the disgust of Sergeant-Major Lewis, who had been wiping away the saliva from his mouth as he watched us go plop-plop into the wadi. There was also a party given to mark the occasion, hosted as always by Captain Hone 'Glenny' Glendinning who, for some odd reason, always chose to adopt a headmaster's gown and mortar board. The success of these parties was usually measured not by how much one could drink, but how many of the female staff of the Army, RAF and Crown Film Units could be persuaded to leave the dance-floor and make use of one of the four darkened preview theatres, where the merits or de-merits of the use of service issue were often discussed.

The heady success of completing the course and becoming full Sergeants was slightly dampened when we were sent to Lingfield Barracks to be given a final 'toughener' by the Irish Guards. This was a real three-week battle school where a great deal of live ammunition was used, not just for atmosphere and effect, but a very successful exercise in use of cover and keeping one's skull in one part. The entire affair was topped off with a 32-mile route march back to the barracks where we tottered to our bunks and proceeded to let the MO inspect our beautiful blisters.

Thankfully, we returned to Pinewood and almost—I said almost—eyed our Sergeant-Major Lewis with some affection and, in retrospect, I believe he had actually missed us. He gave us a short lecture. 'Well, it's obviously done you good, you look fit and you look like soldiers. When you leave here, never forget that discipline comes first'. He waggled his eyebrows, and with a touch of the old malice, 'You *do* understand the meaning of the word—discipline, hey?' It was a question that little Billy Greenhalgh just could not leave unanswered. 'Yes sir, we noticed it especially at the Guards depot. One evening in the Sergeant's Mess the RSM took a 'phone call from the CO and when he finished he replaced the receiver, took two paces backwards and saluted the telephone. That was sure some discipline!' Sergeant-Major Lewis's reply is X-rated and therefore unprintable.

But his departure prediction was correct. Soon we were packing for a temporary move into London, from where we would leave to join the various units that would shortly take part in the largest operation of the war—the invasion of Europe. Just before this happened, two of our closest friends suddenly departed, little Freddie Woods and Bob Turner. At that time all we knew was that they were bound for the Middle East. Their places were filled by two veteran officers, Derek Knight and Martin Wilson who had now received a commission. From Derek Knight we heard how AFPU had fared during the invasion of Sicily and caught a grim picture of the Anzio beach-head. We learned, too, that the apparently indestructible Harry Rignold had died of wounds and, although we had never met him, we sorrowed and prayed that we could be as brave and as good a cameraman as he had been. There was more too regarding Geoffrey Keating playing the role of Public Relations Officer hosting the famous war artist Ted Ardizonne over the rough spots, forcing the surrender of the town of Taormina together with its garrison of one Colonel and 400 Italian troops. Derek was sincere in his admiration for Keating and believed that he had worked hard for his MC. He was pretty convincing until he mentioned that on the latter escapade, Sergeant Bill Jordan, a brave and experienced cameraman, had been left to look after the Jeep like some hired driver and had been wounded by an anti-personnel mine.

Leaving Pinewood was hard, it had been home for over a year and we all had a great affection for it—some would never see it again. The commandeered flats in Knightsbridge we now occupied looked just what they were, a temporary residence for no more than a few weeks. But during that time I was whisked away to do some Top Secret filming off the Isle of Wight. This involved the many new uses of tanks with some extraordinary additions such as new type flails—a

The following three photos are from Top Secret filming I did just before D-Day. They are from the collection known as Hobart's Funnies, (Major-General Percy Hobart), and these adaptations of tanks were shown for the benefit of the War Office. This first, is a bridge-layer, and sometimes referred to as an AVRE.

Left *A Sherman flail-tank, used to explode mines, and referred to as a Crab.* **Right** *The DD, or swimming tank, with flame-proof canvas skirts, surrounded by tiny jets for spraying water. Intelligence sources said there was the possibility of the Germans' ability to set fire to some sections of the sea off the invasion beaches up to 1,000 yards off the beach, the Commander of my flotilla was biting his knuckles! These trials took place off the coast of the Isle of Wight, and around Saxmundham.*

Sherman 'Crab' tank (when at rest, the drooping steel links gave the impression of crabs' pincers) which, when whirling the chain flails, could scythe a path through a minefield (they had been experimented with in the desert), flame-throwers and fascines (large rolls of wood on two projecting arms which could be dropped into ditches and then allow the tank to roll over). There was also the Churchill Mk VIII AVRE which carried a mortar capable of chucking 'dustbin'-sized explosive charges to blast blockhouses, and another bright idea was the Ark, which carried its own bridging device in the form of a double pontoon, one half of which could be extended forward as the tank would settle itself in a ditch and form one half of the bridge. The tank referred to as a Duplex Drive was soon shortened to DD by one and all, and was a cunning little beastie inasmuch as it could take to the water, using underwater propulsion and waterproof screens, which were raised to form a hull. The screens were fire-resistant, and in one spectacular scene which I filmed, about a dozen of them sailed through a sea of fire. They soon became known as Hobart's Funnies. Major-General Percy Hobart was a 'super-boffin', and he created this odd assortment of inventive genius at the request of Sir Alan Brooke, CIGS. The correct name for this diverse and adaptable force was the 79th Armoured Division, and they were to prove their worth time and time again. Oddly enough, the Americans refused to have anything to do with them. At later dates, this decision often proved to be their loss. In all, it was a very successful filming exercise for me and would give me a lot of confidence, for I was to spend most of the campaign in tank warfare.

Chapter 5

Time was running out fast and, early in May 1944, we held several conferences with our CO, Major Hugh Stewart, during which he made it clear what each member would be doing. It must have been a soul-searching period for him when he had to decide who would land with whom in the first wave to breach fortress Europe. Oddly enough, I felt quite elated when I was told I would land with Lord Lovat's No 1 Special Service Brigade of Commandos, and I was happy to note George Laws and Norman Clague would be with other Commando units, and Captain Leslie 'Broken Nose' Evans would be the liaison officer. We soon cemented a perfect working relationship. He would tell me what to do, and I'd go ahead and do it my way. With the 3rd Division would be little Billy Greenhalgh and Jimmy Mapham, and with the Airborne Sergeant Christie—a stranger to the unit as he had been doing most of his training with the 6th Airborne.

Almost before I had time to digest this information, Laws, Clague and myself were ordered by Captain Evans to get our kits together and climb into a Jeep he was driving. We tore off at high speed with 'Busted Hooter' at the wheel doing his man of action bit. To do Evans justice, he looked the part, all six foot of him was well proportioned and his broken nose gave him the craggy look. The only thing he lacked—and this really rankled him—was a row of gongs pinned to his breast. Back at Knightsbridge, a very high proportion of the unit had received things like the Defence Medal, the 1939-40 Medal and we now had a couple who wore the Africa Star. It was the one thing lacking in his image and he had openly declared that he was going for a Military Cross. And I'll be darned if he didn't get it later in the campaign. Evans dropped each one of us separately at a different camp on the outskirts of Southampton. Quite suddenly we were almost strangers to each other and managed only a gruff 'See you' at each stop. But inwardly the conscience repeated 'keep safe—keep safe'.

Confinement within a wall of barbed wire. Lectures; constructional and destructional. Theories, plans and dispersements on large-scale maps which, as yet, showed an undefined shoreline. Boredom; eating, sleeping; sprawling in a tented city. Warm, spring sunshine giving promise of the summer ahead. Beyond the wire, people, cars and the buses turning around at this terminus point, returning to the city—a threepenny ride perhaps—to homes, shops, cinemas and pubs. Was it real—us and them? Alarms, escapees and Military Police with holstered guns. The Commando found talking to his wife across the wire—

Southampton his home-town—the wife politely arrested, confused and confined until a later date. Further lectures on maps showing features, objectives and cross-references—certainly not Pas-de-Calais—guessing games—the Belgian coast—maybe even Dieppe again—Britanny too far—Normandy just an outside bet.

I moved freely around with camera, sensing the moment; filming a group; a rapt individual; Lord Lovat at ease or in discussion, and he, now accepting my presence and status, insisting I wear a green beret—'no helmets on the day Sergeant, as you don't want to get shot up the ass'—eyes twinkling; myself very proud. The day must now be close; Normandy it is; armed guards patrol the wire perimeter; French phrase books and strange scrip money issued and I film men mouthing unusual words, laughing at each other trying to assemble appropriate greetings to girls; wished I could record sound.

Tomorrow, June 4, we move out at 6 am. Myself tense, the others not so, their faces mirror anticipation and confidence. Try to sleep on my straw paliasse in the tent I share with a Commando Sergeant-Major—a POW by D-Day plus One—and other senior NCOs. Light sounds of relaxed sleep around me, and I stare the night away.

We had stood, alert and eager, on this morning of June 4, for more than three hours, and the decision to abort was not accepted with pleasure. Men were sullen and critical of the higher echelons of command. The light breeze that blew on our faces gave no indication what it was doing to the waters of the English Channel. We returned to our tents and relaid the necessary bedding, then broke for lunch. A chaplain retired to his single tent with a borrowed revolver, checked the barrel for ammunition, placed the muzzle in his mouth and pulled the trigger. His death did not create much sensation, just a mild bewilderment and speculation as to

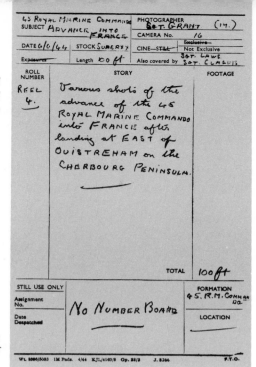

Left *No 5 AFPS just before leaving Pinewood Studios for our dispersal areas. I may be noted wearing a Scottish Glengarry. Lord Lovat later changed that!*

Right *One of the author's 'dope sheets' written on the spot during the Commandos' advance off the beach on D-Day.*

how we stood in the eyes of God at this moment when we were about to kill or be killed. Then the slight tension was gone and we stopped wondering what was over the hill. Probably just another hill.

*   *   *

Next morning there was no hesitation and we sped away in trucks, racing through Southampton's streets, with passers-by knowing full well what was about to happen—blowing kisses, weeping and cries of good luck. Then into the docks and moving aboard the vast LCIs, and I had a busy camera for, as from this moment it was the pattern of history. General views to show its mammoth size, then close-ups, faces, boots, feet moving ever upwards into the yawning bellies of the ships. A bunch of naval Wrens gathered together, a bright clean kaleidoscope of blue and white and as English as the Dover cliffs.

The lines of craft of all sizes had taken some time to swallow the thousands of troops and just before I embarked I looked around for my link-man—a despatch rider—to give him my hastily written dope sheets. For D-Day, cameramen carried pocket-sized note pads requiring written information regarding subject, cameraman's name, date, film stock, camera number, cine or still, footage exposed, exclusive or not, roll number and length, followed by a brief outline of the story, and bottom-lined with the name of formation or unit seen on film, and its location. Later in the campaign, these came in foolscap size with the dramatic 'Top Secret' heavily printed across the top. We were also issued with a slate-board and boxes of chalk, and were supposed to print one's name and roll number of film.

I knew that many cameramen religiously carried out this practice throughout the campaign, but the last I saw of mine was about 15 minutes after landing on Queen Red beach on D-Day. It was propped up against the hobnailed boots of a very dead soldier, and I filmed the darn thing lying flat on my stomach with a vicious salvo of Spandau fire blasting its way over my head, as I focused on the simple message—'GRANT, ROLL 3'. As soon as the Spandau gave up, I said, 'The hell with it', and got off the beach like the 'clappers'. 'Who needs the effing thing?', I shrugged, and from that moment on, my name and roll numbers appeared on walls, tanks, the canvas of my Jeep, and anywhere I could scrawl this earth-shattering information—provided, of course that I could find a grubby morsel of chalk!

I gave my link-man all my exposed film, and received the same number of rolls of fresh film in exchange. So I would sail with ten rolls, 1,000 feet, of unexposed film to last me until I made further contact on the other side. I roughly estimated that I would use no more than two rolls on the departure and whatever else I saw before nightfall, then another at daybreak and from there to play it strictly by ear—or by eyesight.

When we did sail it was worth every foot of film I could spare, and I remained so busy that it was only distance and the fading light which made me realise that I was seeing England disappear for what may be a long time. I thought vaguely of my wife and what she may be doing about this time, but the situation had a feeling of such total unreality about it that my last thoughts before I went below were that I had not eaten since breakfast and I was starving. As I was about the last to go inside, the RN seaman at the entrance handed me the standard sea-sick pills and spew-bag, then clanged the door shut with a terrible finality.

After the scent of clean sea air, the atmosphere below was foul. Not only the diesel which powered the LCI's engines, but its nauseous fumes were well mixed with the smell from the new paint job that had obviously been recently applied to the interior. Some of the early arrivals were already stretched out, their faces the same shade of green as the paintwork, and their recent meal had already been deposited in the soggy bags beside them. My appetite was rather shattered but I attempted a mug of soup, a couple of hard biscuits and another mug of passable

Sergeant Rennison in the Jeep specially fitted for a wet landing.

LCT, loaded with tanks and carriers, preparing to join the convoy.

tea. Within the hour I was headed for the single toilet—sorry, head—and later lay back on my bulky rucksack and surveyed the scene with diminishing faith. My God, I thought, here come the conquering heroes.

Lying there, I thought back to some of the information we had been given in Southampton at a Lord Lovat conference. In this he stressed the dangers we would meet on the landings; beach defences with names like Tetrahedras and Element C—apart from ripping our hulls on their jagged edges, it was a definite possibility there would be mines attached to them. Mines too, dug into the sandy beaches, most of which we hoped would be dealt with by small parties of the 3rd Division, who would precede us.

But worst of all—and this had been very Top Secret—via the French Maquis, our Intelligence had knowledge of a series of underwater pipes, reaching out from concreted bunkers ashore to a distance of at least 1,000 yards out to sea. All of these pipes were fitted with a multitude of jets, and from the shore-based bunkers, powerful pumps could inject a potent mixture of petrol and oil down the full length which, as it reached the jets, could be ignited by remote control. They would then act like a chain of flame-throwers, thus setting up a virtual wall of flame, through which our line of landing craft would have to navigate. This made me think back to the 'wall-of-flame exercises' I had filmed some weeks before. The DD swimming tanks, specially prepared for such a hazard had successfully negotiated this obstacle, but could our landing craft do likewise? Up on the bridge of the main landing craft was Commander Rupert Curtis, and he was to spend an apprenhensive night with this knowledge on his mind. For this flotilla of 12 craft which carried the élite of Lord Lovat's Commandos was under his command and it was his responsibility to navigate a true course to Queen Red Beach the next morning. With these uneasy thoughts in my mind, and the conception that I could be reduced to something resembling a shish-kebab early tomorrow, I tried to get some rest.

Sleep must have overcome me, for I still remember the nasty, recurring dream of fire on water, and wondering how could water burn? But deep sleep must have erased the dreams, for I came awake quite suddenly with a complete nothingness

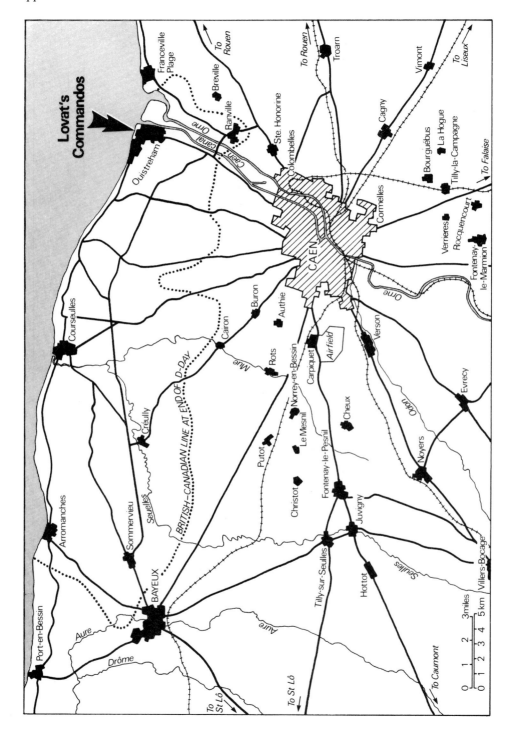

on my mind. My first action was to look at my watch. It was 1 am and, although I did not know it then, Sergeant Christie with 6th Airborne had just passed overhead. Christie would be the first AFPU cameraman to land in enemy territory. The ungainly LCI lumbered through the sea and I looked around to see how the others were faring. Some still slept, but there were quite a few who just half lay against their rucksacks looking at nothing; in the semi-gloom their eyes appeared sad and they did not seem to be the same men I had known back in camp. But in these unfamiliar surroundings it was understandable; these were men of action who preferred to take their chances out in the open. Despite the 'no smoking' warnings, one little chap, head tilted back and a cigarette stuck to the corner of his mouth, kept repeating with little thought for harmony, the same lines from an old song *Show me the way to go home.*

It was a long, long night and for something to do I rechecked my De Vry camera, looking with ill-humour at the makeshift sling made from thickly meshed string. This was really hotch-potch I thought, but I'd had it made so I could keep my hands free for other matters. By 4 o'clock I had had enough so I gathered all my gear and approached the exit where an RN type sat. He looked at me curiously 'No one allowed top-sides until general orders', he grunted. I flashed him my special SHAEF pass which had a copy of Eisenhower's signature at the bottom, then I turned it over so he could read all the special instructions 'that the bearer will be accorded every co-operation by all commanders, etc, etc.' This pass was to prove solid gold in the future and now was no exception. The metal door swung open and with a 'mind your nut' from the matelot, I climbed into the cool fresh air.

Dawn was just starting to take over from night, but the sea had a luminous glisten to it and as my eyes and ears came alive, I was aware we had a lot of company out there. An RN officer recognised me and remarked it was a bit early for photography but I wrinkled my nose and gestured below. He smiled and in the next 15 minutes he had organised a steaming mug of cocoa—it was delicious. As dawn began to yawn and stretch I saw more and more of my horizon and the enormous number of ships around us, but it was still too soon to use the camera.

Very soon the sound of a squawk-box told me that the Commandos had been summoned for breakfast. This startled me and I realised that I had lapsed into a wide-awake day dream, a hypnotic effect created by the quiet of the morning. My mind raced as I realised that within the next two or three hours it would be far from peaceful, and I cursed to myself as I saw that the light conditions were now perfect. Reflexes began to function at once and I grabbed my camera and made for the bows. The churning froth from the props made a natural tilt up to the sweeping armada all around. Stop camera and do cut-away shot of sailor using Aldiss lamp. I was in business.

Lovat's Commandos began to assemble on deck and I tore around shooting their preparations—weapons and ammunition were being checked out; the special knives they carried inspected with loving attention; two signalmen began abusing one another from opposite ends of the LCI through the heavy radios on their backs—and beyond, all those mighty ships crowding the sea, but not sufficient elevation for my camera to do it justice. Soon, the sky became as busy as the sea below—heavy bombers, fighter-bombers and Hurricanes and Spits thundered overhead, claiming our attention, ensuring tht we would now identify our aircraft by the two white stripes on the wings. So much to see and too much to capture it all on the precious ration of film I carried—I was in danger of over-shooting.

An RN rating with two bacon sandwiches and a mug of tea halted my furious drive—'You missed breakfast and there won't be a NAAFI wagon where you're going'. Suddenly I was exhausted and smiled my thanks as I gratefully collapsed on to some ammunition boxes. But I felt happy—the Pinewood training had destroyed that early lassitude which had crept over me—I was ready for the next step.

It was not long before we heard the sounds of the next step from the horizon, the battleships *Warspite* and *Ramillies* were pouring 15-inch shells on their targets and the RAF bombers were laying a carefully chosen carpet. Our eyes strained to see the distant shore which gradually became an indistinct smudge. Suddenly the squawk-box came alive and a cheerful voice announced that the initial beach-clearing parties of the South Lancs and East Yorks had made a successful landing. Everybody cheered and laughed, but this gradually subsided as we realised we now had about 45 minutes to beaching. But there was no sign of nervousness at this moment although one or two hastily knelt with heads bent and murmured their private prayers. A tense silence prevailed and I watched two naval ratings move into position behind the port and starboard Oerlikon guns, one of whom was the lad who had brought me the bacon sandwiches. We waited, and I had thoughts for Norman, Des, George, Billy and Jimmy who were also somewhere in this vast, initial assault. Special thoughts too for Christie who had been on land now for several hours.

I could clearly see the coastline ahead, and tried to judge our distance. Maybe two miles at most and those flame-throwers were just over a mile away. At the speed we were moving, they were only a few minutes away. To take my mind from the thought, I turned my camera on a small group of waiting Commandos. Their faces registered complete calm and a latent toughness, and I wished I could feel the same way. I turned again to look at the coast, and was surprised how near we had come during the time I had consumed taking two film shots. Then it hit me like a flash—we were well inside the 1,000-yard danger zone—and we were safe. At least from the flame-throwers. I was suddenly elated at this realisation and turned eagerly to the job I now had to do.

Ten minutes to go and my elation was abruptly broken as our own firepower in the convoy began its hellish thunder. Broadside followed broadside and we could now see the effect on plotted objectives. Could anyone survive this, I wondered? But when we were about ten minutes from touchdown I suddenly knew that somebody was taking umbrage. Whining salvoes were passing overhead and gouging the water nearby. I swung my camera in that direction and then panned quickly to the nearest LCI which had suddenly been hit and was now burning fiercely. Now, with every landing craft racing almost line abreast, it seemed like every gun the Royal Navy possessed opened up at once. The destroyer to our right had made a slight turn, and from her port side came salvo after salvo of rockets screeching their way towards the shore. I heard a Commando behind me make a nervous comment, 'Christ, what'll they think of next?' As if to give the penultimate reply to that query, the next sound I heard was the weirdest of them all. Lovat's personal piper began playing his bagpipes!

Every detail on the beach ahead was now in clear sight and our approach was free of the dreaded Tetrahedra and Element C obstructions which were designed to rip the guts from approaching craft or, if Teller mines were attached, blow them to hell and gone. As it was, it was obvious from the speed we were travelling, when we hit that beach our LCI would not be on a return ticket. Moments before we grounded the two ramps, port and starboard, were hastily lowered—our bow was some 15 feet above the water level—but due to the speed we were travelling the one on the port side broke loose from its stanchions, which meant we would all have to crowd down the remaining one—or jump!

My camera had been running up to the moment we came to a shuddering halt—no doubt Pinewood would comment that the shot was unsteady—and the Commandos moved sharply to the remaining ramp. As most of the LCIs had touched down about the same time we now came under a hail of small-arms fire and one or two chunks of larger stuff. Hastily draping the camera around my neck I pushed my way into the queue cramming its way to get off in a scramble which, as one Londoner later described, 'was worse than the Underground at rush hour'. I took one fast look backwards and was horrified to see my benevolent rating slumped over his Oerlikon gun, his face and arms covered in blood, then I got a hefty push from the Commando behind me and I was on my backside, thumping down the ramp and into about two feet of water.

The beach was under my feet and I meant to cover it fast, but no, I had to change film. A quick look up the beach and I saw some troops sheltering behind an AVRE tank and I made it in nothing flat. The three men crouched there were from the East Yorks and they had been in this maelstrom for nearly 45 minutes. They watched with no little amazement as I unslung my camera, took an empty tin from my haversack, opened the light-proof door, pulled the exposed roll of film out and hastily threaded in a new one, blowing sharply at the gate in case there was sand, then snapping the door closed. Hastily judging the light conditions I made a slight aperture adjustment, then backed off from the cover of the AVRE, started the camera running on the trio whose attention was now diverted in the direction I panned to pick up the shots of Commandos coming ashore. At the same time I heard Lord Lovat shouting, 'Move it—move it', and I rejoined them to move in double time to the top of the beach and the shelter of a shattered building.

*　　　*　　　*

A sequence of stills; mostly 'freeze-frames' from cine, of the final hour to touch-down. The Commando approach includes material by Laws, Clague and myself. **Above left and right** *Commandos of No 1 Special Service Brigade examine the approaching coast-line.* **Below** *Having chosen my ramp, I rest my rucksack and start filming. Just then, one of the LCIs explodes with a roar; the sound audible over the two-way shelling.* **Above far right** *The beach, only moments away, I don a rucksack and continue the filming. The noise is intense; no time to look anywhere but ahead.* **Right** *A freeze-frame from Laws or Clague. They appear more organised, and had a shallower wet-landing. But no one can imagine the noise.*

Above left *Both my craft and the other came in fast and hard, each losing a ramp in the cross-surf. Too steep for me carrying a camera; I plan to go down like the chap I see ahead—on my backside!* **Left** *Either Laws or Clague. An RN rating about to push out the first ramp. There cannot be a beach-master on this section, that beach is too cluttered for a clean landing and get-away. They've got problems and it could be nasty.* **Below left** *That was mine in the middle. I wasn't the only one to come down on my backside. It was a right mess, and for a while I forgot the noise.* **Above** *Laws or Clague. He appears to have got mixed up with an LCT, and appears also to be filming from cover. It looks a good spot to change a roll of film.* **Below** *Appears to be 3rd British on my right. Des O'Neill or Billy Greenhalgh. Certainly not Jimmy Mapham. He had a rough landing.*

Above left *Could be Jimmy Mapham after he had taken his well-known picture of wounded and exhausted troops. The foreground makes me feel it's 'Mapham's Ridge'.* **Left** *Commando group—at last—just leaving the beach, and the welcome feel of solid ground. Now, on inland, to the objective. Still early in the day.* **Below-left** *The first panic is over. DUKWs, Jeeps and recovery vehicles now roam, and what looks like a section of Mulberry now linked to the shore.* **Above** *The aftermath, and evidence that the German block-house took its toll. The fighting is now much further inland.*

As I took this brief rest I gave thought to what my other colleagues were doing and hoped that they too had made safe landings. Actually, for such a small unit our overall success ran pretty high. George Laws left Southampton with No 4 Commando on the *Maid of Orleans*, and at first light they were transferred to small assault craft and headed for Sword Beach. Their objective was the six-gun coastal battery at Ouistreham, and as they raced towards it George had a grandstand view of the destroyer which had accompanied them receiving a direct hit in its magazine, which caused it to sink almost immediately. Although this did little to cheer him, he filmed some good landing material and then proceeded inland towards the River Orne where, like Lovat's Commandos, the 4th hoped to link up with the 6th Airborne. But it was during this advance that George had the bad luck to have camera failure; the spring drive on the motor picked that moment to pack up. However, he also had a still camera and got some shots of glider reinforcements dropping into the 6th Airborne positions.

Norman Clague, Jimmy Mapham and Bill Greenhalgh all made safe landings, but the latter's success was to be relatively short-lived. Little Billy landed with a Bren gun carrier section of 3rd Division which met with heavy enemy gunfire. Many of the carriers never made dry land (all vehicles for the initial landings had been waterproofed and their exhausts extended and curled upwards like poised cobras), with drivers and crew dying within feet of the land they had come to liberate. Billy says that his smallness must have saved him several times as he could feel the sharp down-draught of heavy stuff just clearing his head. As they crawled on to the sand he leapt out of the carrier and got his camera going, and by dodging from one carrier to another he eventually made the top of the beach. Partially exhausted, he turned and looked down the beach where he could see burning carriers and several dead lying about. It was this scene he was filming when his luck ran out. A mortar shell exploded just a few feet away and fragments hit Billy on his body and severely concussed him. The last thought he had before he blacked out was 'I hope some bastard doesn't nick my camera!' Billy Greenhalgh became the first AFPU casualty of the campaign.

Meanwhile, just a short distance away and still on Queen Beach (this beach had three sectors, Red, White and Green), Jimmy Mapham came in with the 13/18th Hussars who had been supported by a few DD tanks, and he had the good luck and good fortune to be one of the first off the assault craft. He immediately raced up the beach with his Super Ikonta at the ready, turned around and took the picture that was to make history. From large foreground to a misty background the photo shows a straggle of troops, some coming on with shock registered on their faces, the wounded being assisted, and the dying beyond. The entire imprint of what it was all about is registered in that one photograph, and it became the first to be wired to the world and clearly hammered home the message—this is D-Day. Jimmy was fortunate in finding a convenient shell-hole close to the breakwater, for he was forced to spend most of the day there as the Germans zeroed their heavy guns on this small sector which saw wave after wave of British troops come ashore. In AFPU history it became known as Mapham's Ridge.

Norman Clague made a good landing, although some members of his Commando ran into what appeared to be an isolated burst of cross-fire and several fell dead in an instant. There were several knocked-out flail tanks lying about and one burning fiercely which Norman used with good effect as he filmed Commandos dragging heavily, in sodden clothing, two of their wounded comrades to the top of the beach. There was little pause for breath as they moved inland and Norman actually performed the almost impossible feat of changing rolls of film whilst on the move. Minutes later they encountered fire from a German strongpoint which enraged the Commando to the point that, after lobbing several grenades, a small group charged it with knives and bayonets, disposing of the enemy without firing a shot. This short, rapid action shook Norman a bit and he was further despondent as to whether there had been sufficient light for an exposure in the wooded copse which had concealed the strongpoint. They turned and moved off in the direction that would make our paths cross later in the day.

Desmond (Des) O'Neill, whose sensitive photography was, in later years, to weave patterns of fine gossamer in the world of women's fashions, found himself in a terrestrial theatre of crashing mortars and machine-gun cross-fire, as he touched down with the 3rd Division. Houses and DD tanks were ablaze as his feet found traction on sand already strewn with the dead and the dying. But, again, that Pinewood training made him stop halfway up the beach, and he got his cine-camera running. Peering through the view-finder, he filmed LCTs disgorging masses of grimly determined troops who were being flailed by murderous machine-gun fire.

He was surrounded by men of the 3rd British, when he felt his body thrust forward by the impact of a bullet, or stray fraction of a mortar. His knees buckled and, with camera still running, he fell to the wet sand. For Des his immediate war was over, as he was soon evacuated, but there remains a unique piece of film, showing the troops storming past then, as his camera tilted, they appear to be running in a quite impossible position, finishing in close-ups of upside-down boots kicking sand into the lens.

*   *   *

The main objective for Lovat's No 1 Special Service Brigade was to link up with the members of No 6 Airborne who had seized the main bridges over the River Orne and the Caen Canal just after midnight. This was no more than four miles away but the route had many small pockets of confused but belligerent enemy which had to be mopped up very quickly. And when Lord Lovat said 'very quickly' he meant just that. Little quarter was given and very few prisoners taken, for we did not have the manpower to shepherd them to the rear. I restricted my filming to scenes which—at the time—I felt would be acceptable to cinema audiences, completely ignoring the fact that the War Office would require a complete and impartial record of the campaign. Despite the Pinewood training I was still a comparative novice in battle photography and my instincts shied away from the more horrible aspects of warfare. For example, as we continued our erratic progress towards the Airborne's position, we came under mortar fire several times and, although Lovat insisted that we did not bunch together, there was always the fear that one would lose sight of the man ahead when we had to negotiate the many hedgerows and small wood patches. One felt, too, that a German lurked behind every tree and, more important, we were entirely dependent on the section leader who was doing the map-reading. Inevitably, I was with a small group when an air-burst crashed overhead (this is an anti-personnel shell which bursts outwards and downwards, and is very lethal), killing one and wounding several others. I was very shaken by this and as we again moved forward I still remained close to the man ahead. He was one of the signal-men and carried a heavy radio pack on his back and I kept my eyes fixed to him as we dragged along. Then I became aware of an object resting on the pack which was quite obviously not part of the equipment. At every forward lurch the object bounced up and down again, and with slow, dawning horror I realised it was part of a human arm! Except to keep moving forward, I did no more than remain transfixed by this horrible sight, until it gave another bounce, fell off, and was lost in the long grass. If I had not been such a greenhorn and in a state of shock I should have immediately taken a few quick steps to one side and started running the camera on the signaller's back-pack and panned across the faces of the others which were now registering weariness, pain and the same shock which troubled myself. This would have been a grim and harsh picture of the realities of war and I blew it from sheer lack of experience. But I would learn, and I would learn fast, for this was my job and it had to be done.

After all the fields, ditches and hedgerows through which we had scrambled, it was a relief to get on a roadway and it was here that we met one of the other Commandos headed towards their own checkpoint. They had been resting and were just preparing to move off as we arrived, so Lovat decided to call a halt and we were certainly in need of it, but mainly because he did not want to risk the likelihood of any mix-up. I looked around expectantly and sure enough I spotted Norman Clague heaving himself reluctantly to his feet. We were delighted that each of us had made it this far and hurriedly exchanged experiences. Norman confessed it had been a bit rough, then he patted his camera with a grin and said, 'Better than a tin hat—think it saved me a headache at least'. Looking at his De Vry I saw a heavily scored line down one side. Apparently he had covered his head with the camera when he dived into a very shallow ditch. He didn't know whether it had been shrapnel or a bullet. We had a couple of laughs then I asked if he had seen Captain Evans. He thumbed up the road, 'About 50 yards I suppose—he's been wounded'. He held my arm very firmly. 'He's OK—'nother hole in his nose'. This time he grasped my hand. 'Look after yourself, Ian—we're off now—see you'. He had to double for some yards to catch the rear end of his Commando, and that is the last time I ever saw him.

I wandered up the road and found Leslie Evans sitting in a ditch with a medical orderly doing something to his face. A stray bit of shrapnel had hit him, knocked him out for a few minutes and when he came to, he found a couple of Commandos had propped him in the ditch and shouted for a medic. The plan had been that he would try and contact cameramen and collect their film, and I asked if it was still OK. The orderly, anticipating the reasons for my question, told Evans if he walked back down the road a bit he would find an emergency aid station—from there they were ferrying wounded back to the beach. It seemed like a fair set-up and I gave Evans my film and watched him get up, a field-dressing stuck to his face that made him look so darn funny that I laughed. I certainly needed a laugh. But Evans took it very seriously, squared up his shoulders and marched off down the road just as though he was going to turn the next corner and march through the gates of Pinewood Studios. I felt a lot better as I returned to my Commando and we set off for our link-up with the Airborne, even though Lovat set a pretty sharp pace. Our meeting was behind schedule and the pride of No 1 Special Service Brigade was at stake.

Refreshed by their short rest, the Commandos appeared to be a lot jauntier in their stride; cockier, too, their new-felt assurance blossoming with the knowledge of the successful advance up to this point. The major victory of the landings and the subsequent crushing of the opposition had given their egos a tremendous lift and they approached Benouville bridge with confidence, despite the sounds of small-arms fire up ahead.

Lord Lovat was also in better humour—he was a little behind schedule but he was determined to give the Airborne a little show. He summoned his personal piper, Bill Millin, to go to the head of the column and told him, 'just blow, man, anything at all but make it a rousing march'. Bill Millin did as he was told, pumped the bag under one arm and the Commandos swung on to the bridge approach, the bagpipes snarling out *Blue Bonnets over the Border*. This was great stuff for my camera and I raced ahead getting as many different angles as I could—Lovat marching as on parade, the fantastic sight of Millin's red cheeks bulging behind the bagpipes, the red and the green berets mixed up together, the crashed glider so close to the bridge, civilians waving from the nearby café—and over it all came the sound of enemy fire from the woods. Strangely, nobody gave a damn and nobody appeared to be hit—maybe the German gunners were so astonished by this crazy sight, their thumbs and fingers just froze over triggers and the firing went as wild as the scene.

I was delighted by this sequence and I looked around just in case Sergeant Christie should make an appearance, but there was no sign. I studied the faces of the Airborne men; they really looked tired and weary—but far from spent—and now their happiness shone through their beards and the grime. Amongst the officers who greeted Lord Lovat was one who would later become one of Britain's leading film actors—his name was Richard Todd. He was, of course, an unknown at that time, although he had aspired towards a career on the stage in repertory just before the war, and indeed had helped to create the Dundee Repertory Company in Scotland. I had never been aware of his presence at Benouville Bridge on D-Day until a few years ago, when I had to film an interview with himself and Margaret Lockwood in Sunderland. After the interview, we chatted over a drink and the subject of D-Day arose as we discussed the film *The Longest Day*, in which he played the leading Airborne role of Major John Howard. The film also depicts the scene where Lord Lovat (Peter Lawford) crosses the bridge with his piper, and I made the remark that in the real thing I was just ahead of Lovat. At this, Richard Todd chuckled and produced a tail-piece to my story. On D-Day he was with the 7th Parachute Battalion and, as their Assistant Adjutant, was one of the first officers to greet Major Howard who came in with the glider force!

With the river bridge now firmly in our hands, No 1 Special Service Commando had several further tasks to perform and they now split up with two main objectives in mind. The first was the high ground around Le Plein and Amfreville, which would give them a commanding view of the whole area, and secondly, to drive swiftly towards the coastal area of Merville where the Germans had an efficient assembly of heavy guns capable of putting down heavy fire along the landing beaches. I did a mental toss of a coin and decided to go with the latter. By now I was feeling the strain of mounting pressure, the rapid rise and fall of tension and the sheer weight of my 90 lb Commando rucksack plus camera and film was causing me to sag. Never before had I felt so tired, so weary and so damn sorry for myself. Some soldier, I thought.

We got as far as the village of Sallenelles and ran into trouble. Enemy fire appeared to come from all directions and we hit the ditches real fast. If nothing else I was becoming quite expert in the use of ditches as, with the first burst of mortar, I was able to assess the usability of all ditches around within seconds. We would hear the plop-plop-plop as the mortars fired—we were that close to the Germans—and the Commando troop would suddenly vanish, and by the time the shells hit the road there would be a row of green berets sprouting from the ditches like mushrooms. But this delighted our own Mortar Group who were close by and they were soon lobbing three-inch shells in reply. As they had humped them all the way from the beach they were only too happy to dispose of as many as they could, and the opposition was soon squashed.

By this time the light had faded beyond the point of further exposure and I decided to spend the night in the area of Sallenelles with one Commando troop, whilst another pushed on to Merville. I reasoned—correctly as it happened—that any action towards the gun batteries would take place in darkness and my being there would be pointless. This was not an inspired guess on my part—just a quiet word in my ear from an Intelligence Officer. But it would give point to an argument I would have with my CO, Major Hugh Stewart, at a later date on points of strategy and common sense.

We had picked a small deserted house near the edge of the village to spend the night, and I was just arranging some bedding on the floor—the Commando Sergeant had nicked the bed itself—and a couple of sentries had just been posted at the front and rear doors, when there was one helluva crunch just up the street, followed very quickly by about three more which sounded as though they were marching down the street in our direction. The Commando Sergeant was off the bed in nothing flat and hollered, 'It's a fuckin' SP [self-propelled artillery weapon] and they've got this street zeroed.' There wasn't any cellar and we went out the back door like trained monkeys, made for the bottom of the garden where one brawny Commando bent over, using his back like a launching platform. As I was trailing my rucksack and camera and found I was still hugging a couple of blankets, it was no mean feat for me to negotiate the garden wall. I don't believe the brawny Commando thought a great deal of me either for, when he joined us he gave me a dirty look and was about to say something real mean about the Army Film Unit, when our little house plus its outside toilet disappeared with an almighty roar. We quickly melted into the darkness and a line of trees I took to be a small orchard.

It had to be an SP, for after about 20 minutes' silence we heard it start up again, but away towards the other edge of the village on the road to Merville. After hammering that for about ten minutes it finally gave up—and when an hour went by in silence, we figured he'd gone for a sauerkraut supper break. After that, we decided to spend the night amongst the trees—it was as safe as anywhere could be on this night—except, maybe from air-bursts which exploded as soon as they touched a weeny tree branch, but somehow they were rarely used at night.

I borrowed a trenching tool and scooped out a shallow trench, placed my rucksack at one end so I could use part of it as a pillow, eased the laces of my boots—I wasn't taking them off, just in case—and settled down happily with my two blankets. As I lay there, I could just see some stars through the trees and I realised this was the first time I had really relaxed since we hit the beach that morning. I was feeling a bit peckish and reached into my breast pocket for a couple of chocolate bars I had put there—oh, about 24 hours ago. With all the haring about I had done, the jumping into ditches and scaling walls, I found they had broken up and were also a bit mushy. Nevertheless, I began gnawing on the lumpy mess, when a Commando figure appeared—so quietly, I jumped a little. It was the brawny one who had hefted me over the wall and surprise, surprise, he thrust one half of a dixie into my hand which was full of cold beans, a length of French bread softened with a liberal coating of butter, margarine, or dripping—I couldn't tell, it was tasteless—and a bottle of wine! It tasted delicious, every bit as good as caviare on toast and a bottle of Dom Perignon. As I gulped greedily, I could hear other bottles clink around me. Obviously this troop had a first-class scrounger, and—I suddenly realised—they now regarded me as one of them. I felt great, and then just as quickly, ashamed with my earlier feelings—ashamed of being sorry for myself. But now—now I felt I had all the friends in the world right here in this wood in Normandy. I could now see the occasional glow from a cigarette, so, if they felt safe, I reached for my pipe, packed it full and lit up. Never had I felt so good, although I had the sense to realise that the wine was creating part of the goodwill, but after all that had happened to me on this long, long day, I was at peace with the world.

After about half-an-hour I felt myself drifting quietly into a slumber—I thumped out the dottle from my pipe—upended the remains of the bottle and tried to marshal some thought of things I had to do tomorrow. Apart from what I had in my camera, there was only one roll of unexposed film left, and my orders had been to try and contact Film Unit HQ—wherever the hell it was—by D-Day plus One, and that was tomorrow. Trying hard to maintain a balance between wakefulness and sleep, I went over some of the identification areas we had been given to contact with regard to AFPU HQ—military police, first aid stations, DID bases where food supplies would be coming in right now, or any other battalion HQ. There were some more, but I was fighting a losing battle and I allowed the beautiful luxury of sleep to rush over me, and I was 'way, 'way up there with the stars. For me, D-Day was over.

Chapter 6

June 7 began a damn sight earlier than I expected and even earlier than D-Day. About 3.30 am I got a hefty shove and was told we were moving out ten minutes ago—I had nearly been overlooked when the message came through to move back to Brigade HQ at Le Plein. We stumbled our way through the darkness for about two or three miles—I was by no means fully awake—and we got to Brigade HQ about the same time as No 4 Commando. I learned they had taken a bit of a pasting down at Ouistreham and my first reaction was 'where's Georgie Laws?' An officer was taking a head-count and when he appeared satisfied I got really worried and went over to him. He answered my question with a broad smile, 'Oh, him—he's probably halfway back to England by now'. Then he told me about the busted camera and, still wearing the smile, said he was grateful to George as he had learned a new line in abusive slang about the time the camera spring broke. That sounded like George all right, and for a fleeting moment I felt a twinge of envy. Much later I learned how he managed to make the trip at all, after all, he could have been a deserter and got himself slung into the can. But George is a smooth talker, and when his eyes twinkle behind his glasses he could make anyone feel as though his bank manager had just given him an overdraft. He eventually got himself aboard a ship taking German prisoners back to England, and at the other end quietly marched a group of them ashore, made a big show of handing them over to a reception party, and was off to Pinewood. He got back to Normandy about two weeks later and rejoined the unit.

Satisfied with George's safety, I made it known that I now had to try and contact AFPU HQ as soon as possible. I was told to wait a bit—a patrol would be moving out soon in the direction I wanted to go and it would be a darn sight safer. Certainly, Le Plein was no rest centre, the enemy knew where we were and most of my conversation took place in a nice deep trench, whilst salvoes of Moaning Minnies gave us a good stonking. Just before I was told it was safe to move off, Lord Lovat paid a quick visit and asked if I had got any good film. I assured him I had and he looked pleased. Before he left to 'make his rounds' as he put it, he paused and nodded at my green beret, 'Sergeant, you've earned the right to wear that—come back soon, and if you haven't got it on I'll put you on a charge'. With a brisk smile, he was off and, although I did return within a few days I never saw him again. He was very badly wounded during an attack on the night of the 12th, and had to be evacuated to England. Lieutenant Colonel Mills-Roberts took over the command and held it until the end of the war.

It was downhill most of the way and in the distance I could see the beach; the sea with hundreds of ships, some at anchor with enormous balloons floating above and small boats scudding about minding their own business. Clearly, we had established a very firm beach-head and it was going to take more than a few Moaning Minnies, SPs or the Merville battery to make that lot disappear. The Commando group left me at the edge of a wood and pointed at a few marker stakes in the ground. They belonged to 3rd Division, and if I followed them I'd find my way to one of their Battalion HQs. I thanked them and rather nervously made my way down a track, past a couple of orchards, until a small hedgerow materialised into two infantrymen of the 3rd. Their helmets and uniforms were covered with hedge trimmings, and one even had a couple of large apples strung from his belt, hanging in the position a Scotsman's sporran would be. The significance did not escape me!

'You the cameraman?, one asked and, as I obviously showed some surprise— 'We got a signal from HQ on the RT [radio telephone] and one of your blokes is here to meet you'. Let today's Post Office telephone service top that one! I was led to a wood where a Battalion HQ was set up, and the first thing I spotted was a Jeep painted with the Pegasus sign. It just had to be Sergeant Christie from his Airborne outfit. We were introduced and I looked at him with some curiosity and admiration. After all, he had been the first AFPU photographer who had jumped in total darkness, on to enemy-occupied soil. A little on the squat side, with a tough, rather flat but squarish face, which broke into an over-wide smile as we shook hands, but it was his eyes that held my gaze. There was a hint of something more than toughness behind those eyes—a hidden storm. This man was living on the edge of something.

But this was only conjecture on my part, and he indicated I dump my kit in the back of the Jeep then get into the passenger seat. The conjecture soon vanished as he slammed the gear into first, and the rear wheel sprayed dirt as he made a fast half-turn out of the HQ and on to the macadam road. For the rest of the drive it was flat out and no conversation. I watched the trees and hedgerows flash past and I tried to orientate myself from the angle of the sun. Fortunately, we met no other traffic in either direction, although a small section of British troops had to make a hasty scramble into a ditch, followed by a nice choice of English. Eventually we came to the outskirts of a village, with a shredded sign announcing it was called Cully, and turned sharply through some stone-pillared gates, tore up the driveway and halted at a largish chateau, which I somehow guessed was the Film Unit HQ.

It was a reasonably sized place and had obviously just been vacated by the last occupants. Germans, I suspected, from the peculiar smell that pervaded the atmosphere, possibly a mixture of their type of food and cigarettes—the sort of odour you stored away in your mind and always associated with the near-presence of the enemy. A useful sort of memory to store in the think-tank. But the speed of their departure had been to our advantage—plenty of bedding, but in desperate need of washing, kitchen utensils and crockery requiring the same treatment and a couple of good-sized bathrooms which actually had hot water. Last, but not the least, a makeshift bar with several bottles of schnapps, some cognac—and a bottle of Johnnie Walker! Now where the hell did they get that, I thought; as far as I knew that would not be amongst the first priorities to come ashore to the DIDs.

'Like a drop?', and the familiar voice turned me about. Major Hugh St Clair Stewart, my CO, his tall, rangy frame growing out of his neat and clean uniform—making me suddenly aware of the mess I was wearing. Then I remembered Sergeant Major Lewis's trumpet call of discipline and threw up a salute, he returned it with his slow smile and once again indicated the bottle. I nodded and he poured a couple. We chinned each other and he took a good look at me. 'Apart from a bath, you'll need a new uniform—that one positively stinks'. I was now very aware of my body odours and couldn't agree with him more. 'Upstairs then—a bath and any bed you like—the rest of the unit won't be arriving until later today. Then I'll tell you where to change that clobber'. He paused. 'And—Grant—thanks for the good work.' Then he told me about Billy Greenhalgh, Des O'Neill, George Laws—the former of which was news to me, and it slowly dawned on me how slim we were on strength, and I'd probably be back with my Commandos after a night's sleep. But I intended to make the most of it this evening.

I decided to change that order of priorities and, with a chit from Hugh Stewart, went first to the Quarter-Master at the nearest Base Supply Depot, picked out a Canadian battledress (about a size too large, but it felt and looked a better material than the British), underwear, socks and a pair of jump-boots. I left my old stuff lying limply at ease, after snipping off the stripes and AFPU shoulder flashes, and headed back for that bath. Glowing with health, hygiene and two whiskies, I inspected myself in the slightly oversize battledress, and concluded that a few tucks here and there would help.

The only person around was 'Tiny' Shepherd—Stewart's batman—and he produced a meal of tinned stewed steak, potatoes and carrots, followed by tinned Christmas pudding and custard! Over a mug of tea he explained that this time tomorrow the place would be running OK—with the back-up of AFPU personnel, there would be Jeeps and RASC drivers and the Catering Corps would be supplying a number of cooks on permanent attachment to the unit, when it came to full strength and fanned out with the three separate Corps that would be 2nd Army. Stewart had gone out with Christie to try and get a line on Norman Clague, unlike my case, communications with his Commando had been negative. Captain Evans was all right, but I was told he was a real scream to see with one side of his face done up in a bandage, he was with Intelligence Corps at the moment getting movements information. Jimmy Mapham would be in later that evening—his first rolls of film had somehow got to Stewart all right via a 3rd Division officer who had been very impressed by Jimmy's reluctance to leave 'Mapham's Ridge' where he was having a field day. But Stewart had ordered him back to base.

Anyhow, it seemed I had drawn the short straw to have a night out so off I went into the village of Cully. I should have stayed back at base and got smashed on schnapps. Cully, like most the little villages near the beach-head, had taken a pasting from the Naval and RAF bombardment prior to our invasion, causing considerable damage and a few local inhabitants had been killed. To compound this tragedy, when the Germans fled they took most of the livestock—and I mean live, as the shelling had caused a few casualties among them as well. During that crazy ride with Christie, I had seen a few dead cows lying about, but absently accepted the fact that it had to happen. Their presence was to become more noticeable as the warm June weather progressed.

But I was not prepared for the hostile reception from the villagers from whom, in my naïveté, I expected at least a little warmth of welcome. Despite the rumbles of war in the not too far distance, it was a pleasantly warm evening; about 7 pm and the sun would not set for at least another two hours, and I entered the only street the village possessed. There were a few other troops about and the thought of personal safety never entered my head. I carried a .38 revolver on my hip and I knew with confidence that I could hit a door with it if I held it firmly by the handle. This standing joke passed through my head in a flash and reminded me of part of a lecture given to the Commandos back in Southampton about German weapons—'if you get the chance, pick up a Schmeisser machine-pistol—the best goddamned light automatic in the world'—so I made another mental note. Then someone opened an upstairs window and hurtled a pail of water right at my feet— oh, the anguish, the shame, the goddamn Frogs—my brand-new battledress was soaked! First reactions were to go and clobber someone—then I remembered the French do these things in small villages—so, steady now, maybe someone will look out of the window and shoot off a string of French which means 'sorry'. No chance. The sun reflected in a firmly closed window.

A couple of infantrymen who had watched this with great amusement came over and gave me the facts of life. Stay in the middle of the road—the natives are

British troops of the initial landings go for a welcome bath.

not too friendly for the reasons given above for, curiously enough, the French in Normandy had on the whole enjoyed the German occupation—oh yes, they had a small proportion of FFI, but for some reason they had sloped off when we landed—and if you're looking for a drink with about the only friendly native, then there's the Café du Normandie just up the road. They went off with a slight lurch that bespoke the truth of their past preoccupations. As I turned and walked towards the café I carefully noted the attitudes of the few people around, there was a blank look about them—not really animosity, not friendliness, not any-thing—and I made yet another mental note to return to base within an hour, certainly before sundown. It was an odd feeling, we had come to liberate these people, and I resented this attitude.

A blind man with half an ear could have found the Café du Normandie as waves of singing bounced from its interior. I vaguely wondered how they had got the entire 3rd Division in there, until I opened the door to find less than a dozen troops jostling between the small bar and an old piano in the corner. One of them paused in mid-song to look at my wet trousers and laughed, 'Couldn't you hold it mate—piss-house is out the back', and went back to the *Blaydon Races*. There was about six inches of empty bar and I stuck my shoulder in and asked the soldier nearest to me what one drunk around here. 'Calvados—just that—they got nothing else—but jeesuss, it's great'.

Calvados is the powerful brandy made in Normandy and considered by most people to be the strongest in Europe. Almost pure ethyl-alcohol, it even gives the Guy-Lussac hydrometer the shakes and should really be sipped from tiny thimble-sized glasses. But not so the Army, they were putting it away in long glasses, full to the top, and it was showing. Mine host pushed a glass in front of me and I pushed some of the new French scrip back at him, and to show how honest he was he returned a few coins of an unknown denomination. I pocketed the change and took a good belt at my glass (I didn't know about Calvados either), and wondered who had started the fire. No wonder these men were more than slightly merry and the owner of the café was enjoying being the friendly mine host. Someone had obviously explained the value of the money the troops were freely chucking on the bar counter, and a little simple arithmetic was enough to keep his hands rubbing below the level of the counter.

In my very weak French I tried to strike up a conversation with him, but he was far too busy and I made another attempt with a couple of soldiers who had momentarily run out of dirty lines for *Roll me over in the clover*. For about two minutes we exchanged experiences of yesterday's landings, but the lance-jack who appeared to be with them plainly decided that this was no time for chit-chat as he pounded the counter with his fist and launched into the well-known Army ballad *Bless 'em all,* with particular emphasis on the part which proclaims a certain act upon 'the Sergeants and their something sons', as he blearily eyed my three stripes. I'm afraid I'm just not the singing type—the more I drink the less I talk, and prefer just to watch. So, after a few more drinks—and I was feeling their strength all right—I decided it was time to return to base.

There I found Major Stewart, Christie, Jimmy Mapham and 'Tiny' Shepherd

After a welcome rest from his much-lauded beach position, the ever-happy Jimmy Mapham gets out to seek a story, and spends time with the Maquis.

(he was all of six foot two) sipping cocoa and yarning away, so I got a mug and joined them. Listening to Jimmy's north country dialect tell about the remarkable photo position he had claimed on the beach, and watching his expressive eyes bulging behind the heavy magnification of his glasses, I felt a warmth for this professional who appeared to have treated the whole affair as the second half of a football match. Looking at Christie, however, it was obvious that he was not listening to the story but seemed to be wrestling with some inner emotion. He moved his hands for no apparent reason and his whole body seemed wound up like a tight spring, coiled and waiting for someone to push the button. This, I would later learn, was a symptom of what we called being 'bomb happy', or just plain shell-shock.

For some reason, this caused me to query Stewart as to the whereabouts of Norman Clague, and he replied that Captain Evans—at the moment asleep after an injection against infection from his wound—had been in touch with him. Indeed, it was emphasised, I should get some sleep as Evans would be returning me to my Commando in the morning, at the same time bringing Norman in for a rest. This seemed logical—we *were* a bit thin on the ground, due to the absence of George Laws and Billy Greenhalgh, and despite Jimmy Mapham's bubbling enthusiasm, he had earned a respite and, I reasoned, that sometime tonight the unit would be considerably strengthened. I was still curious about Christie, however, but shrugged and made my way up to a real bed.

Next morning, Evans drove me the short distance to where I could pick up the fringe of the Commando sector. He appeared to be quite recovered from his wound and only a small strip of dressing covered the lower half of his face, emphasising his rather rugged expression. I had the feeling that he was anxious that I should make some comment so I obliged with, 'Morning, Captain—how's the wound healing? When I saw you a couple of days ago it looked real messy'. I hopped out of the Jeep and slung my camera gear, then grinned at him: 'It'll be worth a pint back at the Crooked Billet'. He grinned back: 'At least a couple, I'd say—good luck Grant'. I chucked him a quick salute, to which he replied American style—straight out from his cap—and I turned and made my way to Le Plein.

The next two days were far from being peaceful; the enemy knew exactly where Brigade HQ was and gave it little rest. Heavy mortar shells often straddled the area, but the Commando had dug deep and well and retaliated with their own fire and frequent patrols. Le Plein was important and must be held.

My own involvement was entirely my own choice. These men knew me by now and I was able to move freely, using information gleaned from various briefings. I had scaled my equipment down to two haversacks, one with film and the other personal requirements; my Commando rucksack left at AFPU HQ and neatly tagged, should they be required to move to another billet. A courier arrangement was set up so I could send exposed film back and he would return with fresh stock or messages. For resting—there was little chance of a full night's sleep—I used a stretcher and a couple of blankets at the First Aid Post, with the full agreement that I be tipped out should the stretcher be required!

By now the Commando Jeeps had arrived and I was able to make use of them during patrols, but only as somewhere mobile to carry my haversacks, so I could move at speed with just the camera in my hand. That is how I came to lose a six-inch lens! The De Vry cine camera was a far cry from being the perfect battle camera. It carried only 100-foot rolls of film—just over a bare minute of running time, and powered by a clockwork motor which required winding about three times per roll—although we had been trained to re-wind after every shot, which meant that the spring was always in tension and could—and of course did—snap, much to the disgust of George Laws. Only one lens could be used at any time and I invariably used a 35 mm or a 50 mm—over that you would get a shaky picture.

From information I had, the patrol was to attack a small farm holding in which a German strongpoint was hidden. So I thought I might be able to pick up some distant action if I took along the six-inch lens, provided I could brace myself against a tree or a wall. Keeping one haversack tightly held by a crossed webbing across my body, I stuck the six-inch in the other haversack and put it in a Jeep. We had gone about a mile and a bit when we heard the Moaning Minnies coming over and we hit the ditches—the driver of the Jeep doing likewise, which was just as well as it got a nice direct hit. I had my camera running on large close-ups of Commandos looking very tense, and with left eye saw the Jeep go up in flame. This habit of keeping both eyes open whilst filming had been brought up during the course at Pinewood and, although some found it a problem, I used it most of the time. So I immediately panned off the big close-ups, pulled my focus to infinity and got a reasonable shot of the Jeep just as it exploded, with parts of Willy's Jeep and Taylor Hobson lens travelling in many directions. If a little laugh escaped me, no doubt the nearest Commando thought I had cracked—but to be truthful, the six-inch lens had become just a bit of a nuisance. Anyway, that was the only bit of good film I got out of the patrol, as the farm proved to be empty except for about two dozen fresh eggs which made up into a nice omelette that evening.

*   *   *

Shortly after the meal at Le Plein, the courier arrived from AFPU HQ to get my film and dope sheets. He gave me a couple of fresh rolls of film, a closed envelope, a peculiar look and departed rather hurriedly. I pondered the envelope for a moment, lit up a pipe and slit open the message. I had to read it twice before its import hit my stomach. Norman Clague had been killed the previous night. As simple and flat as that, with only the word 'regret' to soften the impact. My first impulse was to return to HQ at once, but the dusk had turned to night and I realised that this would be unwise. Instead, I made my way to the signals section and tried to raise some information, but they were tied up with official transmissions. Then I tried the Intelligence Officer's bivouac, but he had gone off with Lord Lovat. I felt lost—I wanted to talk to somebody—and I sought out a Sergeant I knew only by the name of 'Taff' and just gabbled away at him. When he realised what I was trying to tell him, he motioned me to stop and disappeared for about two minutes. When he returned he brought a bottle of German schnapps, heaved out the cork and told me to take a good belt. For about two hours we talked and drank, then he led me back to my convenient stretcher, made sure I got my head down and left. Very soon, I slept.

Next morning, I got up fast, had a steaming mug of tea with Taff and said I wanted a Jeep to take me into Cully. He just nodded quietly, for last night's conversation had formed a small bond of understanding between us—some place in the past he had lost a friend, but had not elaborated—he had just allowed me to exhaust myself, and now he understood what I must do. No words were spoken, and as I got into the Jeep he just smiled a little, wagged two fingers at me, and was gone. When I reached HQ I realised the back-up section of the unit had arrived, Jeeps filled the driveway, their drivers messing around in the engines, and as I went through the front doors I saw familiar faces, Bill Ginger, Ernie Walters, Carl Sutton and others. Nobody looked very happy and my face must have indicated the rage and fury I felt for, apart from a tentative wave, they just kept away. The only officer present was young Peter Handford and he read me like a book, for he just shook his head and told me that no one present had been there—and no one knew what had happened. He looked so forlorn and helpless that my anger died a little, I had become fond of him at Pinewood and he was to prove to be a very efficient officer and one of the most popular. There was no sign

I take the opportunity to visit the area where my friend Norman Clague was killed on the same night as his section of 48 Commando.

of Evans and I asked 'Tiny' Shepherd if Major Stewart was upstairs. He nodded and I went on up.

Stewart was writing reports when he answered my knock, gave me a hard look and told me to sit down. He did not question why I had left my position, but immediately began to tell me what he knew. And the way he told it seemed to be to the point. Norman had been placed with a small platoon of Commandos in a farmhouse where they were preparing for an attack on a German strongpoint. The farmhouse had come under a mortar 'stonk' and a single shell had penetrated the roof, killing and wounding all present. Norman had died immediately. Stewart then went on to say he had written to his parents and his sister, who had doted on him. Finally, he said, knowing how close I had been to Norman—he suggested a little rest and a change of scenery—I should now consider myself on local leave. Take myself over to Bayeux, which had just been liberated, and have a look at the Tapestry. Great, I thought, as I saluted and went out, just what I need right now—sightseeing. It was not until some time later that I realised how unfair I had been in my attitude of that moment. Hugh Stewart is very tall and lean, with a face still carrying the tan of desert sun—but that day it also held a drawn and tired expression.

My steam had evaporated somewhat as I came back downstairs—Hugh Stewart had the knack of pitching his words at a level which created assurance and, although something still nagged at my nerve-ends, I had come to accept the situation—at its face value. The anger I had felt stemmed from a complex sense of responsibility towards Norman, going back to the Pinewood days when we often argued and shouted over some triviality, and when it became overheated he would take a step back and allow me best. I spent a couple of hours gabbing with the rest downstairs, perhaps they picked a cue from myself and it became two hours of tall stories. We had a meal and I decided to take a run down to see Mulberry, and maybe tomorrow pay a visit to Bayeux. I was beginning to relish my feeling of freedom. Anyway, I drew some pay plus my first bottle of issue whisky which, as I recall, cost me the equivalent of eight shillings and sixpence— or 42½ pence!—piled myself into a Jeep and went off to have a look at our bridge-head.

Chapter 7

However personal Norman's death had been to me, together with the wounding of Billy Greenhalgh and Des O'Neill, the effect on No 5 had been a bit unnerving and Hugh Stewart had his work cut out to knock it back into shape. As more British troops poured into the beach-head, the shattered city of Caen was the single bastion in German hands that opposed the 2nd Army's attempt to swarm over the River Orne and into the plains of Normandy. Stewart and his officers very quickly organised the Film Unit into pairs, who were then attached to the emerging Army Corps.

The organisation was thorough and efficient, Public Relations had done their homework, and the lessons learned in the earlier campaigns had proved to be fruitful. The RASC provided a section of Jeeps with drivers who were so often the unsung heroes of many a battle, our special SHAEF passes were soon recognised, and AFPU gained a high degree of privilege and respect from Military Police and up to all levels of command. From Corps Commander level downwards the world went out to expect a cameraman to pop up wherever any action might occur. They would be recognised by the AFPU shoulder-flash and their pop-eyes as they registered every Moaning Minnie. With a few exceptions, it was to be the most smoothly run propaganda unit within the British Army of any campaign. Much of this was due to the skilful handling of the unit by Major Hugh Stewart—a far cry from Dunkirk, and the lone figure of Harry Rignold.

The organisation went something like this: 12 Corps Section was commanded by Captain Derek Knight; 30 Corps Section, Captain Jack Flack and 8 Corps (my pride and joy!), Captain Leslie Evans. Each section had a junior officer; at least three teams paired as cine and still, and often one spare cameraman who took turn to do 'specials'. These specials would range from visiting royalty, government officials, heads of state and other theatricals such as film actors and busty pin-ups. A toss of a coin usually decided who would do the specials and, despite the fact that at least one member considered he had more experience for this chore, there were to be no exhibitions of one-upmanship, as displayed by some characters. Fortunately, I managed to steer clear of this chore, except for two occasions when I had to film Montgomery presenting medals, and each time he barked at me as I stuck my noisy De Vry under his nose.

Stewart began his operations with extreme caution, giving the cameramen just the scent of the action, allowing them time to acclimatise to the feel of a battle.

None were allowed more than a day, but during those daylight hours they were obliged and encouraged to go with units operating very close to the enemy. At that time, it was the thrust towards Villers-Bocage by the 7th Armoured Division and the 50th Infantry Division, and this was to prove an excellent foretaste of battles to come. The enemy here was the Panzer Lehr, which was equipped with several Tiger tanks, those lumbering monsters whose frontal armour was totally impenetrable by the 75 mm guns on the more speedy Cromwells of the 7th Armoured. So it was lively stuff indeed, and for the first week or so, those one-day-only trips to the front line sometimes felt like a week long. But they learned, and by the time I returned to base they had become veterans.

But there was still a hint of unease in the atmosphere regarding the disposition of cameramen to front-line areas; in some cases, it was being voiced, situations would arise where a cameraman may have to make his own decision to withdraw, and he did not want his section officer looking down his nose and saying 'you should wait for orders'. Clarification on this point was being sought very earnestly. Hugh Stewart accepted this in principle, and even declared he would accompany the next pair of cameramen who were going into a small infantry attack backed by a couple of Sherman tanks the very next morning. This he did, and by early morning they were moving forward with the infantry, chest-high through fields of corn. After two hours they were still wading through the corn and not a single shot had been fired. The thump and rumble of other engagements could be clearly heard—but here—nothing. When they reached their check-point, Stewart was not quite sure how to accept this. There just had to be an enemy, otherwise the object of the exercise would rather fizzle out. It occurred to him, too, that he had not seen any sign of the Sherman tanks, although he had heard the clanking of their tracks. The tall-growing corn had been more than four foot in places and gave an odd appearance to the horizon, rather like wading in sea at the same depth.

At last they reached a hard straight road which kinked off to the left at about middle distance and, probably reassuring to Hugh Stewart, the sound of small-arms fire up ahead. Infantrymen had taken to the ditches—apparently waiting for orders to move—but Hugh, with his long legs now free of the clutching corn, decided to walk up the road a bit. One of the infantry shouted 'Hey!' and Hugh, hardly pausing, turned and grinned and asked, 'Are the Shermans up there?' The 'hey!' man just nodded dumbly as he watched Stewart's long strides take him rapidly up the road. He never quite made the kink of the road as a blast of Spandau fire ripped the hedge about three feet away. Hugh did a smart right-about and came back down the road, at the double, but by the time he came abreast of the 'hey!' man, he had recovered his composure and fixed him with a glare. 'I said Shermans—not bloody Germans', and with complete dignity walked away.

Above left *During a quiet period, I film Monty decorating some airborne troops.* **Left** *5.5 in gun/howitzers in action in Normandy with an attentive AFPU cameraman in the foreground.*

Chapter 8

My first introduction to the 11th Armoured Division was during the Odon
Offensive in the last week of June. Whilst the city of Caen, despite heavy
bombardment from the sea and the air, still remained in German hands,
Montgomery decided to drive a wedge between Tilly and Caen. The 15th Scottish
Division would begin the attack and the 11th Armoured would follow up and
attempt to establish a position across the Caen-Falaise road near Bourgebous.
Stewart used six cameramen for this assault—George Laws (just returned from
England) was paired with Bill Leeson (old 'Stress and Strain' from the loos of
Pinewood), Norman Johnstone (who had been doing a 'special' with General
Dempsey) with Jock Gordon, and I had the unexpected task of working with
Captain Evans.

Just before dawn on June 26 we waited in a thick ground mist as the artillery
barrage began to roll across the terrain ahead. We had been promised an air
bombardment at the same time, but the English bomber bases were locked in with
fog. We began to lurch across country in our Jeep, keeping a respectable distance
from the Sherman ahead, but even with the coming of dawn the mist still held,
and we just prayed the tank commander had the right map. Every now and again,
I would get out and run ahead, using hand signals to guide the Jeep with Evans at
the wheel, around a crater, or at one point, across some railway lines. Sometimes
we hit a road, but I could not even guess where we were.

Wherever it was, the sounds of heavy firing ahead told us we were about to see
some action. I got my camera off the back of the Jeep and decided to stay on foot.
The light was stronger now and I got some weird, ghostly effect of tanks against
leaden skies just at the moment two of them suddenly decided to fire their turret
guns at the same time! I nearly died of heart failure, I was so close, no more than
12 feet away, and my eardrums complained. By now the mist had completely
cleared, although the hedgerows dripped with moisture and I could feel the damp
of my feet where I had walked through a puddle. We were nearing the brow of a
hill which ran down into a village below, and from a lurching sign-post I knew it
was called Cheux. The 15th Scottish had obviously preceded us, for the remains
of two kilted figures lay just at the brow. I wondered why no one had moved
them, but seeing their shattered bodies, I realised that maybe an hour ago, the
brow of that hill had been sudden death. As tank after tank rolled over them, their
remains just gradually became part of the road surface. Sick as I felt, I recorded

the tanks moving over the brow and into the valley below, where, due to heavy mortar fire and mined roads, they soon became immobile in a ghastly traffic jam.

The 15th Scottish had run into stiff opposition, in the shape of the fanatical 12th SS, and, apart from the number of dead, the village of Cheux had sustained much damage. As it lay in a valley, there was an ominous ridge on the far side, and through the lowering clouds I could see the tiny figures of the 15th moving over and beyond. But the scene in the village itself could well have been one created by that Dante merchant; it was unholy chaos as the bulky tanks tried to negotiate the wreckage. Where a corner became too much of a challenge, a Sherman would just back off a few feet, then plough through the gable end of the obstruction. As the occasional German shell sailed into this inferno, it was clear that the tanks did not want to be caught in the valley. The high ground beyond would be heavy going, but they would be able to fan out; right here, they were sitting ducks.

I was running off the footage as fast as I could cram it into the camera, whilst Evans dodged about taking some stills. As the tanks gouged and tracked, the road surface vanished with cobblestones flying, leaving a trail of absolute carnage. When the Shermans eventually began to make progress up the far slope and out of the village, Evans, surprisingly, said we had enough material, so 'let's get the hell out'. For once I entirely agreed, and as we drove back out of Cheux, over the brow of the hill, there was nothing to indicate that two brave Scotsmen had lain there some hours before.

Over on the right flank of this attack, Norman Johnson and Jock Gordon were operating with the 49th Division, supported by the 8th Armoured Brigade. Again the heavy ground mist held down the speed of attack, so Jock and Norman could

For the advance through the village of Cheux, I was paired with Captain Evans ('Old Busted Hooter'), and we both agreed that the village was small, and very, very nasty.

do little but follow as close as they dared in their Jeep. The road had been well traversed by the infantry of the 49th and the heavy armour of the 8th, but as they drove through the swirling mist, wrapped in their own thoughts, some intuition galvanised them both into action at the same time, they shouted the one word, 'Stop!', in unison, and their driver Ted slammed on his footbrake and started to swear. The single shout from Norman and Jock had probably dragged him back from some lecherous daydream, and he looked swiftly around expecting to see a Tiger tank menacing them. But by this time the two cameramen had left the Jeep and were moving tippity-toe to the front, and stopped. Less than three feet away, a Teller-mine had surfaced from the roadway like a rabbit. How did a fair chunk of the British Army pass down this road, and over the Teller-mine, without exploding it? Also, what made them both shout 'stop' at the same moment?

A little shaken by this experience, they drove round the mine and streaked for the rear of the 49th who, when hearing of the incident, sent a demolition team post-haste to blow it. The main objective of their advance was a place called Rouray, and to get there they had to cross the main Fontenay-Cheux road where they ran smack into trouble. Norman and Jock soon realised something was on when they saw the infantry clamber on the backs of tanks and wheel off the road. They ran after them, and got some good shots of grim-looking infantry hanging on round the tanks' turrets, then with a roar of engines at full power they disappeared into the mist. Shortly afterwards there was an unholy noise of heavy tank guns in action and the chatter of automatics, but it was impossible to get the Jeep any further. Norman and Jock proceeded cautiously on foot and eventually came across where the Reconnaissance Regiment had unleashed some six-pounders and knocked out four Panther tanks. With this marvellous brew-up registered on film, they felt it had been a good day. Looking skywards, they felt someone up there loved them.

It was not long before we added another casualty to our list. That very popular officer, Derek Knight, had been working a closely-knit assignment with Eddie Smales and Max Collins. They had been mostly foot-slogging shoulder to shoulder with the Warwick Regiment whilst trying to penetrate Caen. After a very trying day they sought refuge in the usual ramshackle farmhouse and, after a meal, Derek retired alone to a makeshift loft, reached only by a ladder. He still had quite a bit of paperwork to do, but shortly fell asleep, covered only by a very handsome fur-lined leather coat he had 'liberated' from some German officer. Whilst he slept, a ferocious bombardment from the enemy was laid down all round this area. Mostly field artillery, it contained one battery of the deadly 88s. It wasn't long before their shells began to creep close to the farmhouse, and Smales and Collins soon became alarmed for their safety. One of them ran up the ladder and shouted at Derek that they were coming under heavy fire. Derek was soon awake and his ears told him it was time to 'abandon ship'. With that shout, he headed for the top of the ladder when one of the 88s found its target. Derek was blown head first down the ladder, and, apart from concussion, received some leg injuries. He had to spend some time in hospital, but his greatest personal injury was the loss of his beautiful fur-lined coat.

Others too were less fortunate, and indeed it was a black period for the Army Film Unit, and the focal point of it all was Hill 112. Just a tiny pin-prick of a map reference, but important to either side, as it gave a commanding view of the country around it. Both the 11th Armoured and the 15th Scottish Divisions were involved. George Laws and Bill Leeson began their day with a Cordon Bleu breakfast—cold tinned sausages and swishy, tepid tea—so they were in good spirits at 4 am when one of Monty's famous creeping barrages began. They started to hump around 5 am, but progress was very slow through the cornfields, although the traffic of heavy metal overhead was so furious they could not distinguish between outgoing and incoming. But one almighty crash was definitely incoming and George was bowled over. When he picked himself up— 'didn't it blow your glasses off, George?'—he could not see Bill Leeson. Hastily puhsing corn in all directions he eventually found Bill with a nasty mess around his chest. Shouting 'stretcher-bearers' was a sheer waste of time with all that noise and George was worried about the Bren carriers milling about. The nearest first-aid just had to be somewhere at the rear—and somehow he carried Bill and both cameras for about a mile before the familiar Red Cross loomed up. When they stripped Bill off they found a chunk of shrapnel had penetrated his chest, after passing through a very thick notebook that we all carried, and this undoubtedly saved his life. The wound was not serious, but it was a Blighty, and George filmed the dressing of it, then decided to retire to the scene of the action. Bill Leeson eventually returned to the UK and whilst convalescing visited the local cinema where he saw the newsreel of himself at the First Aid Station. It probably elated him at the time, but it never cured his constipation.

Bob Jones and his partner 'Robbo' Robinson had the unenviable task of scaling Hill 112 with the infantry attack. The going was hard and precarious, the well dug-in Germans had a clear view down the hill and, although they were being plastered by artillery fire, maintained a murderous reply with automatic weapons. Bob and Robbo were nigh exhausted but kept plodding, when Robbo— who was ahead of Bob—stepped on a hidden mine, losing both his legs. When Bob partially recovered from the shock, he hurtled himself forward to his mangled colleague. But Robbo was dead and there was nothing Bob could do. A passing infantryman advised him to leave Robbo for the stretcher-bearers, and Bob, now in a state of advanced shock, carefully removed his identity discs, paybook and other personal papers and started off down Hill 112. It was near the bottom where I met him, the colour drained from his face, mouthing words quite beyond my comprehension, other than the three which he repeated over and over again, 'Robbo is dead'. It was a grotesque situation and just beyond my own immediate ability to formulate the right words and make an intelligent reply. Even today I still wonder what I could have said to try and console the stricken Bob Jones. Nothing. Instead I led him back to find the nearest medical assistance—other than that, I just felt empty and useless.

Chapter 9

With the ending of the battle of the Odon, the Army Film Unit withdrew to its HQ at Cully and the inevitable arguments arose regarding the placement of cameramen. But when faced with the logic, that to produce authentic battle material, one just had to be as far forward as those troops taking part in the action, the few dissident voices were stilled. My own feelings on the subject had undergone a few changes since the morning of June 6. On that day I had accepted my role with enthusiasm, but this had changed at the time of Norman Clague's death. Yes, I was bitter all right at first, and the memories of the good times we had spent together at Pinewood gave me some bad nights. Most of all, I kept seeing again my last vision of him walking away from me on that dusty road after the landings. It was odd—he never seemed to disappear, and I kept hearing his last words, 'Look after yourself, Ian—look after yourself, Ian'. Somehow, after a few nights, the dream no longer bothered me, and the tension gave way to a strange, new-found strength. Time had eroded my bitterness and I had unwillingly accepted the conclusion that, if the Army Film Unit was to succeed in its role of producing battle photography, then inevitably some element of risk was obligatory. Perhaps it was something to do with the *closeness* I'd felt with Norman Clague, both in life and death, but I knew I had come to terms with whatever lay ahead.

Hugh Stewart, however, rode out this little storm in his usual urbane manner, ensuring us of every comfort that was available at HQ. We had good food and slept in comfortable beds and, more important, he encouraged us to relax. We learned that replacements were joining us from Pinewood, but they would not arrive until we departed for our individual sections which would be based near each of the three Corps Headquarters. When would this be, we asked. Tomorrow—tomorrow, and we groaned in unison.

One relacement was Dickie Gee, who joined Captain Flack's section in an isolated farmhouse near Bayeux where he was introduced to the resident Sergeants Carpenter, Parkinson, Ginger, Leatherbarrow (who enjoyed the many variations of his name) and Norman Midgley. To ease Dickie Gee's transference from the fleshpots of Pinewood to the haystacks of Normandy, where one could plainly hear the 'bumps in the night' indicating the presence of war, they had a sing-song after dinner. This was always led by Les Carpenter who had a neat finger on the guitar and would usually launch into his favourite *On Mother Kelly's Doorstep*. They were well into the session and their voices reached far into the night, for they had no neighbours to worry about—none that they knew about at any rate—until suddenly there was a terrific hammering at the door. Dickie Gee recalls that he wondered if this was some kind of attack.

Eventually three of the cameramen, with pistols unsheathed, opened the door and came face to face with two dishevelled American GIs—both very drunk—who stood swaying in the dim light. One was in full battle kit with a rifle hanging from his arm, the other was wearing only a shirt, trousers and what they call sneakers. Bottles of Calvados seemed to stick out from them everywhere. The one in battle kit spoke: 'Say, is this a whore-house?' he asked thickly, and fell back into the arms of his companion, who also joined in with, 'Yeah—we're looking for a whore-house'. After a moment, pointing to his stupored friend, he added, 'This guy's supposed to be on guard'. By that time Flack had come to the door and, after hearing further demands to be admitted to 'the whore-house', told the two characters in no uncertain terms that he would put them both on a charge if they didn't clear off. They seemed to understand, and lurched away into the night. Dickie often pondered this disturbance as the Americans were miles away—God knows, he remarked, what the soldier was supposed to be guarding—and God knows where they came from—or went to.

However, it was not all jolly little sing-songs around *Mother Kelly's Doorstep,* and the new boys had to be introduced to the 'facts of life'—a slightly cynical phrase used by we veterans of less than six weeks' standing! Dickie Gee had described it so admirably that I give his description in its entirety.

'The afore-mentioned farmhouse was also the place from whence I departed for my battle initiation—my "baptism of fire". Having been in Normandy only a few days, I was completely green so far as real war was concerned and wasn't unduly worried when a particularly fearless Lieutenant named Handford told me one morning that I was to accompany him "up front". (Afterwards I discovered that Peter Handford had quite a reputation for bearing a charmed life. He'd walk around calmly under fire as if he were at a picnic, and I believe he boasted that he would never stop a bullet. Apparently a mortar bomb had dropped right at his feet a few days before—and hadn't exploded!)

'We set out in a Jeep (he was driving) and made our way along the dusty roads. After a brief stop at Brigade HQ to enquire latest developments, we pushed on through narrow lanes (which looked dreadfully ominous) until finally we met up with small groups of infantry lying flat on their stomachs by the roadside. We shoved the Jeep into a farm gate nearby and Handford marched off down the lane towards the prone figures. I followed him, cine camera at the ready. The blokes on the verges saw us and started to wave—at least, in my ignorance, I thought they were waving, so I waved back. Suddenly, all hell was let loose. At first I thought an express train was coming down the lane—until I realised that we were under heavy shell-fire. It was then that I also realised the significance of the "waving" by the infantry, they were signalling us to get our bloody heads down!

'The unfamiliar sounds of battle set me shaking like a leaf. I plunged into a ditch beside other khaki bodies and felt the sweat pouring down my face. (We hadn't been taught anything like this at Pinewood!) The shells screamed in with a terrifying sound, followed by the really menacing, hollow 'clap' of explosion. One didn't need much imagination to picture the red-hot lumps of metal that were flying around. A few yards away someone got hit, and an NCO called for stretcher-bearers. I started to film more or less automatically, but I doubt if I got one steady shot. I simply wanted to get out. I felt a tap on my shoulder: Handford—looking rather worried, despite his past record—could also see the wisdom of returning to comparative safety at the earliest possible moment. Furthermore, he was cursing the fact that he had forgotten his tin hat. After the next shell we made a dash for an armoured half-track vehicle which was parked about 30 yards away, and flung ourselves underneath. I filmed, from this shelter, a few other armoured units which had arrived on the scene—thinking how unpleasant it would be for our outstretched legs if the half-track suddenly moved on! Then I found myself looking into a face that was upside down. A head hung down at me below the vehicle's framework, to enquire if I knew, "Which direction those bloody shells are coming from". I wasn't able to oblige.

'After half an hour there was a slight lull in the shooting, and—covered in white dust—we made our way back to the Jeep. We were just about to climb in when a noise to end all noises sent us scampering for the shelter of a battered woodshed close by. My greatest relief was to find that this shattering sound came from our own side—a number of low-flying, rocket-firing Typhoons screamed across our heads to blast the enemy lines a quarter of a mile away. It was quite a sight—but I had run out of film!

'Neither of us exchanged a word on the way back to base. I didn't eat much that evening; but Norman Midgley, a battle-hardened member of our section, could see that the 'new boy' had been truly initiated. He poured out half a tumbler of neat whisky. I drank it and went to bed. A week or so later a report on my first piece of filming arrived from Pinewood. It said; "A good beginning. Well photographed story, excellent photographic standard. Keep this up and you won't go far wrong". I'm so glad I pleased them.'

And all I could have added would be 'Dickie Gee, welcome aboard'.

Chapter 10

Early in the second week of July we became aware that a heavy one was about to be launched around Caen. The destruction of the city had just recently been accomplished by the Canadians and the British, and teams of bulldozers, rescue workers and mine detectors were still trying to clear a safe way through the ruins. The task was not made easy by sporadic, long-range bombardment from the enemy, and the omnipresent stench of death. Many of the pitiful survivors would still die, and the promise of the bright new future heralded on the morning of June 6 was still a lifetime away.

This new assault meant a re-allocation of Film Unit members, for Hugh Stewart had been made aware of the concept of the coming battle. With cameramen working in pairs, this would mean direct attachment to those Divisional HQs whose tanks and infantry would be in the initial attack. Since the wounding of Bill Leeson, George Laws and I had paired up, and were living with other members of 8 Corps section in a pleasant farmhouse with a tiny bubbling stream out back. We all pulled long faces when we were told to evacuate and join our Divisional HQs, but we were more than a little huffed when we were told that 30 Corps Film Unit section would occupy the house for a couple of days, before they too were divided. Consequently, a really over-ripe Camembert cheese was purchased for a packet of cigarettes, then carefully concealed in the dining table which had a top in two sections. We also repositioned the table near a window that was favoured by the angle of the sun, and in the few hours we had before leaving the billet, the cheese was coming along quite nicely.

Happily, our next billet was quite adequate for George and me. The occupants went out of their way to make us welcome, and produced quite a marvellous meal from several tins of M and V (Meat and Vegetables), Spam, tinned potatoes and a few tins of soup. Although the farmer had a reasonably pretty daughter, she was also kept at a reasonable distance whilst the farmer regaled us with stories of how he had pulled the wool over the eyes of those *'salles Boches'*, and proudly showed us his now non-clandestine radio used nightly to listen to the BBC. For the next few days we heard the recurring theme *Moonlight Serenade* played by Glenn Miller; this and other Miller themes would be constantly heard from tank radios for weeks to come.

The 'big battle' was now becoming a solid fact. Montgomery was gathering three armoured divisions—the 11th, the 7th and the Guards, plus two infantry divisions, for a mighty break-out thrust over the Orne and code-named Goodwood. The plan was that the three armoured divisions, under the command of General O'Connor's 8th Corps, would smash out the bridgehead across the River Orne, through the narrow corridor held by the 6th Airborne and then fan out to allow the 11th to move to the right, the Guards to the left and the 7th to continue in the centre. They would be flanked by infantry of the 3rd British and 2nd Canadian Divisions.

Montgomery's orders to his commanders were full of the 'old boy' phrases he made famous during the Western Desert campaign. He exhorted them to engage the German armour and 'write it down'—to spread alarm and despondency and discover 'the form'. To really 'hit them for six' and generally 'crack about as the situation demands'. Monty always seemed to give the impression that one was off for a day's duck shooting, but with Operation Goodwood it would be a fair question to ask, 'Whose turn to be the ducks?'

The Army Film Unit's Commanding Officer, Major Hugh Stewart, had no doubts about this being a major tank battle, giving it saturation coverage with an overall emphasis on cine film. The latter decision was a wise one either way for, as the code-name indicated, Monty had high hopes that it would develop into a race. The fact that it did not, does not detract in any way from Stewart's judgement that the sheer weight of three armoured divisions tangling with a Panzer or two would make good newsreel material. So we had Palmer and Jones (now recovered from Robbo's death) with the Guards, Smales and McCardle with the Seventh, Laws and myself with the 11th, and the rest of the unit strategically placed with elements of the 3rd Division right back down to Rear Echelon. Officers had to 'swan' between the whole set-up and maintain the necessary liaison.

'Hoppy' Hopkins—what else?—a cheerful Cockney RASC driver, who was designated to George Laws and myself, drove us in the Jeep to 11th Armoured early on the evening of July 17. The familiar sight of the black charging bull—the divisional insignia—was a heartening one for we had formed a bond with this unit during the Epsom 'do' at the back end of June.

*   *   *

Epsom was a bold attempt by Montgomery to make good his promise of capturing the city of Caen on the first day. Therefore, General O'Connor, a successful leader from the Desert Campaign, was chosen to thrust the British 8th Corps in a flanking drive towards the River Odon. The 15th Scottish Division led the attack, closely supported by the 11th Armoured (I had been whisked very rapidly from my now comfortable relationship with the Commandos, into my first encounter with a tank battle, and I was grateful to see the bespectacled face of George Laws, just returned from Pinewood with a new camera), and elements of the 43rd Wessex Division.

Although I was not aware of it at the time, our immediate opposition was the 12th SS Panzer Group, and the Scots were taking a bit of a beating. The armour of the 11th was immediately pushed forward (it was their first action), and after

From the start of the Goodwood fiasco I was happy indeed to be paired with George Laws. Apart from a slightly up-beat sense of humour, he was a steadying factor in my continued existence.

some bitter exchanges, we reached the River Odon. To me, it was just another river (at this point, I hadn't familiarised myself with the useful material benefits of the map truck, nor had I introduced myself to the Intelligence Officer). In fact, this had been such a hastily put together 'do', that we had not met 'Pip' Roberts either. This was to come later. So, together with the bad weather, all the physical conditions of a lousy cold, and the post-reaction to Norman's death, I must confess that, if it hadn't been for the warm support of George Laws, I was ready to chuck it and seek the refuge of the nearest Medical Officer.

Fortunately, or otherwise, and depending on which side of the fence you were sitting, the Germans had already begun an offensive of their own. No less than the 2nd, 9th and 10th SS Panzers were pushing their armour on a direct collision course with our own thrust. I certainly have vivid recollections of the moment of impact. We had left the Jeep with Hoppy (our first introduction to him, and our mutual impression was—as Cockney as the Old Kent Road, and a fondness for chain-smoking which made him look like a compressed industrial area), and we were crawling through a ruined house, to where a backed-up Sherman was blasting off a steady flow of shells. We wriggled the last few feet until we saw at least two other tanks do likewise, then stood up against a tottering wall. The noise made talk impossible, but George indicated he was going to try and get nearer the third tank. I nodded—my eardrums were popping, and for the moment my cold symptoms had vanished—and George headed for a hole in the wall—when the firing abruptly halted, and so did George.

Our ears re-tuned, and we now heard a lot of yelling and shouting. I screwed the dust out of my eyes and looked across the cluttered wreckage. A small group of infantry, hump-backed with the weight of wounded, were tottering towards the tanks and shouting, 'Tigers!—TIGERS!—gimme a hand mates—hordes of fuckin' Tigers!—come—coming this way', and they collapsed in a heap behind the nearby tank. From there it was just a blur of speeded-up action. George got his camera running on the infantry boys, who were pulling field-dressings from the pockets of the wounded and making hasty bandages and tourniquets. I raced

The 7th Armoured Division, still known as the Desert Rats, assemble their tanks for the start of the Goodwood tank battle.

to the head of the tank and got a quick shot of the commander heaving himself out of the turret and running round to the infantry group.

There was a lot of garbled shouting, until the tank commander pulled a map from his blouse, the shouting died to a more coherent argument with a great deal of pointing to the south of their position. The tank commander stopped the flow of words with a gesture and turned his head back to the tank, 'Hey, Smudger—Smudger' he yelled at the empty turret, and a sooty face and shoulders suddenly popped up. 'Smudger—get on the RT [radio-telephone], an' tell the others to get back to base—then alert base, we have enemy in armoured strength attacking from . . . ', and he reeled off a map reference. Then he turned to the infantry, 'Get your wounded—how many—oh, Christ—three—right, the three wounded on the back . . . ', he thumbed at the tank, ' . . . and one other an' try hold 'em on—right?' They accomplished this in double-quick time, and the commander scrambled into his turret, gave a last look to see whether everyone was aboard and holding on, and the tank churned away through the rubble, with George calmly 'shooting' off the end of his film.

We turned and started back to the Jeep, the four remaining infantry going with us and giving us funny looks. 'Hey', ventured one, 'what the hell are you— photy-graphers?—we'll be in the papers—will we?' He turned to one of his mates: 'See Joe—your photy in the noospapers—what d'you think of that?' But Joe couldn't care less—he had that glazed look in his eyes that indicated the first sign of 'battle shock'. As they linked arms with him, we offered a lift if they could hang on, but they said no. 'Our mate's a bit sick—we'll be OK—we haven't far to go—I think', and with a thumbs-up they made their way across a field and out of view. I'll never know if they ever made it.

Just before Hoppy started the Jeep we heard the long, drawn-out singing sound that came from heavy artillery, and the resounding crash of shells hitting somewhere in the area we had just left. The Jeep swung away in a hurry and we raced back to our base HQ, with George advising me on how I should treat my cold. My cold symptoms had long gone. The shakes I now had were the reactions to the game of war I had seen, and I wondered at George's almost indifference to the scenes we had just witnessed. In fact, I was very relieved when we got back to HQ, to be told that 'Epsom' was finished, as far as we were concerned. Hugh Stewart was using other cameramen for the finale.

*   *   *

Thus, having 'bitten the bullet' on a major tank battle, I realised that too many of those were going to play hell with my mental stability unless I made some firm contacts with someone who had read the bottom line. Being pushed into the deep end might be all very well for some people, but I wanted to sleep happy at nights! So, recalling the co-operation I had received from the Intelligence Officer with the Commandos, I decided to approach the IO of the 11th Armoured Division, and was pleasantly surprised to be received with the attention usually bestowed on visiting Commanders. Mind you, it was also the first time I had flashed my SHAEF (Supreme Headquarters of Allied Expeditionary Forces) pass signed by General Eisenhower to an officer and I've no doubt that it helped to fill in the unspoken words.

As it happened—and despite his very Oxford—or could it be Cambridge—accent, he was to be one of the most helpful officers of the 11th Armoured that I mixed with. As soon as he realised my problem, he arranged for both George and myself to meet the Commanding Officer. General 'Pip' Roberts was the Commander—a most likeable but tough little man who had learned a few tricks in the Western Desert. He had also taken the trouble to find out what the Army Film Unit was all about and we were assured of every co-operation that he could muster. This meant we had privileged access to the map truck, a large pantechnicon with inner walls covered by maps, photographs and other illustrations giving precise details of the area now in use. Although Very Top Secret, such Commanders as Roberts never hesitated to allow the Army Film Unit to make use of this heavily guarded vehicle. After a short briefing within the hallowed walls, we were then issued with copies of the maps; this was usually done on a daily basis, thus keeping us well informed as to the flow of events.

The first stage of Goodwood was to get across the Orne Canal at the now named Pegasus Bridge, which had been bolstered with the addition of two Bailey bridges and named by someone with a strong affection for England's capital: London, Piccadilly and Euston. They were certainly about to live up to their names for traffic congestion. The obvious flaw was, of course, that the enemy had a very precise range of the area.

And he knew we were coming.

There was no moon that night and you could cut the darkness with a knife. The Germans used heavy artillery.

With the 11th Armoured in the lead, we began to make the dash across the bridges in twos and threes, trying to guess the opportune moment between shell-bursts. Incredibly, vehicles and tanks passed over the three bridges at the rate of between 150 and 200 vehicles an hour for each bridge. But it was as hairy as hell. How Hoppy kept cool, wedged between two Shermans, I will never know. I soon found there is no such thing as an opportune moment as we trundled across 50 miles of bridge with crashing shells all around and I kept pleading for the tank right ahead to move, move, move. Then suddenly, we were off the bridge and moving slightly upwards across open country. I sighed with relief, but I sighed too soon, for without warning the whole area was as brilliant as daylight. The Germans had fired dozens of magnesium flares and the jumble of tanks was clearly defined. I could see the tanks all around. their squat shapes decorated with additional bogie wheels, spare tracks and rolls of barbed wire. This, no doubt, gave the crews a feeling of extra protection but in that brief illumination I felt as naked as Lady Godiva.

Hoppy still appeared quite unperturbed, although his sideways look at George and me was a bit lopsided, but he used the light from the flares to pick out the pennant of the Command tank and homed on to it like a honey-pot. After a brief discussion with an Intelligence Officer, Hoppy somehow found his way to drop George with the Royal Tank Regiment and myself with the Fife and Forfars, then turned the Jeep around, gave us a two-fingered salute and vanished into the night. I wondered at his apparent coolness and tried to conjure up the method he would use to get *back* across those bridges in the face of three tank divisions. But then, I would never cease to be amazed at Hoppy's abilities. A great little Cockney.

There is nothing like total darkness for dark thoughts. Since the shelling had ceased and the squadrons assembled, I was now in proud possession of a scout car loaned to me by 'Pip' Roberts, and with its two-man crew we were now huddled

Below *Myself (left), with the crew of General 'Pip' Roberts' personal scout car. After a brief use, I gave it back. There is only one way to film a tank battle—on your own two flat feet. This I did until the end of the war.* **Above right** *Tank crews and infantry watch as the RAF lay their carpet of fragmentation bombs, before the tank assault.* **Right** *The smoke, flames and dust caused by the RAF bombardment.* **Below right** *Shermans of the 11th Armoured Division on the Goodwood start-line.*

under the wing of one of the many crashed gliders which had preceded our arrival on D-Day. Conversation was practically nil and we left the scout car only to take a pee or have a smoke in the shell of a shattered Horsa. I suppose we all had our own private thoughts of what the dawn would bring and we chose to remain silent through the hot, dark night. To paraphrase Tolstoy, our most powerful weapon during the long wait was the weapon of ignorance, and it was just as well.

The Germans had three infantry divisions of 86 Korps, plus the 21st and 1st Panzers with around 230 tanks, about half of which were the formidable Tigers and Panthers. In addition, there were nearly 400 pieces of artillery, from the well dug-in 88s to free-wheeling SPs and batteries of the terrifying Nebelwerfers. This curtain of very penetrating steel had been organised to a depth of about ten miles. How much of this was known to Montgomery is difficult to tell, but tactically the whole object of Goodwood was to draw as much of the enemy's firepower as possible into the British sector and allow the Americans to revitalise their own areas. Monty, too, felt that he also had a few more aces up his sleeve which he could lay on the table come the dawn and shout 'nap'. These aces were the overwhelming air support of 4,500 Allied aircraft and the powerful heavy guns of the naval ships *Roberts, Enterprise* and *Mauritius*. Together, they were to lay a 7,000-ton carpet of hurtling and plunging steel upon which Monty hoped his armour would 'crack about'. So finely had this been planned that, in consultation with Air-Marshal Leigh-Mallory, the bombers had been directed to use only fragmentation bombs over the area to be used by the armour.

Very slowly, reluctantly, the hard darkness began to lighten, until I became aware that I was now able to see, rather than feel, the vast array of tanks around me. Nervously I checked my camera—yes, I had a fresh roll of Kodak Super XX—and made sure I was at a wide aperture. At 5.45 the skies began to rumble as the heavy bombers started to arrive from their English bases, and with dawn now rapidly pulling aside its curtain, all eyes were turned upwards to watch this stupendous sight of Allied air power. Tank crews jumped to the ground and cheered madly. All the pent-up emotions of the long dark night burst forth. Tons of hardware poured from the sky and the explosions created a billowing wall of smoke, fire and dust. I had my camera running now, but the aircraft were just tiny blobs until one, and then two, were hit, plunging towards the ground in flames and vanishing behind the curtain. The heaviest attack lasted nearly an hour, then there was a pause and the smoke began to disperse in the gap ahead. Then the medium bombers came in with their fragmentation bombs—deadly stuff if placed correctly—and they had no sooner completed their run when the long drawn-out whines from the sea indicated that the 15-inch and 6-inch guns of the three naval ships were doing their stuff.

It was all very impressive, but nearly impossible to capture on film with the

Top left *A camouflaged Sherman of the 3rd RTRs, crossing the Caen-Vimont railway line early on July 18.* **Above left** *Guards Armoured Division armour is directed by Military Police during the Goodwood push. MPs were key-men during any battle—they taped routes, placed indication boards and directed a route as UP or DOWN.* **Left** *The initial assault destroyed large numbers of enemy tanks. This is a Panzer IV near Emieville.*

hand cameras we were using. Nevertheless, our spirits were high, and as the lead tanks of 11th Armoured set off at 7.45, I looked forward to getting some closer material of what must be a scene of devastation up ahead. After about an hour of spine-shattering movement in the scout car—the driver was feeling a bit skittish and showed his skills of driving by hitting every ditch and pothole at maximum speed—I declared enough and started off on foot. This way, I found, was to be my 'modus operandi' for all future tank assignments—wearing, as I did, my green Commando beret I was soon identified by the tank crews of the 29th Armoured Brigade. I would very quickly run ahead of any tank—they were only doing about three or four mph across country—and put myself in view of the driver peering through his visor, and give him a quick two-finger exercise, let him see the camera and then point to the ass-end of his tank. Over a period, the message soon became clear: 'Don't for chrissake back up, I'm right behind'. When dealing with Churchill tanks, this was simplified by the use of a direct 'phone plugged into the tanks' rear hulls—an extra no driver should ever be without when some dumb cameraman chooses to follow on foot!

I felt exhilarated; intoxicated almost, as the armour began to move through the gap created by the bombardment. There had been nothing in the way of a reply from the enemy and our hopes ran high. By mid-morning we had reached the railway crossing at Demouville and it was here that I got some of my best cine material. Part of the railway station was burning fiercely and it made a good backdrop as the tanks reared up the tiny embankment and teetered across the tracks. There was one anxious moment when someone declared there *could* be an 88 somewhere along that dead straight track of railway line. If there had been, it could easily pick off the tanks as they crossed in single file. Progress was still good and by early afternoon the 11th was in the area of Tilly Le Campagne and La Hogue, the Guards at Cagny and Cheville, with the 7th slowed down by traffic congestion between Cuverville and Demouville.

Then the enemy recovered his breath and suddenly several shades of hell were let loose. Six Tiger tanks very methodically began to pick off the leading tanks of the Guards Armoured and on the railway embankment leading to Bras and Hubert-Folie, a group of Panthers from the 1st SS started to hit the tanks of the 11th Armoured. Very soon scores of Shermans were 'brewing up', most of their crews dying in their flaming coffins. By this time, my own sang-froid had taken a bit of a beating as well. Gone was my early morning enthusiasm, but I continued to trail the tanks, sometimes getting yelled instructions from tank commanders. I could sense they were scared too; this was a helluva sight different to exercises on Salisbury Plain. This was killing-ground. Once I was close enough to one tank that got hit on its offside track; it was moving slowly when it happened and it spun on the other track on impact, the severed track peeling off its bogies, twisting and writhing like a huge metallic snake, the jagged edges swinging upwards and backwards, taking the turret and its occupant with its momentum. It happened so fast, not a scream or a yell emerged from the tank man and I raised my camera when it was all over.

With the coming of nightfall, the remains of the 29th Armoured Brigade went

Above *A rare shot of a Sherman 'Firefly' during Goodwood. If we had had more of these 17-pounders on our tanks, I feel sure the Goodwood battle would have had a different finish.* **Below** *Fred Palmer and Bob Jones, one of the best teams under Stewart's command, filmed the Goodwood tank battle, riding the backs of Cromwell tanks. But during enemy 'stonks', they often found themselves hugging the sides of tanks for protection, whilst the tank crews sat it out under closed hatches!*

into laager and the costs were added up. The 11th Armoured Division, having spearheaded the attack, had taken the brunt of the opposition, but numerous records give different totals as large numbers of tanks were recovered during the hours of darkness, and were fighting fit the next day. Chester Wilmot, in *Struggle for Europe,* gave an overall total of 521 tanks destroyed on July 18 with the 11th Armoured's share as 336. The conclusion from that being either the 11th were overstrength at the kick-off, or they declared a minus total at the end of the day. My own guess is that the 11th lost about 125, the Guards between 50 and 60, and the 7th about 40. Not all were write-offs and the recovery sections had a busy night knocking a large number back into shape.

The Army Film Unit was able to declare a good day's work with Eddie Smales turning in a fantastic 1,370 feet of film. In all, the footage totalled over 6,000 feet of exposed film for Day One of Goodwood. Fred Palmer and Bob Jones had a hairy time as they took their chances and their pictures riding piggy-back on a

Above *Cromwells kicking up the dust during Goodwood, before the rains came.* **Right** *Flail-tanks of the 79th Armoured Division during the Goodwood assault.*

Cromwell tank. It took a lot of courage to cling to this roaring, belching thing with 88s punching out this most deadly and penetrating shell—and shoot film at the same time. No doubt the enemy fire was completely drowned by the noise of the Cromwell itself but, even when they halted and clambered off to unscrew their legs, Bob Jones, who was having a bit of camera trouble, very calmly spread his black changing-bag on the grass and became absolutely immersed in what his hands were doing with the mechanism of his camera.

Hugh Stewart, never one to be left out of the action, went along with Sergeant Connolly and the 3rd Division. Connolly was built like a 3-ton truck with hands the size of dinner plates, and the De Vry camera appeared much like a toy in them. He shot nearly 600 feet of film that first day, but Hugh Stewart had the slight problem of finding where Connolly kept his film, for he never had it on his person. As soon as one roll of film was exposed, Connolly would hesitate and pat his pockets, then a slow beam would encircle his massive features and he would answer to Stewart's uplifted eyebrows that he had stashed his film back in the ration truck. Whilst his Commanding Officer remained to shoot off some still photos, Connolly would amble to where the ration truck was located, stuff himself with food he had hidden then grab his film and get back into the action. To say the least, Stewart was mildly annoyed when he found out, although for Connolly, it was just a question of keeping the priorities on an even balance. Like I said, he was a big man and needed lots of nourishment.

This forbearance on Major Stewart's part should not be misinterpreted, for Connolly's actions could easily have been seen in quite a different light. Stewart had learned a great deal during the Tunisian campaign and his administration in

Europe was as light as a soufflé. He had studied his team and rightly assessed that no two could be alike in character, but he could implement the Pinewood training—most of which was his idea anyway—with the use of a light rein, yet adroitly encouraging any choice of movement used by one or a group of cameramen—provided they produced results. It was this kind of thinking that made No 5 AFPS the most successful of any in the Army Film Unit. There will be many members of other sections who will beg to differ, but there was no other campaign as tough as the European Campaign. No doubt they will argue that one also.

The weather next day gave a hint of what was to come. Heavily overcast with a hint of rain, and not the best light in which to work. Whilst the recovery units were doing their restoration job on the armour, it was mostly a day for the infantry of the 3rd Division who kept hacking away at Troarn. Around four o'clock in the afternoon the 11th launched another attack and the 3rd RTR managed to get into Bras, despite sustaining very heavy losses of tanks. They had kicked off their attack with about 65 tanks, and by the time they got to Bras they were down to less than a dozen. With the atmosphere choked with dust and the heavy overcast, George Laws had a hard time getting through 200 feet of film. Like myself, George had the use of a scout car belonging to Colonel Silvertop of the RTR, and he also had to endure the confinement of such a small vehicle. He was grateful for it at one stage when they came under some heavy Spandau fire, and he moved from an exposed filming position to a closed-up, hatches-down emplacement in nothing flat. The heavy bullets raked the side of the car so noisily the driver promptly snapped his visor closed and in his mind's eye aimed the vehicle for a clump of hedgerow, then promptly drove into a ditch. Now, George, who wears glasses and is slight in stature, gives the impression that he would be more at home sitting with his feet up, drinking hot milk and wondering if he had locked the back door. No chance; he is as tough as old boots. So he unhatched and jumped out, had a look and decided he needed a tow. The first tank he approached already had its hatch opened and the tank commander was looking at him as though he was crazy. When George asked him for a tow, the commander ripped off a few choice words to the effect that he wasn't getting out of his tank with all that hard stuff flying about, but if he cared to untangle that roll of cable at the back and hitch up he would gladly do so. Thumbing his glasses firmly into position, George, with a resigned sigh, did as he was directed and the scout car was soon back on its four wheels. First giving the tank commander a nasty look and the darkening sky another one, he got back into the scout car and drove into Bras.

At dawn on July 20, the 7th Armoured Division made its second attack on Bourgebous and found to their surprise that the enemy had abandoned the place. There was still a great deal of German armour in the area, mostly of the 1st SS Panzer Group, and the recently arrived 2nd Panzer Division, in all well over a hundred tanks and it is debatable if the now well-flogged Shermans of 8 Corps could have endured further hammering. Mother nature was the deciding factor when the skies opened up and heavy rain turned the tortured ground into a sea of mud. The 2nd Canadian Division had just launched an attack on the Verrières ridge held by the 272nd Infantry Division, but the rain was so torrential that all movement on both sides just stopped. Tanks glued themselves to the stinking morass and the infantry had to leave trenches and bomb craters for fear of drowning. Goodwood just expired like a spent match, with Monty accepting the fact that 'you couldn't crack about in weather like this—could you old chap?'

Crack about!—in less than two hours we could scarcely move about. Never have so many humans found themselves up to their chin-straps in a goo-goo sludge of unrequited hopes in such a short time since the Great Flood. A line from Song of Solomon sayeth 'Many waters cannot quench love, neither can floods drown it'—but it sure as hell swamped enthusiasm for further action. With all the makings of a 'snafu', I began to hump my way down the route sign indicating Rear Echelon and came across George Laws doing likewise. He was scraping wodges of mud from his glasses, and the rest of him looked as though he was trying for a new battledress. I didn't comment, but just squashed into line with him and, before we had gone half a mile, we saw a Jeep approaching, mostly in a series of sideways movements. By all that was holy, it was our driver Hoppy, also mud-bespattered but grinning like a Cheshire miaow. George said he would drive; he also said a lot of other things, but it boiled down to one basic, he wanted a bath—and fast. So we settled in and hoped for the best. Once we got on to a travesty of a road, he just belted past lines of Shermans, slithering close to ditches and rapping a few backsides of equally unhappy tank crews who happened to choose that moment to inspect—or rather, look for the tracks of their tanks. We made it all right and George, shedding his mud-stiffened clothes as he headed for the bathroom, was heard to mutter something about depositing said clothing in some QM's physical parts. I settled for a couple of large cognacs and waited my turn for the bath.

Chapter 11

I don't give a damn what the history books say, but the Battle of the Falaise Gap was a balls-up from start to finish. By the end of July, the Allied bridgehead in Normandy had, with relentless progression, extended their positions and increased their operational strength in overwhelming numbers with the 1st Canadian Army, the 2nd British Army and the 1st and 3rd United States Armies, so that the area was bursting at its seams and positively screaming for a breakout. Naturally, the Germans were only too well aware of this situation, and their Generals were equally aware of their own deficiencies. Their losses had far exceeded the replacements and, although Hitler was stamping around and demanding that his commanders fight a war of attrition, von Rundstedt and Rommel realised that the 'old man' was piddling against the wind—again. Von Rundstedt had actually suggested a major withdrawal, and got the proverbial bullet, thus being replaced by von Kluge who, after a few days in the field, soon arrived at the same conclusion. From his map, he was able to see that the US forces had begun a wide enveloping sweep that was rapidly closing the back door. Von Rundstedt had been right, and von Kluge very quickly informed Hitler of the situation, then sat back to check his cyanide pills.

But there was no way that Der Führer could be wrong—wasn't he the Commander in Chief of all Germany's Armed Forces?—so why not counter-attack? Thus 'Operation Liege' was born. Intention? Reseal the US Forces within the Cotentin peninsula by breaching the gap at Avranches. Mein Gott, he fumed, could anything be more simple! Coincidental or not (Ultra at Bletchley Park were reading the German Enigma code signals loud and clear), Montgomery was in the middle of putting his own super-plan in order. It read in clear, 'destroy the enemy west of Seine and north of the Loire rivers', and Monty rarely fumed. His message also made the point that it would be frightfully naughty if the Hun were to reach the rivers and escape. With quiet assurance he only asked for the total annihilation of the German Army in the West!

Ready or not, von Kluge dropped the flag at midnight on August 6-7, and the attack moved forward, with Panzer divisions and detachments going straight over the start-line, with a bare halt for fuel, after long and hairy journeys from various parts of France, thus putting Montgomery's forces on a red alert defensive footing, with the other foot still under the blankets. The Battle of the Falaise Gap had begun. The first strike by the enemy hit Mortain in the American sector, and

A pause for humour and fun; two qualities which were sadly lacking during Goodwood. Taken in Caumont, George and I try to forget there is a Falaise Gap coming up.

part of the 30th US Division was dislodged and the town recaptured. As 8 Corps area was adjacent to that of the Americans, this was the first indication to AFPU—although we had been alerted regarding Monty's attack—and this effectively screwed up the initial plans to disperse cameramen to their own operational 'jump-off' points.

George and I had been moving forward with the 11th Armoured Division on a preordained line. Caumont—Le Beny Bocage—Vire, and up to Beny Bocage it had been a pleasant little romp, giving us our first experience of a liberation. The locals swarmed the streets, climbing on to the backs of the tanks and invading our Jeep. It was cheerful film-making and we didn't mind one bit as the female population hung around our necks smothering us with kisses. It was great therapy for battle jitters, and I let my film and adrenalin run to their high-water marks. After much passing of the bottle we decided that was enough for one day and looked around for some place to kip. Oh, we had plenty of invitations from both sexes of the happy population, but as I mentally tagged the females to be a shade over-enthusiastic, and the families bursting to tell us how it had been under German occupation, I reckoned that either side of the coin would add up to an all-night session, and with the rigours of the day plus one helluva intake of cognac, all I wanted was a good night's sleep. So it came down to the usual farmhouse barn, some distance from the 'knees-up-Mother-Brown' caper going on in town, and we just rolled out our bedding and literally 'hit the hay'.

When I woke at daylight, George was already up and moving away from a window with his finger stuck to his lips. Knowing that George never makes 'shushing' movements for no good reason, I edged forward and looked cautiously out of the window. In the field outside was a German Panther tank with its crew going through the motions of packing up and moving off. Luckily, we had taken our usual precaution of running the Jeep into a stall and covering it with straw. We had been using barns for some time now, and we'd had stuff nicked before. But it was a chilling thought that we had shared our nocturnal bliss with the enemy only a few yards away, and I must admit it made me wonder just how far away the Germans were. I was relieved when the Panther clattered off, and although we had a few chuckles, I could see that George, too, was giving the incident some serious thought.

But what happened next day was entirely our own fault. We got back on to the main road where the traffic was heavy and the warm air—thick with the fumes from passing tanks and troop carriers—made the open Jeep bloody uncomfortable. We noted that most of the traffic was from the 11th Armoured and *assumed* that the previous day's briefing still was that Vire would be the next town on our advance line, where we would link up with an infantry unit who had thoroughly mopped it up. So, to get away from the slow-moving traffic, creating its own noxious brand of chemical-warfare, we decided to take a few back-doubles around Beny Bocage, and with George, who was a damn good map-reader, giving 'left here a bit, then right and right again' instructions, we eventually hit a cross-roads with a decrepit old sign pointing the way to Vire.

It was one of those long, seemingly never-ending French roads, which soon has you nodding off in the heat of the day, with Hoppy making his usual comments

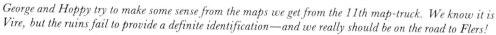

George and Hoppy try to make some sense from the maps we get from the 11th map-truck. We know it is Vire, but the ruins fail to provide a definite identification—and we really should be on the road to Flers!

that 'it's all very well for you buggers, but—' and that's about as far as he got, when there came two separate 'whoosh—whooshs' over our heads, that soon jolted us wide awake. The three of us had been around long enough to realise what that was. German 88s! Our immediate reactions would have got us jobs with Barnum's Circus no bother. Like a perfectly trained trio of acrobats, we took a header over the side of the moving Jeep and rolled into the ditch—our thoughts of 'mined verges' could just hang about! As we popped a careful head over the side of the ditch, we watched, fascinated, our poor Willy's Jeep continue for a short distance then, realising it had suddenly been bereft of ownership, decided it must be part of the general plan, and plonked itself in the same ditch about 50 yards away. Sure as hell, I thought, that machine has a mind of its own. We waited a bit to catch our breath, then turned and looked at each other, contemplating who would ask the obvious question. It was real nice in that ditch—the sun pleasant and warm—and the birds had begun to twitter again. Then Hoppy voiced the vexing question, 'Who ever slung those milk-churns at us ain't too friendly—and the bloody Jeep ain't gonna come to us—let's stick to the ditch and go heave it out'. It was the longest statement I'd heard from him for many a long day, and the hell of it was, he was right in both assumptions. It was too bloody easy, and we were soon racing back the way we had come—Hoppy whistling off tune—George polishing his glasses—and me scraping the dirt from my finger nails—an air of nonchalance that you could have cut with a—well—an 88 for instance, that didn't prevent the hair on the back of my head twitching a little.

My equilibrium didn't return until we were playing footsie with the command tank of the 11th Armoured, and at the first halt we both made a dash for the map truck to find out what had happened. The situation map of the day and the information given to us by the Intelligence Officer, told us that our escapade had occurred during a little exchange of real estate, and at that particular moment the 47th Panzer Korps had taken over the mortgage, but if we cared to return to the area we could probably cadge a good, stiff bourbon from the 29th US Division, who were now in possession! I had always been impressed by the amount of first-rate information one could gather by a close inspection of the Top Secret communiques available in the 11th Armoured Division's map-truck, and I was eternally grateful to 'Pip' Roberts, whose command it was, for allowing us this freedom of access which, I must point out, was limited to his own section commanders. After the Vire fiasco, I promised myself to use it more often and curb my restless temperament to 'do my own thing'.

As I studied the maps and up-dated signals I tried to evaluate the pattern of the battle to date. Clearly the Germans were taking a thrashing and the Canadian Army were doing the thumping with the help of the 51st Highland Infantry Division, although they had the bad luck to be on the wrong end of a US 8th Air Force bombing run. Furthermore, the Yanks in the south, although they were creating merry hell with the Panzer formations of the German 7th Army, were racing forward in their 'F— you Jack', nose-to-tail technique, allowing the RAF Typhoons and USAAF Thunderbolts to protect their flanks. But the gold medal goes to that inimitable Lone Ranger of the US Army, George Smith Patton and his 3rd Army, currently belting towards Le Mans. Now, a wide-sweeping right hook, was tactically correct and necessary, to help close the gap which the overall pincer movement was hoping to achieve, but this was just a mite far south. But Patton reckoned the roads were better and faster, and hell, he was bound to hit the enemy somewhere, and if it came as a surprise to either side, that was OK with Georgie boy. As a precaution, he was maintaining a strict radio silence with his boss, Omar Bradley, and it had nothing to do with security, he just didn't want HQ yelling at him, 'Hey Patton, hang about a bit, you're gonna have to turn north pretty soon'. This was not all guesswork back at Signals HQ—the 'Patton method' was fairly predictable, and you could be sure of one thing, Bradley was no fool.

Fascinating and heady stuff, I thought, when the Intelligence Officer re-entered the map-truck with a fresh batch of signals and maps, and began pinning them up in a series of overlays. 'Come on, out you lot—we're moving'. 'Where', I asked, and he thrust a couple of maps into my hands. 'Flers', he said, 'and this time stay with the column'—then he paused, and with a half-cocked grin, 'Maybe you'd like to take the lead—as a couple of recce scouts?' We passed up this sardonic suggestion and headed for our Jeep.

That simple statement declaring our intention to drive to Flers must surely rate as one of the *under-statements* of the campaign. As it involved the entire British 2nd Army, with all related divisions having different objectives, we were to be a small cog in the relentlessly crushing wheel of three tank divisions, several infantry divisions, and the might of the Allied air forces.

As with the Americans in the south, the northern section of the giant pincer had already taken shape with the Canadian First Army's attempt to capture Falaise, and the operation, named 'Totalize' was to be made in three phases: first, take out Fontenay le Marmion and La Hogue, second, ditto with Hautmesnil and St Sylvian, and third, give the Canadian armour a free hand to punch holes where they could. The first was to be achieved by the Canadian 2nd Armoured Brigade and 2nd Infantry Division on the right with the British 3rd Armoured Brigade and 51st Highland Division on the left. In the second phase* the Canadian 4th Division was to pass through the 2nd Division while the 4th Armoured Brigade captured high ground at points 180, 198 and 200 some three miles further on. The Polish Armoured Division on the left was to make a similar advance. Army Film Unit cameramen would be working with the British elements, but the Canadians had their own film unit, and I assumed the Poles had the same. Lieutenant Tony Keyes had trained a bunch of them back at Pinewood for just this eventuality.

The night assault, together with a tremendous 'stonk' by 1,000 RAF bombers, and the thrust achieved most of its objectives, but a second assault in daylight was less fortunate, inasmuch that the US 8th Air Force, carrying out a support attack, inflicted more casualities on the 51st Highland Division than did the Germans,

*Information based on *Caen, The Brutal Battle and Break-out from Normandy* by Henry Maul published by David & Charles.

and the Canadians failed to take Falaise. Thus it came to pass that George, Hoppy and myself got our Jeep wedged one down from the command tank as the 11th Armoured pushed on towards Tinchebray, our first watering-hole before moving on to Flers. But if we thought it was going to be a cake-walk, we were sadly amiss. The 11th Para Korps and a battle group from the Panzer Lehr Division were 'swanning' the area, but with the Guards Armoured Division moving on a parallel line towards Vassy, just north of the 11th Armoured's advance, they had to strike in both directions or be trapped in their own little pocket.

Suddenly there were some god-awful explosions up ahead and the column came to a halt. Now you could hear the pattern of the shoot-out that was taking place, and I winced at the unmistakable ker-r-r-lunk of 88s penetrating the hulls of the Shermans. I didn't like it much, but a job was a job, so we pulled out of line and cautiously poked the Jeep forward, passing tanks whose commanders were straining to see ahead with their binoculars. Very slowly now—from tank to tank—until we came to the first with its hatches closed. That, so far as I was concerned, was Hoppy's limit—although he usually protested otherwise—and from that point it was 'shanks-pony' for George and me. By a mutual consent agreed upon some time back, we never followed one another, but, and according to the lay of the land, began our moves down opposite sides of the column.

I took to the ditch after careful inspection, but the worst I came upon was the bloodied half of a dead horse and the remains of two men, possibly farming types, because a few yards further up was the matchwood of what could have been a cart. Sad, I thought, probably early that morning they had set out on some farming chore, and we come along and in a flash send them to hell and gone. Very soon I came upon the receiving end of the ker-r-r-lunk I'd heard. I was wrong, it had been a half-track and it had been carrying about half-a-dozen men, judging by the grisly torsos strung around, and the lead tanks had zapped off in pursuit, crashing their way through the hedgerows. I could hear their MGs slamming away from the right, then the thump-thump of cannon fire. They had found the enemy. I was tempted to follow, but there was a good visual story right here, so I got my camera going and wondered where the hell George had gone.

Soon the area was swarming with infantry, their faces grim after one look at the blazing half-track, and they piled their way through the gaps in the hedges. They must have hit the enemy fast—I could tell the difference between the Sten and the Schmeisser. At that moment the petrol tank on the burning half-track blew and the concussion on my back slammed me into the ditch. I didn't see any pictures of my past life, so I guessed I was alive. A couple of infantry lads picked me up, gave me a quick going over and announced I would live. 'You're OK mate—a bit of shock—but check your pants, you might've crapped yourself', and they were gone. I flexed my back muscles a bit—painful but whole. Then in next to no time, the shooting ceased, and soon they were streaming back through the hedge—a couple of wounded carried piggy-back fashion, and I could hear the tanks returning. My camera seemed OK, so I rolled across the road to get a shot of this—my clobber *was* 'crapped', but it was only mud, oil and soot and I made a mental note that was more than enough for a new outfit at the first DID.

They came crashing through, and it looked good—more so, when a couple of figures cadging a ride were jolted off the back and hit the road with a thump. Then I quickly shut the camera off—one of them was George! His glasses had come adrift in the fall, and he didn't spot me. Besides, he was doing his best to do several things at the same time—adjust his glasses—inspect his camera—and tell the tank driver just where to go, and it was the latter that was rousing his dander—the tank and driver were long gone! I was stiff with laughter, and that revealed my presence. He saw how I was holding the camera, and the penny dropped. Very carefully he spaced out the question 'Were-you-filming-that-tank?'. I nodded, but when I saw he was on the boil again, I told him I'd switched off at the crucial moment. The boil adjusted to a simmer, then be began to question 'just where the hell were you when . . . ' which drifted away as he began to focus on my appearance—the burning wreckage and the bodies—then the knowledge penetrated. He went very quiet and reflective. George was back to earth, and he sighed. 'Guess you had a bit of trouble, huh?' I told him and he nodded quietly. 'Let's get back to the Jeep,' I nodded again and looked at my watch. At lot had happened in less than an hour. Many people had died in that short time—on a warm summer's day—driving to some village called Flers.

Meanwhile, the rest of the Army Film Unit had been very busy, and their own particular drives had been as dodgy as ours, with the assault on Mont Pincon being harsh and brutal, but an initial, though bloody victory, going to the 43rd Division when they seized the town of Ondefontaine where Sergeant Norman Midgeley and his cine colleage worked under the same precarious and vulnerable conditions that George and I had to—from their very soft-skinned Jeep, or the simple shanks-pony—and when it came to searching for snipers in Ondefontaine, that was about the best way to do it—but not to be recommended. But the job didn't come with built-in guarantees—risks had to be taken, and that was the name of the game for front-line photography. By the end of the war, our casualty rating was fairly high, and I have always been surprised that it did not escalate far beyond the final count. Much of the Pinewood training, and certainly all the advice handed on by the Western Desert and Italian campaign veterans had to be thrown out—the European Campaign was on a far larger scale—a war being fought with superior weapons against an enemy who were, more or less, on their home ground, and every inch lost was a step nearer defeat. Thus, the skills and techniques of No 5 Army Film Unit were conceived and utilised on a greater scale which reflected the self-reliance of the men involved.

As the British 2nd Army's involvement in the attempt to close the Gap ebbed and flowed, the same applied to the cameramen. Fortunately, Hugh Stewart had also become aware of the differences in the tactics that should be applied to this new style of warfare, and was allowing his cameramen to be the best judges of where to move in the rapidly changing conditions. Thus he had a steady stream of film arriving from all parts of the front, and it was all good stuff. 'Jock' Laing came up with action material of the new Challenger tanks armed with 17-

Left *Another Scot, Jock Gordon, and his partner Norman Johnston, took a big risk, when they featured a Bren gun carrier attack, using flamethrowers for the first time, during the closure of the Falaise Gap.* **Right** *Sergeant Jock Laing, was your original dour Scot, but he was a great little photographer and is seen taking action material of the new Challenger tanks.*

pounder guns, and some brief shots of the flame-throwing Bren carrier, but it was Norman Johnston and 'Jock' Gordon who got a very good sequence of this new acquisition. With the flamethrower attachments, this deadly and vicious weapon had found a good home in the nippy carriers, whose drivers had obviously been learning some new-fangled strategy. When those fiery ferrets went into action they were able to make a pot-roast of any concealed enemy positions in a matter of minutes. It was a very impressive sequence as the carriers, in line-ahead formation belched enormous jets of liquified fire into the German positions. Norman and Jock had to get real close to this action to ensure results and remained with it long enough to film the after effects. Norman admits it was bloody horrible—it was the first time he had seen humans incinerated so fast, and to be honest, he was as sick as a dog afterwards. The sequences were much praised by Pinewood, but I wonder if they really appreciated the courage and the dangers involved just to capture it on film.

The unit attached to Horrocks' 30 Corps had to operate a very hectic schedule with cameramen belting from one sector to another as Horrocks played hocus-pocus with the enemy. Whilst Midgeley had been in Ondefontaine, Bert Hardy had been doing a similar job in Montchauvet, only a few miles away, where snipers were even using burning buildings as hideaways. However, when the harassed AFPU section officers finally managed to get the message out to all the cameramen that the 30 Corps bulls-eye was to be Condé and the crossing of the River Noireau, they did a smart about-turn and prepared to home in on the target.

On the map, the German front line began to look like a bad month on a salesman's chart—more lows than highs, with the 50th and 43rd Divisions making full but bloody use of the lower bulges. Every day a few more hard-won kilometres were gained. As they neared Condé, Norman Midgeley met up with Dickie Gee

Above *This is the sort of thing Johnston and Gordon were able to get. Although the picture only shows one, there was an entire squadron of carriers fitted with this deadly weapon, and they created havoc with the enemy.* **Below** *The RAF did what they could during the Falaise Gap; keeping the sky free of the Luftwaffe. The pilot of this aircraft escaped with shock.*

who had been pushing from Vire, and when they reached the blown bridge of Pont Erambourg, where it crosses the River Noireau, they spent some time with the engineers who were erecting a Bailey bridge. They filmed this operation up to the point where 30 Corps began streaming across, hotly pursuing the tail-end of von Kluge's forces, now retreating towards Argentan. This now brought 30 Corps into a line-abreast formation with 8 Corps approaching Flers, a little way south on the D924. George and I had kept our promise to stick with the 11th Armoured, but it had been a real grind. Oh, we had seen a bit of action—more than enough to get the cameras and ourselves well and truly ingrained in the permanent dust-clouds, which was unavoidable as the tank tracks ripped the roads apart. Then there was the overpowering stench of death—from cattle to men—and by now, it didn't seem to make much difference. In this killing ground of the Falaise Gap, the methodical massacre of everything that got in the way began to taste sour, and I was in an obnoxious mood the day we got to Flers.

Despite his mild and inoffensive appearance, it was plain that George was no better off—and when George got into this sort of mood, I knew it was time for a change of something. But what? Our first sight of Flers didn't help at all— scarcely a building was left standing, and the Shermans were not hanging about, bulldozing their way through the rubble, and what had begun as a sharp left turn round a lone building still standing upright had proved to be too much bother for the tank drivers to change down to a lower gear, so they began using the front door set on the corner, and very soon had it in a condition of straight-through access. For a time this kept us happy, it made damn good pictures—but it also increased the pall of dust. I turned to George and said I was bloody thirsty. He agreed, and we tasted the warm, brackish water from our water bottles. Ker-r-r-ist!—we'd have done better draining our radiator. Although George is no tippler, I reminded him of all that lovely wine back at Beny Bocage and firmly declared that in future we carry some with us, and for once, he saw my point. But where,

Left *Well, mostly by instinct, as opposed to map-reading, we reached Flers and by now George and myself were covered in dust, and very, very thirsty!*

Right *The oldest inhabitant, a 1914-18 veteran, elected himself to be the 'town-crier', and is seen doing his stuff, whilst I (right of photo with camera) wonder how to slake my thirst. Later; after the others had disappeared, our veteran led us to a hidden cache of wine. But, I must add, he did not know!*

he asked, looking around the rubble that was Flers. The few remaining locals who had emerged to watch their property being mangled to hell, had, nevertheless, decided this was the price to be paid for 'la liberation', (and hadn't the Maquis given them that sales promotion bit—snatch a few Germans by the cobblers—help us and the Allies free our country—and the prize would be free homes for all)*, but after a few cheers and a couple of 'Vive de Gaulles' they had vanished into their burrows like moles.

One snaggle-toothed veteran of the '14-'18 War had remained—the medals on his best, but dusty jacket, jangled to prove it—and he cackled across at us, 'You want fic-fic' George gurgled, and I replied 'No fic-fic—ahh—want wine—oh hell—du vin—', then with increased confidence—'Oui, beacoup du vin'. More cackling and a shake of the head, 'Café kaput—allus kaput'. We were on three languages now and I was getting angry. A whisper from George behind me, 'Try bordello', he suggested. Snaggle-tooth must have been 80 if he was a day, but there was nothing wrong with his hearing. 'Bordello—bordello', he cackled, 'You want fic-fic'. This slick music-hall patter was beyond me, but I dipped into a pocket and produced a packet of cigarettes. He grabbed them and I said 'Oui, bordello, fic-fic'. So it was just possible, I reasoned, even a busted brothel might have the odd bottle. We walked all of 20 yards to a heap of red brick that still had a jazzy-patterned tiled ground floor, and the old so-and-so left us, happily smoking a Player's cigarette and giving us his signature tune, 'Fic-fic, fic-fic'. I'll bet he'd had some too in his lifetime—the old buzzard.

The ground floor proved negative—that's all it was, just a ground floor with a few fancy tiles—no walls, they were in the roadway—not even a dirty picture;

*The RAF had dropped hundreds of pamphlets asking the French population to give all co-operation to the Allied Armies, *suggesting* that we would give them all kinds of assistance towards their rehabilitation, but I suspect that the Maquis had printed up a few with their own catch-phrases.

George pointed downwards. Cellar? We humped some rubble and there was a swing-back flap. Light? George went into the roadway and shouted for Hoppy to bring a torch. It was cool down there—musty, damp—and Hoppy shot the beam of light round the walls. Nothing, but a pile of anthracite. But there was a shelf with jars of preserves—and a few bottles. I scrambled up the anthracite and grabbed one—empty. Another—ditto, and I angrily threw it against the far wall. Whoaa!—the anthracite was slipping under my feet and I came down with it. Hoppy turned the torch on me as I began smacking the dirt off, and George whispered gently in my ear, 'There's cases under that stuff'.

There were. About two dozen, and by the time we ferried them up to the Jeep, we were as black as niggers. But happy, and a few bottles later—very happy. Hoppy was happy—he cracked a bottle and poured it over his head. Washed himself in the stuff. We were merry all the way to the billet we had picked for the night—in one fell swoop, the promises we had made to stick to the column, literally went down the hatch!—and we staggered off, with George croaking a line from some ditty, 'You never miss the water until the well runs dry'. The way Hoppy packed the bottles into the Jeep the next morning assured me ours wouldn't run dry for some time. It didn't. It lasted all the way up into Belgium.

After that little side-step from the prearranged plan to stay close, it was partly good luck and a fervent 'thank God' for the maps we had acquired, that we managed to hit the 11th Armoured a bulls-eye, although we had to take a bit of a rocket from the Intelligence Officer, and a heftier one from Captain Evans when we reported in with our film. But the squeeze on the Germans was now so critical, and Allied forces were now becoming so intermingled on the ground, that most of the cameramen were having a helluva job finding a section HQ which never appeared to be static for more than a few hours at a time.

When I got the chance to have a look at the 'overall strategy' map in the truck, it seemed to me that the Allies were as confused as the Germans. As I was now 'off the hook' with the IO, I voiced this opinion and, although he did look down his nose, and with a touch of asperity, 'The 11th Armoured Division certainly knows where they are, and exactly where they are going—but I'm afraid some of those Yanks—well—'. 'Like old blood and guts Patton', I offered. The IO chewed his tongue, and I knew I'd overstepped my mark. 'We will not discuss personalities—' and he eased down to his old self—'and you better get out and take some photos'. The so-and-so knew where to hit me—I had always taken pains to explain that 'photographers took pictures'—I 'shot' film.

As I walked back to the Jeep, I speculated on what I'd seen on the 'overall strategy' map. We might be closing the Gap, but there had been too many lost opportunities. If it hadn't been for the tremendous efforts of the Spits and Typhoons, working closely with the Lightnings and Thunderbolts of our air forces, that Gap would be much wider. As it was, what was left of the German 7th Army was trying to link up with the 2nd SS Panzer Korps, and although they were committed to leaving all their transport, the German effort was now simply how many men they could get out. Nevertheless, the hard-working unit under Captain Derek Knight continued to film and photograph every aspect of those final days, often under the most appalling conditions, and even after the cease-fire, they were still hard at it. Therefore, today, there exists the most complete record at the Imperial War Museum, of the carnage and destruction of those days and nights of mortal terror, followed by a stampede of panic-stricken men, whose only thought was survival.

The 11th Armoured now came under the command of 30 Corps, and we advanced rapidly, overcoming pockets of fanatical paratroops who had obviously been ordered to fight to the last man. Nevertheless, we pressed on to Briouze, where we made contact with the Americans, then Ecouche. Now that 30 Corps had been enlarged, it was able to expand its front and I found that we were now 'swanning' at some speed. But the zing had gone out of the operation, and when the troops on our left reached Putanges on August 19, we heard that the Polish Armoured Division of the Canadian Army had linked up with the 5th US Corps at Chambois. The Gap was closed, but I didn't hear any cheers. A great deal of hoo-hah was made that more than 3,200 German vehicles, tanks and guns had been destroyed, and that the German Army in the West was utterly crippled, and I couldn't help but smile at the tentative use of the word 'crippled'. No one could truly say the German Army was dead, and it would be many a long day before that word could be used with confidence.

I began this chapter by stating that the Battle of the Falaise Gap was a 'balls-up', but I did so with hindsight, although during the actual campaign, there were several incidents witnessed by myself and my AFPU colleagues that could establish this statement. But obvious reasons, eg, the rules of libel, forbid such personal revelations. Thus, I will merely quote those now established by the Ultra Section based at Bletchley Park and simply known as 'Hut 3', or 'Station X'. Ultra was the most effective system for reading the enemy's mind ever employed in World War 2. By enciphering a multitude of high-level signals on their

An example of the damage and destruction caused by long-range bombardment, and the mines strewn by the Germans in our path, as the enemy evacuates and looks for a way out of the hell of Falaise.

complicated Enigma machine, the Germans thought they were invulnerable, but their system was broken by 'Station X' at Bletchley Park. Their services were a vital link—often the only link—providing information via their SLUs (Special Liaison Units working in the field), to Churchill and Army Commanders.

Take the following: Field Marshal von Kluge (Army Group 'B') sent a signal to General Eberbach of the 7th Army, ordering him to send three Panzer divisions (with which the latter was desperately defending Falaise) to Mortain, (to comply with orders from the Führer) and, although von Kluge tactically disagreed with it, ended his message with, 'the order from Hitler was unequivocal—it must be obeyed'. This was on the eve of General Simonds' famous Canadian onslaught to try to cut through the German armour guarding Falaise. If the attack had been delayed by 24 hours, the three Panzer divisions would have departed. But the Canadian attack went ahead on schedule and was stopped eight miles from its objective. This, of course, left the German troops fighting hard around Mortain, expecting the support of three more Panzer divisions which did not arrive. The resulting signals, intercepted by Ultra, which crackled between OKW, von Kluge, Eberbach and Hausser (General of the Waffen-SS), made it quite clear that the whole situation was out of control—a situation which could have been developed to the advantage of the Allies.

Later, when the Americans reached the outskirts of Argentan on the 13th, signals were sent by the 7th Army and the 5th Panzer Army warning von Kluge that they should be withdrawn immediately. The Allies knew that Eberbach's armour was virtually immobile, being short of ammunition and fuel. The Americans, at that moment, could easily close the gap. Ultra waited to hear Eberbach's report on what was expected—the battle for Argentan by the Americans. Nothing came, and it was much later they discovered that, just as General Haislip was preparing his 15th Corps to attack Argentan, he had a signal from Bradley telling him to

Left *British armour streaks from one boundary line to another, in the constant shuffle of units whilst closing the Gap at Falaise.*

Right *In completing the Gap of Falaise, British armour finds that the fleeing Germans have weakened some French bridges, never intended for the heavy traffic they endured.*

stop the offensive and assume a blocking position. Haislip had every reason to be puzzled. Even if Monty couldn't make headway from the north to close the gap, what was stopping Bradley doing it from the south? It later transpired that in the plans for Overlord, a line dividing the operational zones of the British and American forces had been drawn and it passed through Argentan!—which meant that in normal circumstances, Monty would have to give Bradley permission to cross the line! As Eisenhower was with Bradley, no doubt he had to advise Bradley to stick to the agreement until Monty suggested it, but nobody *supposed* that either of them thought that Monty would fail to do so! This wasted 24 hours. It is a great pity that Ultra's facts and figures were also destined to be ignored prior to the Arnhem operation. If they had not, an enormous waste of life could have been avoided.

On August 15, signals intercepted by Ultra told them that the 7th Army could not get in touch with von Kluge. A further signal from von Kluge's HQ informed Ultra that 7th Army had no idea where von Kluge was. Von Kluge was lost! Eventually, on the 16th, he turned up, stating he had spent the day in a ditch with a broken radio! For 25 hours von Kluge's armies had been leaderless! And it was shortly after this incident that poor old von Kluge decided that the cyanide pills had to be the answer after all. It was on the same date—the 16th—that Monty finally proposed to Bradley that they should now close the pocket by meeting half-way between Falaise and Argentan. The Canadians captured Trun on the 18th—the village suggested for the above meeting—but the Americans were only reaching Chambois, a few miles away, and the point where the Gap would be finally closed. But on the night of the 19th in heavy rain and early morning fog, thousands of trapped Germans were stealthily escaping through the Gap, and even when the fog lifted on the morning of the 20th, the Gap was still packed by the escaping enemy. Only by midnight on the 20th was the Gap finally sealed.

Chapter 12

The race to the Seine was one of the most stimulating experiences I have ever encountered. The 11th Armoured roared through Argentan, Gace, Conches and Evreux, bypassing many small pockets of resistance and the demands on the map-truck were heavy. Sometimes it would take no more than an hour to run across a single map, and when it became obvious we were about to thunder our way clean to Vernon, maps of a smaller scale were being issued.

In the early hours of August 25, we entered the agreeable town of Vernon with its many splendid apple-groves which backed on to the River Seine. These were soon taken full advantage of, although some not too choosy pickings led to a few tummy-aches. The Film Unit section soon established themselves in the local railway station, then I went off, ostensibly to get some fresh milk, although I had glimpsed a comely female tending the cows in the yonder pasture, and George said he would take the Jeep and have a look at the river. Well, everyone to his own tastes.

But of the two light-hearted missions, George's one became the more serious. He left the Jeep in a secluded back yard close to the river, took a look round this placid scene and the wooded escarpment on the far side which could have hidden

After severe difficulties, endured by most members of the Army Film Unit during the Falaise Gap story, Bert Hardy prepares a chicken dinner.

a battalion of the enemy, then turned back to the Jeep. He got within a few yards of it, when several carefully placed shots zapped off the ground and George hit the nearest cover he could find. The fact that neither he nor the Jeep had been hit soon assured him that a sniper—probably with a telescopic finder—was playing a little game with him. This conclusion was confirmed when he made another attempt to reach the Jeep with zinging shots making a neat half-circle round it. The game was played for nearly an hour and now George had his dander up—he was going to get that Jeep. Retreating along the bank and using all the cover, he managed to get back on the road and approached the now lonely-looking Jeep, on his tummy, from the sniper's blind side. He managed to crawl right up to it without any reaction, then he realised that being a left-hand drive, the Jeep's steering wheel was in full view from across the river. Nevertheless, he snaked into the vehicle and, still lying full-length on its floor, managed to pull the steering-wheel on to a full right-hand lock, reach up to the starter—Jeeps do not have ignition keys—prayed it would start first time and at the same time pushed down on the accelerator. As the engine sprang into life the Jeep shot into motion and George jumped half-way into the seat, now able to use his hands and feet. But the sniper still had the last word and managed to pump two shots into the bodywork before it reached safety. When he got back to the railway station, George was positively animated about it; the words rushing out and his eyes sparkling like gems—until the reaction hit him and he sat down with a thud and asked for some strong tea. Tea!—I thought. Trust George.

*   *   *

The Seine crossing was a hazardous one for three reasons; the first and now obvious, being complete observation from the other side, the others were wide muddy banks and a fairly stiff current towards the middle of the river. In order to compensate for the latter the initial attempt was made from up-river under a light coating of artificial mist. George and I piled into one of the assault craft and my first impression was of being hurled into a vortex. Our propellers thrashed the water and we began to crab our way into the mist with heavy fire lashing all around. The mist and the uncertain movement of the craft made it very difficult to shoot much film.

Voices screamed as other craft were hit and I had just vague impressions of boats, partially hit and unable to cope with the current, being swept away into blank nothingness. Suddenly we hit a hidden sand-bar and stuck, the racing propellers pushing us in further. George, myself and some others leapt out, immediately knee-deep in sluggy goo, and on someone's command began pushing the craft around. With a distinct slop it freed itself and vanished into the mist. If ever there was a moment of truth, that was it. We were stranded in the middle of the river, vainly trying to lift our feet from this giant glue-pot, machine-gun fire crossing our heads from both directions and in the confusion and smoke I wasn't too sure which way we were facing. George looked at me helplessly, but I was all out of suggestions. Dear God, I thought, what do we do for an encore.

Above *Infantry moving towards the banks of the River Seine, for the assault crossing under a light smoke-screen.* **Below** *One of the first boats away on the assault crossing of the Seine. Due to the strong current, the assault began up-river. But when they entered the smoke-screen (which was patchy), many were lost in the heavy current and came under withering fire from the opposite bank.*

But like in the movies, the Marines were coming. Or rather, the Engineers who were strenuously ferrying the assault troops across, now returning to pick up another load. We yelled louder than any machine-gun and the ghost of an empty craft nosed just enough in our direction for us to heave our top halves on board and let the drive of its engine unstick us from Devil's Island. How we made it to the friendly shore and back to our railway station base I will never know. But one thing was for sure, I was going to wait until the REs had completed their Class 9 bridge, now under way, before I attempted another crossing of the River Seine.

Tanks of the 8th Armoured Brigade were the first across the bridge and we worked our cameras at both ends as the armour bobbed across the light pontoons one at a time, with enemy fire still splashing the water between this and the heavier Class 40 bridge near completion alongside. One small incident sticks in my mind. I was filming on the Vernonette side of the river and a few shell bursts had hit some of the 50-odd pontoons on the smaller bridge. Some REs had been wounded but others carried on with their repairs, whilst I had taken cover under my end of the bridge. When it appeared that the firing had ceased, I was just about to move out from my cover to resume filming, when I was approached by a young Engineer, his arms locked across his middle. Briefly, I thought of the earlier effect of eating some over-green apples, then through clenched teeth he asked, 'Have you a fag, mate?'. I produced a packet and handed them to him. His arms unlocked as a hand reached out to take the packet, and I now saw a jagged and bloodied hollow where his stomach had been. He was dead before he hit the ground.

*   *   *

Further up the River Seine, the liberation of Paris was being enacted in a manner, 'très extraordinaire'. The German garrison commander, General Dietrich von Choltitz, had no intention of carrying out the gist of Hitler's last telephone query, 'Is Paris burning?'. A man of great feeling and eternal admiration for the beauty of the capital of France, he now sought a solution to surrender the city in a manner befitting an officer and a gentleman. For several days now, the French Resistance, knowing the Allies were not many miles away, were performing their own liberation movements. From roof-tops, this drama was played out; isolated groups of Germans suddenly finding themselves under small-arms fire, or troop-carriers being quickly engulfed in the flames of petrol-bombs. There was never any great strength behind these occurrences, but if any further message was required to enhance the already shaky feeling that now enveloped the troops of the German garrison, this did at least provide the necessary postscript, and in dribs and drabs the Germans were making their own evacuation. Paris was, by now, clamouring to be liberated.

In the mind of de Gaulle there was no question whatsoever who should initiate this move—General Leclerc and his 2nd Armoured Division had travelled and fought their way from the Normandy beaches for this specific occasion. The only snag was that they were still more than 100 miles away from Paris, whilst the US

Left *General de Gaulle in conference with General Leclerc, Commander of the French 2nd Armoured Division. Despite the fact that the US 5th and 3rd Armies were at the gates of Paris, de Gaulle persuaded Eisenhower to allow Leclerc's 'flying column', to enter Paris with General Gerow's 5th US Corps. Paris wanted de Gaulle; and he headed the victory march.*

Below right *Captain Roy Boulting of AFPU, was aware that the Americans were about to steal the show of the Paris liberation and, with only two Jeeps and a large Union Jack, he infiltrated his cameramen into Paris and, by carefully watching every move made by de Gaulle, managed to steal much of it back.*

1st and 3rd Armies were at the very gates. Whilst Eisenhower and de Gaulle argued the finer points of logical tactics and national pride, Leclerc sparked off the finale by hastily dispatching a flying wedge of light tanks and armoured cars—plus about 200 infantry—with orders to let nothing stop them until they entered Paris. Eisenhower capitulated, and ordered General Gerow's 5th US Corps to proceed towards the city, accompanied by Leclerc's flying column and to show it was a truly Allied force he included a small British contingent. General de Gaulle, however decided to keep his powder dry and began preparing his script for 'The Saviour of France'.

Scripts, in the true connotation of the word, were being prepared by the world's press and information services and the object of this exercise was to be the question of who got there first. Ernest Hemingway and his hard-drinking 'irregulars' tried to jump aboard the Leclerc cavalcade but were rebuffed with the admonishment, 'Buzz off you unspeakables'; not a literal translation, but my French is lousy. From that moment, Hemingway would refer to the General as 'that jerk Leclerc'.

The US Signal Corps, with their superiority in gear and other camera equipment, also produced several camera cars for 'dolly' shots. Frank Capra, who was then a Major with the Signal Corps, certainly had his priorities right. But Captain Roy Boulting of the Army Film Unit, making one of his rare appearances from Pinewood, was not to be outshone. Under his guidance he assembled a unit consisting of Captain 'Lofoten' Malindine, Lieutenant Peter Handford, Sergeants Bert *'Picture Post'* Hardy, Ernie Walters and Max Collins, the latter being fluent in French and German. All in all, a very sophisticated unit.

With a little careful juggling and use of SHAEF passes, Roy Boulting's unit made their way through the lines of the US 15th Corps then, briefly connecting with the US 20th Corps at Chartres, they eventually reached the outskirts of Rambouillet and linked up with the French who were preparing an advance on Paris early on the morning of August 24. There was considerable resistance during that day and the Film Unit section had to play tag until the forward elements of the French reached the Hotel de Ville late at night.

But the day of August 25 was the one that mattered for the Film Unit. A large Union Jack was mounted on one of their two Jeeps, whilst in the other were placed a camera and tripod. This left a roving hand-held cine camera plus two stills— a small enough unit, but adequate for the purpose Boulting had in mind. Then they homed on to the columns of the 4th Division moving steadily through the happy, screaming, hysterical Parisians towards Nôtre Dame and the Rond Point des Champs Elysées. To create the authenticity of British involvement in this rapidly developing band-wagon, the Jeep bearing the fluttering Union Jack was instructed to maintain a certain distance from the mounted camera.

It was classic liberation coverage and the small but effective unit made the most of it, doggedly ignoring the grandiose efforts by their counterparts of the US Signal Corps. When the big parade began the next day, the Film Unit, with their more manoeuvrable Jeeps, were able to maintain a plum position just ahead of de Gaulle as he walked from the main station in that memorable procession that filled every throat with an emotion that knew no bounds.

The sniper shooting from the rooftops put AFPU in an excellent position to obtain the scenes of scattering crowds, many of whom were taking refuge behind the now halted tanks. The tank commanders were in a lively mood and swung their guns towards the direction of the fire and opened up at point-blank range, chipping off corner-stones of buildings and so adding to the impression that German snipers were trying to kill de Gaulle. This, later, proved to be a wrongly assumed impression. Those responsible for the shooting were members of Joseph Darnand's 'Milice' or Militia, a French collaborator in charge of Anti-Resistance Security Forces. One exuberant tank commander was so carried away by the excitement—and no doubt recalling lectures he had been given earlier about the existence of the sinister Fifth Column—that when he espied one particularly

Above *When members of Joseph Darnand's 'Milice' or Militia (a French collaboration of the Anti-Resistance Security Forces), began shooting from the roof-tops, the French thought they were German snipers.* **Below** *During the sniping, the many Parisians who had gathered to see de Gaulle either tried to melt into the ground or took refuge behind the tanks, whose gunners added to the confusion by blasting at the nearest roof-tops!*

famous building with an equally impressive colonnade as its main feature, he halted his tank and ordered his gunner to swing his turret. With shining cognac-brimming eyes he counted the stone columns from left to right and when he reached the fifth shouted 'Fire'. Happily, he resumed his procession, satisfied that he had blasted the Fifth Column into eternity.

Meanwhile, the Film Unit were having a field day and had reached the point where they too felt like joining in the fun. But Roy Boulting was determined to screw out the film coverage to its maximum, and he laid on a small sequence at the Tomb of the Unknown Warrior, which had AFPU and a US Sergeant perform the ritual of a smart march up to the Tomb—halt—salute, hold for a count of five—a smart right about and march off. After this piece of epic footage they wrapped up the cameras and prepared to leave, but Roy Boulting was still hanging on to one of the cine cameras, and suggested that they should sign the Visitors' Book, especially as all the French brass appeared to be preparing to do likewise. In the general excitement, this was a moment of protocol which had

nearly escaped them, and only Roy Boulting had managed to follow the rapid-fire flow of French between the main body of VIPs.

Thus, hastily, but with as much dignity they could muster, each AFPU member scribbled his signature in the book, with Bert Hardy being last to do so, and just a little uncertain whether to throw up another salute or not! Boulting, with one eye on the viewfinder and the other on the top brass, made impatient signs to his Sergeants to get behind him, and not a moment to soon, as the top-ranking French officers suddenly divided, and the tall, angular figure of General de Gaulle strode firmly through their ranks and made his way to the Visitors' Book which he signed with a lengthy flourish.

Therefore, somewhere in the vaults of the Elysée Palace, there rests this historic book, whose final page for this equally historic day ends with the two named— Bert Hardy, Sergeant, followed by Charles André Joseph Marie de Gaulle, General! The full signature has, of course, to be sheer supposition, but everyone present can testify that it was indeed a lengthy signing, but immediately after the ceremony, the book, was removed, presumably as an act of 'the end of an era', or 'the beginning of a new one'. But as many ex-AFPU members, who didn't hear the story until after the war, have made much the same remark without any malice. 'Well, I guess that figures—Bert Hardy's name tapping shoulders with de Gaulle's!'

Nevertheless, this little episode must have added much sparkle to the evening's fun and games. As Ernie Walters has related to me—the fact that they appeared to be the only group of British soldiers caused great excitement wherever they appeared, and they were fêted with champagne at every turn. Where they went, he cannot remember, but the night was filled with glitter, and song, and magic. As he recalls, 'After the dust and smashed orchards of Normandy, the colourful summer dresses of the girls, trimmed with masses of red, white and blue, was a sight not to be forgotten'.

But his best story of those exciting days belongs to the post-war era. When Ernie left the Army, he decided to become a film editor, and has been involved in editing feature films ever since. He was preparing a film for MGM which was to be called *The Liquidator*, and the script called for the opening sequences to be set in Paris at the time of the Liberation. The obvious source of any suitable stock was the Imperial War Museum, and he made an appointment to see the film librarian without telling him of his previous connection with the Army Film Unit.

As he relates, 'I told him I was looking for scenes shot in Paris at the time of the Liberation, and the next thing I knew was that the records he pushed into my hands were my own hand-written dope-sheets of the period. Then, for the first time, I began watching my film of that crazy run up to the Champs-Elysées. I got so damned excited about it, that I had to force myself back to the present, and ordered up prints of this and that.

'So—*The Liquidator* eventually opened under the MGM Logo, then the title sequence sung by Shirley Bassey, followed by shots of our Jeeps going up the Champs-Elysées, with our Union Jack flying very proudly indeed! Thus, I finally got to edit my own film which I had shot as a cameraman!'

Chapter 13

After the Seine, it was Belgium or bust. We raced through Flanders, and in one crazy but heady 24-hour period the 11th Armoured Division came within a few miles of Amiens. As was his wont, Hoppy slotted our Jeep between two squadrons of tanks—a safety measure—and we had one scary moment during the night when a German aircraft dropped chandeliers of brilliant flares, momentarily blinding Hoppy as he nearly wedged the bonnet of the Jeep under the back-end of the tank ahead. The lone aircraft kept this up for some time—he must have been carrying a bundle—and the column froze. It was a heavily wooded area and we could see every tree as a potential aggressor. The tanks ahead must have had similar thoughts as we observed several gun turrets move in a half circle. I stood up in the Jeep and glanced backwards over the canopy to see what action the others were taking. Nothing. There was not a damn thing behind us. We were tail-ass Charlie.

One of the forward tank commanders approached, map in hand and indicated a fork in the road about two miles back. In the dark, the rear column must have made a boo-boo and, 'Would you nice cameramen care to nip back and have a look-see?'

'We would', George replied before I could stop him, and we did. But it was hair-tingling as we turned about into the now solid darkness and I was relieved to find after about a mile we nearly hit the lead tank, now going flat out after discovering their error. And I mean flat out, with the rest nose to tail and Hoppy did a terrific job getting the Jeep turned about before being flattened by the churning tracks.

'George', I said on the way back, 'don't volunteer will you—you know the first rule in the book—never volunteer'. 'But the man asked me', says George, 'it was an order—you can't turn a ruddy Sherman around on roads like this'. George was miffed—dead miffed at me—'Shut up', he said, 'I'm going to sleep'. And he did. Hoppy lit a cigarette. 'Good idea', he replied, 'you both shut up—I'm doing the driving and it's a long night'. I lit my pipe and stared darkly into the dark.

*　　　*　　　*

Amiens seemed pleased to see us and we had a gay, gay time with the natives going noisily berserk. Word came back by bush telegraph that Captain Leslie Evans was setting up a one-night HQ and if we would be good enough to stop by with our exposed film we would be nicely rewarded with hot baths, good food and other little goodies. I was still a bit broody about the dark night back there, but the thought of a good bath and maybe the chance to nick a bottle of whisky finally overcame my rancour and I did as was asked. I kid you not, fate is indeed a very fickle thing. If there hadn't been a jolly old liberation ring-a-ding going on back in Amiens, I would really have enjoyed the Captain's little party, and at the end, would probably have been shovelled into bed in a more or less sensible manner. That, as the saying goes today, is the way the cookie crumbles.

No messing, it wasn't a bad little 'do'. There was a good choice of booze and grub, and AFN (American Forces Network) was blasting away on the radio, with Glen Miller proving he had the best in brass. It was good to see some of the old faces and swop a whole mountain of lies, then I got lumbered with a Major 'What's-it' from SHAEF, not knowing if he was a guest or had just barged in from the street, and he was going on about the strategy of the war. I plucked his empty glass from his hand, mumbled something about a 'refill', and slipped out through the littered kitchen into the back street.

Then Amiens awaited my pleasure and I gave it all I had. British troops engulfed with carousing females. Troops with the staggers. Dancing wildly in the cafés to *Mademoiselle from Armentières*. Wrong war, I said to no one in particular. Any case—this is Amiens. Try another café. Wasting my time, I thought, all the good-lookers already shacked. Time wasted talking to old 'busted-hooter' Evans. One more, I said, just one more café—and just one more drink and—yawn—bed. Tired. Maybe too tired—but that barmaid there is quite fetching. Yes, fetching. So, about 3 am we made it to her room, and after a few squirms and grunts, I fell asleep.

I hoped it was just a bad dream, but it wasn't. Her face was no more than eighteen inches from mine and she was pouring out a stream of vitriolic abuse like a gusher that's just hit oil. She was also trying to strangle me. The latter I took care of simply by socking her in the mouth. It also halted the flow of tongue-lashing. She bit it. Then I dived off the bed and produced my .38 revolver from under my clothes and waved it uncertainly in her direction. At that moment I don't know which of us was the more scared and I began to edge my legs into my trousers. But in the next few minutes she recovered her voice and I gathered that I was a filthy *cochon*, a septic *schwein-hund* and she was a very resentful collaborator. I had also been a bloody fool.

About a month ago an Intelligence bod had issued a statement to the effect that 'certain French women had, for a variety of reasons, lived freely with their German occupiers, becoming their mistresses and camp followers. Four years of their domination would, in many cases, have made them ardent Nazis'. With a dry pause, the Intelligence report ended with—'So keep it in your trousers until you are very, very sure'. With little attempt at dignity I hurriedly dressed and got out of that house and back to section HQ just as fast as I could. My return escaped notice, except for the cook preparing breakfast, who paused in his preoccupation to remark, 'Somebody's had a good time'. I decided to leave it at that.

After we crossed the River Somme, the Guards, the 7th and the 11th, rode their armour at full throttle for the Belgian border. We bypassed Arras—the one-time home of the original Army PR Section in 1940, from which they had hastily departed in their retreat to the coast—and suddenly we were on the frontier. Such was our speed, that there was just time to stop and film the two signs indicating France/Belgium with tanks pouring past as though it was a green light.

We all seemed to hit Tournai at the same time and the sweaty MPs had hell's own time keeping the various units on their own advance lines. The Club Route sign was a good basic for 30 Corps but, after a smart hook round Lille, and a diversion at Tournai, 12 Corps were up and away for Ghent and the River Scheldt. The other two objectives were now plain, the Guards would take Brussels and the 11th go into Antwerp.

All this racing about in the Jeep, whose springs are very tough indeed but not exactly cushioned to give one a comfortable or fluid ride, was playing hell with our cache of Flers wines. A cork would pop and if the contents had not completely disappeared, the nearest hand would grab it and we would quickly sink the remainder, irrespective of what time of day it was. Via the tank radios we heard of the reception the Guards received on their entry into Brussels, and we were confident of getting the same treatment from Antwerp. We also planned to restock our mobile off-licence.

We were, therefore, strategically placed close to the Inns of Court and the 3rd RTR when we reached the outskirts of Antwerp. Through the suburbs we raced, one of which had the wonderful name of Boom, and minutes later we ran into a lot of boom-boom coming from a copse on our right. Many civilians had gathered to give us the big cheer, but when the shooting began they made for slit-trenches, no doubt dug for air-raids, whilst another group stoically shrugged and went back to hacking up a dead horse which they had begun before our arrival.

There was plenty to film, George covered the horse item and I concentrated on close-ups of civilians in trenches and those of our own troops belting away with all weapons at the enemy. At the height of the shooting, George came over and said he was going in with a platoon of infantry to settle this hassle, and he wondered if I was coming along. I looked over his shoulder at some elegant houses across the avenue and shook my head. George turned to have a look and observed the focus of my interest. A woman was framed in one of the tall windows and by her motions it was obvious she wanted us to join her. To make the point clear she held

Left *After crossing the River Somme, the three major armoured divisions of 21st Army Group went full speed for the Belgian frontier— except for short detours around busted bridges, or other delaying tactics created by the enemy.*

Right *We often found the odd mine or two, seeded by the enemy—like they were planting corn!*

up a magnum of champagne. George just grinned, gave her a grand sweep of his arm and told me to help myself—but don't forget Amiens.

The interior of the house was rich and stylish in a manner which positively screamed money and I wondered how this was possible under a German domination. Even the chic maid who came to the door wasn't wearing last year's 'hand-me-downs'. As though reading my mind, this gorgeous creature, began to explain in flawless English that her husband had been in charge of all the port facilities when the Germans arrived, but due to his technological expertise they had asked him to remain to assist in running the port. With tongue in cheek, he had accepted, and many a German ship had sailed after a refit with leaking bilges. Even now, he was down there with a team of saboteurs ensuring that every German ship that sailed today would eventually sink when it was clear of the mouth of the River Scheldt.

Dream woman then turned to the maid, spoke rapidly in Flemish, and soon the maid re-appeared with an ice bucket which now held the bottle she had displayed at the window. She picked it out and I now saw a faded label attached to its neck which read very simply—'To the first Englishman when we are liberated'. It was signed, presumably by she, and dated May 1940. Carefully I broke the wire seals and prised out the cork, poured three glasses and, in complete silence, we toasted one another and drank. I could sense there was some great emotion attached to this moment and with as much dignity as I—unshaven, tired and dusty—could command, took her hand and gently kissed it. There was just an indication of tears in the eyes of both women and, after a second glass of champagne, my dream woman hurtled the empty glass to the floor, where it shattered and, completely out of character, said, 'Damn all the Boches'. I bid her a courteous goodbye, and left. It had been a strange moment and I got back into the Jeep in absolute silence, in the wake of the now moving column. Today, and not very far from that house, a tank of the 11th Armoured Division still rests, in comme-moration of Antwerp's Day of Liberation, September 4 1944.

There is no book of rules relating to liberation but the City of Antwerp reached into its heart and gave every man of the 11th Armoured a piece of it. A lot of men and a lot of pieces, but there was more than enough to go around. Tears and wine flowed without inhibition, streets became so crowded that tanks had to move with caution, and every vehicle was loaded with the people of Antwerp. The floor of our Jeep was soon awash with squashed fruit and spillage from the many bottles thrust into our hands. We were filming like crazy men, there was so much to record, until, late in the afternoon, with mutual accord George and I decided to stop as it became mere repetition. From that moment, we had one hell of a time.

Eventually the tanks reached the dock area and soon discovered German resistance. We were glad we had saved some film as this was in stark contrast to the reception in the city. Not heavily defended but enough to make the Charging Bull (11th insignia) stomp around with fiery nostrils. Even in these moments of joyous celebrations, men were dying. Come sundown, we decided to return to 11th Armoured's HQ the other side of the city on the road to Boom, and we turned back into a strangely quiet Antwerp. At 'Pip' Robert's command, only the tank squadrons had made the crawling dash through the city and on to the docks.

We now moved through empty streets and tried to recall the route taken earlier—but we were stumped and utterly lost. And where were the thousands of people who had greeted us earlier? We were beginning to feel very conspicuous as our lone Jeep hesitated at every crossroad, until a couple of Belgians offered to show us the way out. We had only gone about 200 yards when we were halted by a group who were obviously Belgian Maquis—they bristled with small arms and grenades hanging from their belts—and with a few sharp volleys of Flemish to our guides, we were then told that we had been in the hands of collaborators and were no doubt being led towards the enemy. As it was not quite dark our Maquis friends said they would take us to a 'safe house', and as we moved away we saw the two collaborators being forced to their knees and a Maquis member hastily dispatched them with a shot through the back of the head. I felt sick to my gut until I realised this could well have happened to us.

The 'safe house' proved to be a small family hotel in the Amerikalei where the generous Belgian hospitality soon spread into an all-night party, although I do believe I hit my pillow about 4 am. Not until late the next day did we venture from our 'safe house', and wheeling through the city devoid of British troops was oddly exhilarating, until we reached the 11th HQ and eventually our own. Whilst we handed in our film and replenished with fresh stock we received an unholy 'rollicking' from Captain Evans for not doing so sooner. We tried to explain our lucky escape of the day before, but this was dismissed with two words, 'Stupid bastards'.

All right, Captain, I thought, have it your way, and contrary to orders George and I returned to the Amerikalai where we engaged in much carousing. The fact that we were the only British troops in the city of Antwerp didn't occur to me until I later gave some thought to the strategy of the campaign. Why, then, did 'Pip' Roberts restrain his troops from occupying the city and make further advances towards the mouth of the River Scheldt? For, although he had secured the port and many of its installations, what use was it if he did not also control the entrance? My curiosity in this matter was but a mild one, and when I put it to my friendly Intelligence bod who had a wonderful way of dragging out the word 'frightfully' as though building it letter by letter, he merely shrugged and told me to 'go play with that Brownie of yours and let the Generals get on with it'.

Chapter 14

North of Antwerp, the war returned with ferocious intensity and with the rest of the Army the Film Unit were again faced with the realities of warfare. Fred Palmer and Bob Jones were soon involved with the Guards' advance on the Albert and Escaut Canals, which would bring them within a short distance of the Dutch border. The opposition consisted mostly of tough parachute troops to whom orders had been issued to fight to the last man. It was at the town of Hechtel that Fred and Bob nearly came to grief when the enemy resisted with a heavy counter-barrage. For a while the shelling had been mostly from the Guards and, thus encouraged, they moved from tank to tank, using their cameras when the action permitted, when down came the enemy barrage. Without any ado, all the hatches on the turrets clanked shut, leaving Fred and Bob feeling rather naked and vulnerable.

Now Fred Palmer is on the slim side and was able to crawl between the tracks of the nearest tank, but Bob Jones has the figure that is sometimes referred to as 'comfortable and cuddly', and there was just nowhere for him to hide. As the German shells ripped the tank column, Bob sat in resigned fashion with his back to a tank, produced his changing-bag and went through his Goodwood performance of doing mysterious things with his camera. Fred has a few theories on this approach—it could be the ostrich one, y'know, head in the sand—or maybe it produces some kind of therapy. Who knows—maybe he had a ouija board in there—but whatever it was, Fred and Bob outlived the war together.

Norman Johnson and Jock Gordon were having similar problems with 50th Division at the Albert Canal. The opposition here was of fanatical proportions as the assault boats loaded with infantry began their crossing. There was a railway line running alonside the canal, and it was under a railway wagon that Norman and Jock plus Ted their driver, who had pleaded to have a look-see, took shelter from the heavy small-arms fire pouring from the opposite bank. Now, it is one thing to photograph a battle where lots of tanks brew-up and buildings get shattered by shells, but to film a line of assault boats crossing a canal under heavy machine-gun fire with mute or silent cameras—and not a single assault craft being hit—just does not have impact. There was nothing either Jock or Norman could do, they were pinned to the one reasonably safe position where they had a good view of the river. But it was galling to get Pinewood's report later which read, 'exposure correct and in focus—but looks like a Sunday afternoon on the

Left *After the liberation of Antwerp, with supply routes running back to the beach-head, the tanks began to run dry. But it does not appear to be any problem to this mortar platoon—who have strong legs and a set of wheels!*

Right *The AFPU heroes of Arnhem—from left to right Sergeants D.M. Smith, G. Walker and 'Mike' C.M. Lewis. Their cine cameras are Bell-Howell Eyemos.*

river. You really must try and get more action and a greater variety of angles'.

Naturally, we all took those reports with a pinch of salt or a sip of cognac, but when, after the above action, the trio returned to the Jeep they found the driver's seat neatly stitched by a line of machine-gun fire. Driver Ted turned a little pale, but he soon had a straight answer when he arrived at the nearest RASC repair unit and was asked what had happened. 'Well, I didn't fart!', was Ted's reply.

After the securing of Antwerp, the 11th Armoured Division passed to the command of 8 Corps and with a very secure bridgehead across the Escaut Canal it was envisaged that another dash across Holland would now be made. Unfortunately, this fever of success was not to materialise. Six weeks of non-stop dash and more than 200 miles covered since the crossing of the Seine had stretched our lines of supply to their utmost. Petrol, food, spare parts and supplies of every nature were still being hauled over the Normandy beaches or, even further, from the only workable port of Cherbourg.

Despite the massive efforts made by the famous 'Red Ball Express'—immense convoys of trucks making non-stop round trips of up to 800 miles, the tanks' momentum was dying of thirst. Army Film Unit sections in all areas were turning in almost exactly the same film material. Columns of tanks straggled out without a pint of petrol between them. Everywhere, the order was passed, 'no unnecessary driving', and our own Jeeps were restricted to very limited areas. More often than not, if you wanted to get a film story, it was a question of 'shanks's pony', or no story.

Whilst we enjoyed this period of quiet and comparative comfort, a great deal of argy-bargy was going on in the higher echelons of command. Patton was trying to corner the market in supplies and petrol, and furiously making his much-quoted statement that, 'My men can eat their belts, but my tanks have gotta have gas'.

At the same time Montgomery was issuing directives to his superior that Eisenhower must halt all other advances and give him priority. Monty's view was that, given every support, the 21st Army Group should now make a rapid thrust across Holland and, together with a massive airborne drop seize a bridgehead over the Rhine, and race like the clappers for Berlin.

*   *   *

This, then, was the idea behind Operation Market Garden—or the battle for Arnhem. Broken down into two separate parts, it consisted of a massive airborne operation named Market and a fierce armoured thrust called Garden.

Much has been written about the Arnhem affair—the arguments regarding the time factor—so little time to put the necessary plans together and a two-three day maximum for the ground forces to cover about 70 miles. So I will concern myself only with the Army Film Unit's involvement with Arnhem. There is no doubt that the three cameramen who went in with the 1st Airborne Division were going to handle the rough end of the operation. Sergeants Smith and Walker landed with the gliders, whilst Sergeant Mike Lewis parachuted with the 1st Parachute Brigade. The latter was no mean feat as Mike was jumping with normal paratrooper's survival equipment plus an Eyemo cine camera and many rolls of film.

At about 2 pm on Sunday, September 17, Mike Lewis hit the Dutch soil and as soon as he rid himself of his harness, his camera was recording similar landings by hundreds of grim-looking paratroopers. When they had shucked off their own harnesses, they regrouped and made off in the direction of the main objective, the Arnhem bridge. As yet, there was no sign of any opposition and in fact, some of the locals had made a great show of welcome, and even gave medical attention to those who had turned an ankle or received injuries landing in trees.

Lewis made his way to the DZ allocated to the Air Landing Brigade and, as the gliders made their spectacular run in, he not only filmed their arrival but was very quickly joined by Smith and Walker. They congratulated each other on their safe arrival, and Smith managed to commandeer one of the many Jeeps that were being off-loaded and they moved off down the road in the direction of Arnhem. But they were not to get very far. Near the village of Oosterbeek they met up with the paratroopers who were pinned down by fairly heavy fire from German SPs. With their cameras recording what action they could get, they remained there until the gathering dusk made further photography impossible. They then decided to return to some safer spot and spend the night, but even as Smith turned the Jeep their departure was hastened by bursts of machine-gun fire. They have Smith to thank for their safety as he barrelled the Jeep in a jinking manner down the road.

The moment Horrocks, Commander of 30 Corps, heard of the successful landing by the Airborne Forces, he dropped the flag for his overture. Three hundred field guns poured out a creeping pattern of destruction as the armour of the Irish Guards began to move, nose to tail, down the single-track road towards Valkenswaard. Overhead, seven squadrons of rocket-firing Typhoons powered ahead at five-minute intervals, their missiles screeching groundwards at anything resembling German opposition. It was a pity the tanks didn't enjoy the same freedom of movement that the aircraft had, as, on either side of this single narrow road, the ground consisted of wet shingle and sand barely covering a potential death trap to anything weighing more than a hundredweight.

Film Unit Jeeps had been positioned near Command HQ's pennant-flying tank, which limited their immediate area of filming. Only by loping ahead by 'shanks's pony' did the cameramen manage to get different angles, and away from the tell-tale number stamped on the tank immediately in front of them! And if the one right behind did not show a number on its nose, it did have its personalised signature 'Smellie Nellie' inscribed boldly in white paint. Any thought of a fast run into Valkenswaard was soon dispelled when eight tanks were rapidly hit by 88s, and in the ensuing chaos it was some time before the column once more got under way. Film Unit cameramen managed to record the 'brewed-up' tanks, but were mystified as to the siting of the concealed 88s. According to their maps, they must have been resting on ground that would scarcely take the weight of a man.

Due to the hold-up, it was dusk before they reached Valkenswaard and the Film Unit prepared themselves for another night run (like those before Brussels and Antwerp) up to Eindhoven and beyond, for, according to their maps it appeared possible to cross the Wilhelmina and Willens Canals. From the numbers of Germans who were now coming in to surrender—the cameramen cursed the fading light, used a full aperture and hoped for the best—there didn't appear to be a fearsome opposition. It was, therefore, with great surprise that

AFPU were told the armour was going into laager for the night and would proceed again at dawn.

This overnight stop has never been fully accounted for—but at this juncture the race for Arnhem was already lost. The general explanation was that the bridge at Son, north of Eindhoven, had been destroyed and engineers would first have to reach it to assess what bridging equipment would be required. It is with one of those revealing twists of hindsight that 'had we but known', and due to the success of the US 101st Airborne drop in that area, it would have been possible to pick up a telephone in Valkenswaard and, through the automatic exchange system, call SON 244 for full details of the blown bridge.

Stranger still that the penny did not drop, for an unknown British officer was actually in the Post Office in Valkenswaard when the 'phone rang. Tentatively, the officer picked it up—he fortunately understood German—and received a demand from the German Commander at Eindhoven that Valkenswaard must be defended at all costs. The British Officer assured him this would be done and hung up. Not until late the next day did the Guards reach Eindhoven where they linked up with the US 101st Airborne. It became a scene of liberation that was now a familiar one to the British and vast quantities of Bols gin was consumed by the now orange flower-garlanded troops. What these good people of Eindhoven did not realise was that they were slowing the advance, and again it was not until the evening the leading elements of 30 Corps reached the Son bridge.

Although 8 Corps and 12 Corps had both established a foothold over the same canal on both flanks, this did little to help the plight of 30 Corps, and more especially, the Airborne at Arnhem. Whilst Horrocks's men fretted, and the weary engineers with a host of German prisoners laboured to construct a Class 40 bridge over the canal, the men of the 1st Airborne Division were boxed in by an increasing strength of infantry, tanks, SPs and flamethrowers.

The three Army Film Unit men were, like the Paras they were with, totally exhausted and were now sheltering in a house with the owner, his wife and two

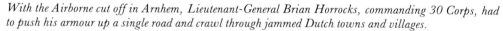

With the Airborne cut off in Arnhem, Lieutenant-General Brian Horrocks, commanding 30 Corps, had to push his armour up a single road and crawl through jammed Dutch towns and villages.

children. Many attempts had been made to drop supplies, but more often it was to the enemy's advantage than to them. However, they had sufficient food to feed them, but it was becoming increasingly more difficult to do the job that had brought them here. As Mike Lewis recalls—'I made attempts to get pictures but it was hard, and frankly at times out of the question with an enemy who was rarely seen but often heard. The whole of the box was bombarded by guns and mortars, no one place was safe. Men were hit by strays and ricochets in the most unexpected positions. Eating a meal in the house was a precarious adventure— enemy fire would come through the windows and down the passages and the three of us were particularly lucky when a burst of fire carried a window on to our meal without harm to anyone'.

A second supply drop was even more disastrous than the first; heavy ground fire and drifting smoke plus a lack of ground recognition signals (some were hastily displayed when the aircraft's engines were heard—but the supplies had already been released), and the Airborne watched in dismay as most of this much-needed food and ammunition drifted into the enemy's hands. To retrieve even a small proportion of supplies the paratroopers had to run a gauntlet of heavy cross-fire, and Sergeant Smith remembers with great clarity the shivers that ran up and down his spine as he was forced to halt and adjust focus and aperture on his camera, then photograph the pitiful few parachutes falling in their direction.

For the first two crucial days, the Airborne were without their Commanding Officer, General Urquhart, and they feared he was either dead or a prisoner. In fact, he and two other officers were safe and well in a house less than five miles away. Unfortunately, they were surrounded by the enemy (who had no idea that such a prize was so near), and particularly by the crew of a self-propelled gun who appeared to have taken up permanent residence. But with or without the General, the Airborne were now in dire straits, and the same question was asked over and over again—where is the British 2nd Army? Where indeed? The lack of radio communications between the two groups was a major factor; the highly trained teams of experts with their specialised equipment had completely broken down and 30 Corps had received little in the way of hard news.

For the AFPU cameramen dispersed amongst the forward echelons it was a particularly non-productive period. Whatever news that came our way was damn little, and it wasn't until two days after the actual Airborne drop that we even learned three of our colleagues were with them. We chafed, fumed and made irrational suggestions. From the limitations of our worm's-eye view we could not understand why the hell we did not get on with it. As pigeon-droppings of news began to piddle through (and I do mean pigeons, for the Airborne Signals did have airborne letter-carriers), we began to formulate a picture of the hell in which our three cameramen were operating. But just before we began to let off steam, we heard that leading elements of the Guards had linked up with the US 82nd Airborne Division at Nijmegen on the south bank of the River Waal. There was a general 'hip-hip hoorah' at this news and expressions of 'good show, the Guards'—until—.

We learned that the Americans had made a brilliant assault crossing of the river—using British boats—and Old Glory was now proudly flying on the northern end of the bridge. The way was now open, but Horrocks still hesitated. Bitterly, he weighed the plight of the men at Arnhem, against the fact that most of his armour was dangerously low in supplies. The narrow, single road from Eindhoven had delayed their appearance, and his infantry were far behind, their advance slowed by the nose-to-tail tanks, making their movements woefully slow. This decision by Horrocks to slow the advance must have been a difficult one to make. For the beleaguered 1st Airborne—so close to the main bridge at Arnhem—it was practically a death sentence.

Smith, Walker and Lewis of AFPU were now huddled in a cellar near Divisional HQ. They were tired, dirty and hungry. Their unshaven faces were etched with the agony of stress and tension; their eardrums assaulted by the non-stop hammering of shell-fire and explosions that brought down plaster from walls and ceilings. Less than an hour ago they had been taking pictures of a gun crew in action near the river, when they caught the full blast of a German attack—they were less than 20 yards away—using self-propelled guns and flamethrowers at point-blank range. A British Officer was incinerated where he stood, but the six-pounder gun was quickly wheeled and very rapidly eliminated the flamethrower.

Wisely, they decided to return to the comparative safety of their cellar, and had no sooner gone a few yards when the area where the gun crew had been was obliterated by savage fire. Mike Lewis says he was never sure if any of them were still alive. On the way back they passed several paratroopers who were now in an advanced stage of shell-shock—they shivered and trembled with every concussion—and some who had become so numbed they appeared to be asleep over their weapons. Mike now contemplated their plight and the grave shortage of food and water—that particular source, an old water-well was under heavy fire. A box of food, originally for 14 men, had recently been shared out amongst 70. But if their thoughts were on food, their stomachs rebelled and necessary functions were taken at grave risk in the open. It was on such a foray that Smith was later hit in the shoulder by a sniper's bullet, and it was now, in such a state of disarray, with Smith grey with shock and a field dressing seeping red, the three Army Film Unit cameramen lay and looked at each other with hopeless eyes.

It was a new rhythm in the outward sounds of gunfire that made them realise that they could now hear the artillery of the 2nd Army. The heavy guns of the 64th Medium Regiment of the RAs were now within range and giving every support they could within a very limited target. So precise was this fire to be that the Film Unit trio were told they had to evacuate their cellar as the area was about to be blasted. Mike Lewis had the unfortunate task of telling the Dutch family they had to leave, and with the wounded Smith they made a hazardous journey down a shell-torn street, stumbling over fallen trees and wreckage of all kinds, to a house where they were told they would be safe, 'at least for a short time'. The sound of those guns brought partial hope to the 1st Airborne, but they were not to know it would be the only ground-to-ground support they would have.

Having now crossed the Nijmegen bridge the narrow Club Route of Horrocks was to be a tenuous one. As the route was a mere causeway through low-lying,

marshy fields, he ordered the entire 43rd Infantry Division to strike forward. This they did in heavy rain and against some very stiff opposition. They were later joined by a mobile column of Light Infantry riding on the tanks of the 4th/7th Dragoon Guards and with a magnificent dash made their way to the banks of the Neder Rijn where they also contacted the Polish parachutists dropped at Driel. After all the previous wallowing, they had made an advance of ten miles in less than 30 minutes!

With this sudden burst, a small section of AFPU went with them and were rewarded with some good material on the link-up with the Poles. But getting that film back to base was a different matter. The single route was cut on several occasions, and the AFPU Jeeps had a hairy time getting back to Nijmegen, one driver being badly wounded, whilst a despatch driver had his motorcycle shot away from under him. He was only slightly wounded and was piled on to the back of one of the Jeeps.

A sigh of relief came when they spied the girders of the Nijmegen Bridge, but this changed to expressions of near-disbelief when they reached the comparatively safe end of the bridge. A mobile Church Army canteen was set up amongst the trees, and three dear old ladies were dispensing tea and buns, as though it was a bright afternoon at Henley regatta! Although this route suffered many such infiltrations, 30 Corps were able to get a large number of tanks and troops up to the Neder Rijn, but due to the impossible time factor, they could only function as a survival link with the 1st Airborne who were now preparing to evacuate the area around Arnhem.

When the Film Unit section on the north bank of the river were told of the projected evacuation they were amazed. It was their understanding that 30 Corps were now drawn up in strength on the south bank, so what was to stop them from crossing in strength? Their awful plight was then explained. The main Arnhem bridge was firmly held by the enemy and their own pocket of resistance was now reduced to less than one square mile. Horrocks had wanted an assault crossing to be made, but with appalling weather nullifying air support, Dempsey had rejected the attempt. All that now could be done was try to save the remnants of the 1st Airborne Division.

On the evening of Monday, September 25, a small party of three AFPU cameramen, two War Correspondents, censors and signals led by Major Oliver of PR—also one of the walking wounded—made their slushy way to the banks of the Rhine. There they waited for two hours in pouring rain and shattering machine-gun fire—during which Major Oliver was again wounded—until a boat materialised from the darkness. Lewis, Walker and Smith grimly clutched the film they had exposed in the inferno of Arnhem and dourly watched the flaming holocaust recede as they crossed to the south bank.

Above left *Using DUKWs to ferry General Horrocks' troops and supplies near the blown bridge over the Lower Waal. With such obstructions, it is not surprising Horrocks' schedule kept slipping back.*
Left *Trucks and Carriers of 30 Corps cross the Nijmegen Bridge.*

Chapter 15

The wet bleakness of what threatened to be a grim winter was now fast approaching. With all due respect to the finer qualities of Holland, the particular area in which we now found ourselves was hardly stimulating. The vast machinery of our type of war did little to help, and often did unaccountable damage. Tanks, transporters, heavy bridging equipment and the non-stop movement of supply vehicles played hell with many Dutch roads, and the countless numbers of cobbled minor roads were often reduced to an unusable shambles. Traffic experts thus devised a vast one-way system, which at times slowed supply columns but, with some hard work endured by the Engineers, did help a great deal.

The Allied armies were now massed along the German frontier, but it was mostly marshy areas, peat-land and orchards. It only required a minimum of rainfall to bring the tanks to a halt. Before a firm foothold could be attained for a strong thrust into Germany, the River Meuse had to be crossed in force. But between the American and British forces there were 60 square miles of the Peel Marshes. This was made up of swampland, canals, drainage ditches and two very important towns, Overloon and Venraij.

The Americans were first into the attack and ran into heavy resistance created by infantry of Hans von Obstfelder's 86th Korps and tanks of the 107th Panzer Brigade. Despite the determination of the Americans, the German counter-attacks were so heavy that, after six days' fighting, the US 7th Armoured Division was halted after an advance of only two miles, with the loss of 35 tanks and 542 men. Montgomery now decided that the British 3rd Division, with the US 7th Armoured in support, should now have a crack at it. Hugh Stewart of AFPU also decided to allocate at least six cameramen with the leading attack element, the rest of the unit playing a secondary role in rear echelon movements. This was one of those occasions when the cameramen were not paired in the initial stages. It was good strategy on the part of Hugh Stewart, for he wanted as much and as great a variety of coverage during the early part of the attack as was possible. For a time I found myself with Dick Leatherbarrow, then he would hare off and up popped 'Slim' Hewitt.

The usual heavy barrage preceded the attack, and as the infantry moved forward they were supported by a 4.2-inch mortar team and a line of heavy Vickers MGs. These latter made for some good film sequences, though they were

With the Allied armies massing along the German frontier, the approach to the River Meuse called for stealth and steel-lined nerves.

bloody noisy, as the Vickers were on continuous rapid fire. Every now and again, a few of these MGs had to be halted and the water-cooling system pumped madly, whilst another operator would thread in what looked like a half-mile belt of fresh ammunition. To preserve a little sequence on this end of the story, Dick Leatherbarrow and I would sit at a reasonably safe position ahead of the muzzles, run the cameras when we heard the troop Commander shout fire, then, if we heard his voice way down the line shout halt, we would race for the group that were reloading. The fact that we usually ran the length of the MGs ahead of the muzzles scared the hell out of the machine-gunners—we just forgot!

For the advance on Overloon itself, our section officers advised us to mix it a little. Being mostly an infantry assault, I chose the 1st Battalion Suffolks who had several Churchill tanks in support. I guess you could say it was an added protection—but tanks I understood and respected their ability to get to places where infantry on their own would often be exposed unnecessarily. Dick Leatherbarow had a go with the Royal Warwicks, and he too had Churchills in support. Dick was another fond of tanks—he actually left the Tank Regiment to join AFPU—so his knowledge of their abilities was often of great use.

He spotted some Churchills carrying fascines, and knowing of the vast number of ditches in this area, he followed them and came out with some good film on their use. Briefly, the fascine is a large roll of heavily pressed timber, wood-falls and compressed tree branches. It is carried ahead of the tank on two protruding arms, and when it arrives at a ditch which might be a problem, is simply popped into the ditch to allow the tanks to move over this obstacle.

Dick was a bit of a perfectionist at this sort of thing. Whilst I satisfied myself filming the fascines dropping in the ditch, and the tanks sagging themselves across, Dick thought it was a good idea to get close-ups of the tracks biting into the fascine, so he jumped into the ditch—muddy one at that—and got to work. Four tanks made it all right, although the fourth had a distinct lean over. Apparently Dick hadn't noticed this, until the fifth began to churn large sections of the fascine in all directions. Fortunately, this alarmed Dick in good time and he hastily ejected himself from the ditch just before the port side of the Churchill caused a total collapse of the fascine, and several tons of hardware slithered into the spot our Dickie had occupied. The so-and-so just laughed and hared after the rest of the tanks headed for Overloon. I followed suit.

About this time, Dick and I went our individual ways when 9th Brigade and 3rd Division did a leapfrog action over the 8th Brigade, and for no particular reason, we both decided to remain with infantry. We had a clear view of the ruins of Overloon by now, and the tanks didn't look too happy at this point, especially when they ran into a minefield where they encountered a new type of mine called a Riegel—very powerful and able to penetrate the heavy base plates of our Churchills. I continued into the shell of Overloon with the Royal Warwicks, whilst Dickie did the same with the 2nd Battalion King's Shropshire Light Infantry. It is strange; I have never felt at home working with infantry by themselves, but after seeing those brewed-up Churchills, I can say that Overloon was the exception.

Not far behind were that eminent, respected and inseparable pair of cameramen, Bill Gross and Vic Watkins. They had the unenviable task of filming house-clearing with a battalion each from the Royal Warwicks and the Suffolks. Such was the havoc in Overloon that most houses had been razed to street level, but there was always that hidden cellar now covered in rubble. What made the task more difficult was always posed by one dreadful doubt. If Germans were hiding there, were there any Dutch families with them? This problem did not actually affect Gross and Watkins—there being no light to film in that area. But the two cameramen had become so attached to their infantry, that they feared for their safety—together with that of the Dutch.

They had worked out this straightforward system of staying ahead of the troops engaged in house-clearing down both sides of the street. Therefore, there was a camera covering both sides of the street. That way, there was a camera covering both groups, but Bill and Vic would be about half-a-dozen cottages in advance, one using a 35 mm lens for a wide angle coverage, and the other using a 50 mm lens to bring the action closer.

The troops were 'hitting' two cottages at the same time on either side of the street—using the simple method of crashing the doors open with their boots—spraying the interior with sub-machine-guns and, for good measure, lobbing a hand grenade inside. As there were no upstairs rooms, it was the general theory, 'that lot had been eliminated—so keep going'—and they would race to the next pair of cottages, whilst Bill and Vic would back up, filming as they moved. But one cottage had survived this fast onslaught, and both cameramen saw the familiar uniforms of a couple of Germans suddenly emerge from behind the fast-moving troops, and they both yelled at the same time.

There was no mistaking the warning, and the British whirled about and fired from the hip, long before the Germans—dazed and bloodied from the grenades—could untangle their weapons. Both cameramen moved fast—Bill closed on the scene, and ran his camera until he felt the slight bump indicating the end of his film. He yelled at Vic, 'Out!' and he, with his 50 mm lens, jumped towards the centre of the street and thumped down on one knee to steady himself. Vic could only have had about 15 feet of film left, and he too had soon run out, cursing the inadequacies of his equipment. Bill had managed to make a quick reload, and filmed the brief aftermath of the British checking the Germans' pay-books—or rather, what remained of them.

The whole sequence had taken less than ten minutes, but Bill and Vic were satisfied they had covered the fast-moving and bloody sequence adequately, despite their film shortage, and with cross-cutting between the two cameras, the Pinewood editors would be able to edit a satisfactory story, provided the War Office censors didn't puke at the sight of Germans with holes where their stomachs had been!

Chapter 16

It was now that I got myself a new partner, Sergeant Peter Norris, with whom I would continue until the end of the war. Peter was reasonably fresh from Pinewood, although he had spent a short time with George Laws. Peter was to make a first-class partner, although, as a stills photographer, he had his own idea how a picture should be composed. He also displayed a certain resourcefulness in acquiring camera spare parts and other impedimenta from the depths of complete devastation. I also found that I now had a permanently attached section officer, to whom I took an instant liking (this was unusual for me as I was strictly for the guys who took the kicks—the Sergeants) but Lieutenant Martin Wilson, who had made a considerable name in Tunisia, could not be faulted. First, he was a Scotsman and, second, he was just as free-wheeling towards AFPU regulations as I was. In short, he was one of the boys. I didn't know it then, but it was to be a great team. In agreement with Wilson, we decided not to push on to Venraij that day as it was being ably covered by Bill Gross and Vic Watkins.

After Peter Norris got the smell of the aftermath of battle—and there was definitely plenty to smell in Overloon—he suggested that he should go off alone to photograph some pretty-pretties of the ruins. We did not object. There were still a number of British medical teams roving the ruins, and the tanks were now rumbling through en route for Venraij. We did warn him about mines (now

With winter blowing cold, and due to the need for some replacements, George Laws left me, and I was given a new 'stills' partner who, after a brief period with George, came to me on a full-time basis until the end of the war. He was Sergeant Peter Norris, and he was very good.

clearly marked), and possible booby traps. So he eagerly scrambled over the ruins and was soon out of sight. Martin Wilson and I sat down and smoked. He told me about Tunisia, and I told him about Normandy.

About an hour and a half had gone by before we realised that we hadn't seen hide nor hair of Peter. The day was drawing to a close, and we were both a bit worried. So we split in two directions and our voices carried quite clearly, 'Peter—Peter Norris'. Nothing. 'Peter—Peter, were the hell are you?' Still several minutes of nothing; then Peter reappeared, looking a trifle warm and very, very dusty. But he was grinning happily. I looked at the cameras round his neck. There was the regular Ikonta and two others. I wondered. Tried to remember. Most of the 'still' boys carried other equipment than that issued by AFPU. But had he been carrying two or three cameras when he went into Overloon? So what business was it of mine? But he did bring back something that is still very alive today. A collection of photographs now specially exhibited at the National War and Resistance Museum of the Netherlands. The museum is just outside Overloon and off the main road to Venraij.

* * *

The middle of October is never the best time of the year to push an offensive down a single road in Holland. This had been clearly pin-pointed during 30 Corps' advance towards Arnhem. The weather had worsened and the enemy knew the ground conditions much better than the British, they had mortar and machine-gun positions everywhere. The verges at the side of the road were strewn with mines, and those deadliest of tanks—the Panthers—popped up in the unlikeliest positions.

Bill Gross and Vic Watkins were having a rough time on the road to Venraij, and much of their material clearly shows the stubbornness of the German defence. Churchill tanks were brewing fiercely from direct 88 mm hits, their crews charred corpses as they made vain attempts to escape from their fiery tombs. But as our Royal Artillery regiments found positions to lay down their guns, a steady barrage of 25-pounders and 5.5-inch shells began to break the resistance—yet it was to take British units all of five days to enter Venraij on October 17. Pity we hadn't kept forward with Gross and Watkins, then we wouldn't have made such damn fools of ourselves as we did.

We got the word that Venraij had fallen and, apart from that anticipatory gleam that crept into Peter Norris's eyes, we were just as anxious to get there as anyone. From the smoke and fire that appeared to be coming from the centre of the town, it had all the makings of some good pictures. As we neared the outskirts we could hear the usual spasmodic MG fire and the odd crump of a mortar. Quite normal, we felt, it always happens. But we left the Jeep at a comfortable distance and decided to walk. Right down the middle of the road, no mined verges for us. Then a bit later we came across a platoon of infantry hugging the ditches, obviously cleared of mines and now they were resting. Best infantry rule in the book, if your feet hurt, get your ass down in the ditch and stick your feet up, preferably higher than your heart. All a matter of circulation.

Good pictures though. Infantry foreground and a burning village in the background. Peter and I went to work, until we noticed that some of the infantry were not just resting, but were taking a decidedly defensive observation of Venraij. Then a couple of officers from the ditch began telling us to, 'get the hell out of there', and pointed towards a ruined church, explaining, 'That's a bloody OP'. The penny dropped very sharply—we were giving the game away. We turned, and doubled back up the road, but it was a shade too late. A salvo of mortars straddled the road behind us, and from the infantry in the ditches came a stream of profanity, not all directed at the Germans. We got back to our Jeep, to find it surrounded by a section of flail tanks and our driver enjoying a cigarete with a troop commander. He grinned at us, 'You should have been here half-an-hour ago. This lot—', pointing to the tanks, 'had a right old beat-up in that field over there. Didn't find any mines, but it looked smashing. Would have made great pictures'. We sat down—deflated—and decided to smoke this one out.

*   *   *

By the start of November winter was beginning to put its bite in deep. My section had taken over an old single structure school-house made of seasoned wood in the tiny village of Deurne. There was one central stove in the middle of the only room in which we ate and slept, and in what passed for a kitchen there was a cooking range. Both burned peat, which was in plentiful supply in the field out-back. The peat burned well and we kept relatively warm, even its strong odour was not unpleasant. Sleeping was directly on the floor, but during the day, bed-rolls were put in order and there was sufficient room. We also had the satisfaction of knowing that as the Army was now drawn up practically along the line of the River Meuse, that Deurne would probably be our home for the winter.

But the 2nd Army was never still and small probes were made at different points (a) to gain just a little more ground, and (b) to impress on the enemy that we had no intention of sitting out the winter squatting on our duffs. Such an attack was made on the town of Geilenkirchen, but I want to use this in an entirely different context in relation to previous actions. I once asked our CO, Major Hugh Stewart, if he ever had any problems in the administration of the unit. He laughed and said it was practically nil, that No 5 AFPS was a very fine section and by now, with all our past experience, the section ran by itself. But Major Stewart had to carry on a constant war with the War Office DDPR back in London, who were apt to read about the course of the war from the daily newspapers. And very often came up with the wrong opinions with regard to the abilities of AFPU.

This began in the very early days of the campaign, during one of our early tank battles of the Tilly-Caen thrust. The newspapers carried diverse reports of this battle, and there was a bit of a moan from the War Office that AFPU photos did not match up with the stories. The reason for this was that most of the reporters sent in their copy from the hotel in Bayeux which they had requisitioned—and didn't even see the Tilly-Caen battles. For the attack on Geilenkirchen I am going to quote directly from Hugh Stewart's report to DDPR, War Office after a great deal of criticism from the Publicity Officer in charge of the Press.

'12th Corps attacked on the night of 14/15th November with 51st Highland Division. The enemy pulled back at once and at a very small cost in casualties, three canal crossings were made at Weert. 53rd Welsh Division attacked shortly after, but made no effective contact with the enemy, who withdrew gradually, leaving the few tracks in the area heavily mined. The ground off the road was very boggy and often under water. No tanks were committed to the battle. The fighting, such as it was, was virtually over by noon on the 15th November and I am informed by my OIC 12th Corps Sub Section, that the Corps attack resulted in the capture of 80 POWs in the first three days.

'30 Corps put in an attack on the 18th November with 82nd U.S. Division and 43rd British Division up. The objective was the capture of Geilenkirchen. This was to be effected by the 82nd U.S. Division, on whom depended the fixing of the attack by 43rd Division. this, in fact, went in about 1300 hours, from Gillrath, and the infantry went steadily forward in tanks as far as Rischden. It was only a one Brigade attack, with two battalions up, and the objectives were reached before the estimated time, with very light casualties. Next day the advance continued to the wood near Tripsrath and tanks and infantry entered Bauchem. There was little British artillery involved as the attack was such that the U.S. troops were in danger of being shelled.

'I was in Geilenkirchen within an hour of the first U.S. Infantry, with many mines still unexploded in the roadway, as I hoped to get a photograph of at least one British soldier in the town. I did in fact find one scout car, and its crew were the sole British troops in Geilenkirchen that day. No sign was found of any enemy although I went all over the town. Next day six POWs were taken, but it is presumed they had either lain low the previous day or re-entered the town during the night. On the 20th November most of my Sergeants went round to the Geilenkirchen area as it was recommended by Corps H.Q. as the most promising sector. Sergeant Seaholme obtained shots of SP guns firing. An attack by 43rd Division was cancelled, but during the night 20/21 November, the enemy put in a sudden counter-attack and captured most of a Company of 5 OCLI, which resulted in us falling back slightly. The POWs taken in this two day attack by 43rd Division were 300. Incidentally, VENLO 'captured', according to the evening newspapers some four days ago, is still in enemy hands.

'8th Corps are still advancing bit by bit, and yesterday reached the Meuse at all points. They never made contact with the enemy, who withdrew over the river in good order.

'G3(1) Second Army had asked me before the beginning of the attack to be prepared to photograph the 100,000th prisoner. About 4,000 were needed, I believe, to attain this number, but the results of the attack still leave this target intact—by a very comfortable margin.

'The reason why no operational film was sent between the 9th-18th November is because there were no operations. Even the most optimistic War Correspondents will support me on this. It should also be borne in mind that the weather for the last three weeks has, with a few intervals, been rainy and over clouded. The rivers are in their highest flood for ten years; movement in many sectors of the front is impossible during the day time, and in some cases rations and ammunition are supplied by boat over what were fields two weeks ago.

'These then are the facts of the 'great offensive'. It is not surprising that the photographs were lacking in action. I too cannot blame Mr. Deverson [Publicity Officer to DDPR] for his dissatisfaction, as he is not privy to intelligence summaries and situation reports. However, I am bewildered that the War Office are not aware of the real state of affairs, and that such a memorandum could have been written on the 22nd November about an attack that started on the 14th November. This should have given ample time to check on the facts, and the whole discrepancy between headlines and pictures would have been explained.

'It is to meet such exigencies that I have my whole Headquarters forward at an operational level, so that I am constantly in touch with the latest information as it becomes available from Corps and Army, as well as urgent letters from the War Office. Were I not to do this I too might well have been dismayed by the news headlines (written mostly in Brussels as McCarthy says) and caused considerable despondency among my Sergeants by my reproaches.

'I hope that an explanation will be given to Mr. Deverson as I would be sorry to lose his confidence.

'Regarding the complaint about the poor quality of the Armistice Day coverage, Pinewood reports on this material as follows:

Sergeant Parkinson material ''Remembrance Day''—11th November 1944
Good story, well covered. Judging by the material you were not in a position to move your camera much, but by change of lenses you have made the material interesting. Good steady panning.

Sergeant Johnson ''Remembrance Day''—11th November 1944
High quality photography, well covered story. One or two close-ups of General Erskine are slightly back focus, but extremely good just the same. The incident of Prince Charles talking to old soldiers is very well covered. Your camera is working perfectly.

'In any case, it will be appreciated we can only photograph what we can see, and the celebrations were admittedly dull.

Signed— H. Stewart, Major
Commanding No. 5 A.F.P.S. (PR)'

I have quoted this document in full to demonstrate the fact that Stewart was a first-rate officer with his finger on every pulse. We too—the cameramen—were equally annoyed by some of the reports in the national press which were, sometimes, openly critical regarding the part of AFPU in relation to good propaganda. In the above report, Stewart makes it clear that some accredited correspondents filed copy from Press HQ Brussels on the latter stages of 1944, without even moving from the Belgian capital. Much worse than that was to follow in later months. It is a fact that certain correspondents would later report the assault crossing of the River Rhine without moving from the Metropole Hotel in Brussels.

Chapter 17

The beginning of December began to give us some idea of what winter in Holland was really going to be like. Thermometers dropped alarmingly and despite an issue of winter clothing, there were great problems in covering the most simple of stories. Cameras had to be nursed and kept well oiled, and specially thick and woolly lined carriers were distributed to ensure the warmth and well-being of cameras and film. Just when I was wondering if the cameras were getting a better deal than ourselves, Hugh Stewart gave me a longish assignment, coupled with a week's leave in Brussels. The assignment was to travel down to the French coast where the 11th Armoured Division were doing tests on the new Comet tank, and also make a tour of the D-Day beaches to see, and get stories, on how they were doing in the way of reconstruction. When I got through with that I could take a week off in Brussels.

I welcomed this with my woolly-mittened hands, and with a little mental arithmetic figured I could make it last about three weeks and be back in Deurne for Christmas, where we were planning a real old-fashioned shindig. It was pleasant to reacquaint myself with the members of the 11th Armoured Division, who were quite enjoying being a long way from the front line. They put the new tank through its paces for me. It was a heavier job than the Sherman, its armour was thicker and it had a heavier calibre gun. But one sensed that not all of the crews were totally happy with it, and my own feelings were mixed, for we had somehow become attached to the Sherman.

After that I made my tour of the old beach-head. Not a lot had been done in reconstruction, roofs, and walls had been replaced and the Allied Military

An advance through a wintry-looking Holland. Nice on picture post-cards, but not for a war. At least it was not Stalingrad!

Sergeant George Laws films a lonely, and very wintry outpost in Holland. George was always a perfectionist; right down to using a tripod. Nice work, George!

Government had siphoned off funds and a small reconstruction unit to help the French. But I somehow sensed the same sullenness that I had felt on D-Day and for some time afterwards. I wondered what they expected of us: an immediate bright new and happy future? Yet, with most of the 2nd Army's supplies still coming in over the beach-head, the local tradesmen were doing very well.

This thought took me to where Mulberry was still in action—or most of it was, for the Americans had been loaned or pilfered parts of it for their own use. Some of it had been used in a sensible fashion, to shore up gaps in the sea-wall. Entrances and exits for heavy vehicular traffic now covered roadways from beach up to land level, some of which were precipitous to say the least. 'Dougie' Wolfe, another member of AFPU on roving commission, later told me of a slightly hair-raising experience he had whilst filming US operations on that beach section.

The Americans were using DUKWs to ferry stores and Dougie noticed that when a DUKW was returning to the base ship, they used these ramps as though they were launching a lifeboat. Dougie thought this would make a good film item and he approached the first DUKW driver making the return journey and asked if he could film from the rear of the DUKW. The driver was coloured and a great hunk of a man, but his face split in a wide grin as he replied, 'Well sho man, it's my pleasure, but hang on tight'.

Dougie took up his position at the rear, braced himself and got his camera in position. The negro slipped into neutral gear whilst some of his mates gave a shove to start the DUKW on its journey seawards. Unfortunately, it gathered speed down the slope all too quickly and the negro was unable to get the damn thing into gear. It began to career downwards like a bat out of hell, its speed multiplying with frightening momentum until finally it hit the water with a sliding, skipping impact not unlike that of the Barnes Wallis bouncing bomb. The entire framework of the DUKW took a terrific hammering, but held together. Dougie had braced himself so thoroughly that the worst thing that happened was, on about the second bounce, he was hurtled forward—camera still running—and found himself slightly tangled with the driver.

The negro half-turned, his massive face split ear to ear in sheer delight, and said to Dougie, 'Well man—we sure made it. If you all got that on film you've got a real honey. Compliments of the U.S. of A'. Dougie thanked him and made his way back to the Jeep and examined his camera. It was in good shape and he reckoned he might have got a good piece of film. The report from Pinewood merely commented, 'please, no fairground sequences required, suggest you concentrate on more serious matters'.

But, for myself, I was rather disappointed with my 'return to Normandy' trip; in fact, I was even unable to pin-point the beach on which I had landed on June 6. The journey back to Holland via Brussels had its pleasant moments, but it was odd, I was looking forward to returning to my friends back at Deurne. True, I had missed most of the British involvement with the Ardennes push, and it had been interesting to hear some of the comments in Brussels, as they feared the Germans would succeed in driving a wedge between the British and Americans. They even expressed disappointment that Montgomery had not committed more of his own forces to stop the rot. I put all this down to the overall feeling I now had that most of the areas liberated by the Allies presupposed that there would be a return to a much easier way of life. Brussels and Antwerp were particularly critical of this point, especially as they were now coming under the fire of Germany's V weapons.

*   *   *

I did manage to return to Deurne a few days before Christmas and I won't go into details regarding the so-called festive day, other than it was darn cold and both the turkey and pudding tasted of peat.

That week prior to the New Year could have been pretty miserable, but for the demands from HQ to supply material of 'how the troops were making merry with Santa Claus'. So we ploughed our way through the snow, to some of the outlying positions, fully expecting to find them huddled in makeshift dug-outs. Not a bit of it—they had worked on the theory that any 'brass' over the rank of Major wouldn't venture too far from their snug little quarters around Eindhoven. There wasn't a barn between Deurne and the River Meuse which hadn't been made comfortable with beds, easy chairs, settees and those thick, warm overlays we now refer to as Continental Quilts, which had been carefully removed from bombed-out homes, and renovated by simply getting in touch with the nearest Mobile Steam Laundry!

One barn I visited clearly displayed the handiwork of the opposite sex, who were obviously being rewarded—if my ears weren't deceiving me—in the loft above! Apart from the ground floor being entirely covered in a passably good carpet, of no mean dimensions (I refrained from asking about its origin), there were drapes fronting every stall, and curtains on all the windows. A long table ran the length of the barn, covered by three separate tablecloths, and on it there were half-eaten turkeys, chickens, some sort of beef and a couple of hams. I didn't bother to count the variety of bottles, and the glassware was spotless and unbroken. Someone obviously ran this place with the firm touch of a 'maître d'hôtel' and, after I'd been introduced to all who lived here, I found that the sole officer in charge (a First-Lieutenant), had indeed been a 'commis-waiter' at one of London's leading hotels!

The officers made me very welcome, but requested that I shouldn't take any pictures. This was clearly impossible anyway, as the lighting—supplied by a portable generator outside the barn—had been kept to a warm spread, by covering the naked bulbs with some material I couldn't identify. He did suggest a small gathering around a real Christmas tree (these firs grew in profusion in this part of Holland), which had been under-lit by a small array of headlamp bulbs—stippled with daubs of coloured paint—and running from the same source. Obviously, there was a skilled electrician in the group, and I had to explain about the lack of exposure. But the officer was not going to be put off. He turned to the group and shouted, 'Hey—Digger—open those double doors and get your scout car in here at the double'. Digger looked a bit worried. 'You mean, right in here on the carpet—sir?' The officer was now in full stride, 'Don't worry, just get the bloody scout car . . . ', and he looked round the group, 'and you lot—spread out and roll the carpet up as far as the table . . . '. He spun round and looked up towards the loft, 'Sergeant Baker . . . ', he roared, 'Ba-ker—just stop what you're doing—do you bloody well hear me?'. There was a hasty commotion from the rafters and a face appeared at the top of the steps. 'All right Sergeant—you won't need your trousers', the officer grinned maliciously, 'get into that nice Santa Claus outfit—and I mean now—and down here on the double'.

Just then, the scout car rolled in, the driver keeping the throttle down to allow the monstrous thing to ease forward and stop at the edge of the rolled-up carpet. The headlamps were on full beam, and he jiggled the vehicle until they covered the area round the Christmas tree, then he cut the engine. I admired the spontaneous ingenuity of the operation, and I took a took through the viewfinder (I no longer relied on the extinction exposure meter we had been issued with—I'd found that my own trained eyesight gave a more exact exposure than a row of graded circles), and told the officer 'only just'. He merely smiled at me in a manner which many a future film director would produce for recalcitrant cameramen, and yelled at Digger, 'Hitch up the lamp'. The driver bobbed down and produced what appeared to be a theatrical spotlight, stuck it on a bracket and flicked a switch. A brilliant shaft of light hit me right on my face, and I ducked away. 'Spread it, Digger—spread it', shouted the officer, and to my amazement the shaft broadened to an even distribution of soft, but effectual radiation of light. Although entirely frontal, it was a damn-near perfectly lit set-up, and I looked at the officer with growing admiration.

He dug me gently in the ribs and said, 'We did a few day's guard duty at Philips in Eindhoven—nabbed a couple of looters—and this boss-man . . . ', he clilcked his fingers, 'oh hell—de Witt van something-or-other gave it to me—honest, Sarge—I didn't nick it', and he gave a chuckle, 'he told me it was some new experiment in stage lighting—and thought—well—a bit of a gift which we could put to some use . . . ', he paused, 'so there you are—let's put it to use.' He stopped and turned, 'oh, there you are Baker', stepping back, 'yes, very handsome—very good indeed Baker'.

Sergeant Baker moved into the light, and I certainly couldn't fault his Santa Claus outfit (wherever it had come from), it would have done justice to anything Selfridge's could produce. Baker breathed a faint jet of whisky in my direction, and smiled with the assurance of a star about to give a first-night performance.

I just asked them to repeat whatever they had done on Christmas Day—which was received with hoots of laughter, and I looked questioningly at the officer. His eyes twinkled, 'We had our Christmas on Boxing Day . . . ', then they hardened, 'Christmas Day we spent mopping up a few Jerries who'd slipped across the river . . . ', he looked down at the ground, 'we lost a man—Purvis—bloody good man . . . ', then he looked up, 'there weren't any Jerry survivors', then to me, 'let's get on with it—we learned how to forget those things way back in Normandy'.

So we all got cracking, and I used two rolls of Super Double-X on a hilarious display of Santa handing out his Christmas gifts. The way he did it got bursts of laughter all round. The line of troops would move towards him singly, and Santa would pick up a tin of Spam, or Corned Beef, or even a packet of 'hard-tack' biscuits, gravely handing it to the surprised soldier, who would react in an offended manner—then Santa would reach under his voluminous robe and produce a bottle of whisky or gin, several bars of *milk* chocolate (an unheard-of luxury), and a card with brightly painted Santas, gnomes, fairies and a single gleaming star up in the top right hand corner. After this they gathered in a tight group and sang carols—which didn't mean a lot without sound—but the close-ups on their faces more than made up for that. They were obviously a very closely knit group, for they hung to to each others' shoulders, and their expressions were by no means forced. There was a strong feeling of camaraderie between them—and it showed very vividly through my viewfinder. This was a strong bond of friendship.

Then I had to explain to them that by the time this film got back to England, the cinemas would probably take this as a block 'Festive Season' item and they should now appear as though they were 'bringing in the New Year'. Without sound, this would be very difficult to show, but the Lieutenant said he had 'a glimmering of an idea', but it would take a short time to arrange. So he proposed that I should feel free to enjoy the 'goodies' on the table, and he disappeared with his Sergeant and a Corporal. The rest of the group gathered round me, ensuring I never had an empty glass, and 'noshing' me with some excellent ham. I was aware that something was going on at the end stall, but the troops kept shooting questions at me about the film business, and the particular operations of the Army Film Unit. I wasn't loath to 'tuck in', as I was both hungry and thirsty, and my accounts of AFPU kept my attention within the happy group. They were getting quite a kick from the idea of being 'fillum actors', and I was happy that my visit was going so well.

The Lieutenant eventually returned and said all was ready. Making sure I had a fresh roll of film in the camera, I was escorted—a little unsteady—towards the stall. The scout car and the portable 'spot' had been angled on the end stall. The drapes were on some pulley arrangement, and were closed, and I was asked to take up a position just outside. (The Lieutenant had really got himself into the role of Director!) He gave me a nod and I started running the camera. A hidden hand pulled a string and the drapes opened. The stall had been really 'done up' to look like a bedroom. There was a bureau down one side, where an assortment of greeting cards and 'family style' photographs, together with a small bowl of 'real'—I couldn't be sure—flowers, were carefully arranged. Above the bed was a picture of the Royal couple, and below was a good-sized calendar, which I suspected had come from the officer's domain, and it very craftily showed 'December 31'! On the bed lay a figure wearing a straggly beard of cotton-wool, and it had been extended to cover his head. The figure was covered in a long white sheet and 'nipped' at the middle to look like a gown. There were a few very visible tears, and with the addition of some sooty streaks, really gave the impression of age. Propped against the wall was a real farm scythe (a prop which would have been easy to acquire in this back-water farming community of Holland). Beside the bed was a small table with a battered alarm clock, whose hands indicated a few minutes to twelve. The figure was writing in an obvious, standard-issue, Army ledger, but someone had painted the bold figures of '1944' across the cover.

It didn't take me long to absorb the impression of the idea they were trying to convey, and I moved forward to take it in close-up, pulling focus and praying I had enough 'depth' at f 5.6. There was just time to establish this close-shot, when I felt a tug on the back of my uniform, and a voice asked me to move back a bit. I did, and another figure appeared from my right dressed in a clean gown and carrying *another* scythe painted white. I suddenly realised how the end result of this mime was about to be revealed, and I automatically shouted 'Cut!' as I switched off the camera. They all looked at me with a touch of annoyance here and there, and I hurriedly explained, that this particular camera only ran a certain time on one full wind of its clockwork motor, and I could anticipate pretty accurately when this was going to be—right in the middle of their pay-off scene. Furthermore, I explained, the sequence would be better if I changed my camera-angle and, incidentally, you've got drips of white paint from the scythe down the back of your neck! They hooted with laughter, and the officer thanked me for the lesson in film making. So I took up a fresh position, cranked the De Vry as far as I dared, and the cleaned-up soldier began his entry once more.

As he approached, the recumbent figure looked up from his diary, then, with a glance at the clock, reached up and pulled the page from the calendar to reveal the printed words 'Happy New Year'. He closed his 'diary', swung off the bed, picked up the old scythe, then, without a glance at the newcomer, he passed out of camera range. The new arrival picked up the clock and altered the hands to show just after midnight, placed the whitened scythe (a trifle gingerly!) against the wall, and lay down on the bed. To my astonishment and hoots of laughter from behind me, he reached into his gown and withdrew a cigar and lit it with one of those 'home-made lighters', which was basically a .303 cartridge case! A very neat touch, I thought, and told him to hold it whilst I moved in for a close-up. There was a shout from behind, and I cut the camera. The officer told me what he had arranged, and I moved back to the stall entrance, giving the camera another hasty crank. I re-focused, and on a cue, the group approached him one at a time, then arranged themselves as best they could, either sitting or standing, with the last man bearing a tray holding a bottle of whisky and several glasses. Quickly now, measures were poured all round, then they first toasted the recumbent figure, now juggling with a lighted cigar and a brimming glass, then they all turned towards me and toasted the camera.

I switched off, then just fell about, helpless with laughter, and the whole scene fell into bits as everyone else did the same. Somebody thrust a glass of whisky into my hand and I put it down in one, then turned to the officer and thanked him profusely—and I wasn't kidding when I told him he had a future in the film business. He shook his head and indicated the Corporal. 'No—it's Corporal Harris here—he's the brainchild. Was just getting into amateur dramatics, when he was called up . . . ', he gulped his whisky, 'we've done a few sketches with ENSA—an' we did a big one in Brussels after the liberation'. He paused, and a reflective frown crossed his face. 'Yes—that was when we had Brown—an' little Jimmy Crawford—an'—oh hell, let's drink up.' And we did—for about another hour or so—then, rather shakily, I made a quick round, shaking each man firmly by the hand—and somehow, but not too clearly, drove the Jeep back to Deurne. My mind was cluttered with too much whisky, but I knew I would remember those troops for a very long time.

I never did get a report from Pinewood, and when I asked about it, they just said 'Sorry, but we had a welter of Christmas and New Year material and—well you know how it was at that time—with the Ardennes ''push'', and the panic it caused all the way to Antwerp—well, I said I'm sorry'. He was right, of course, for I forgot about it also—but during my many years working television, and watching some of those awful rehearsals—the memory of that Magic Barn would come back, and I wondered if they all made it safely through to the end of the war.

New Year's Eve was the usual 'drink to a Happy New Year' and door-to-door tipples with the Dutch we had befriended in Deurne. No doubt the women of Deurne today have other memories. I retired at the reasonable hour of 1 am January 1 1945, but there was little sleep as other besotted members stumbled about in the dark seeking their paliasses, and they were none to careful where they planted their feet. At dawn on New Year's Day, the Germans presented us with their compliments of the season. The Luftwaffe gathered every aircraft they could fly and launched a remarkable attack on every position we held. It was a full-hearted effort and did quite a lot of damage, also curing a few king-sized hangovers. Their attack ranged as far as Brussels, but mostly remained on a low-strafing level.

There was a convoy passing through Deurne at the time and they were not maintaining proper convoy distances, so there was a dangerous snarl of traffic in the narrow street. We all grabbed at the nearest weapons, but the only useful ones were a couple of Schmeissers. Windows shattered with ricochets and we made a hasty exit outside. The cook for some reason thought he would be safer in the outside latrine, but maybe the smell drove him out, and not too soon as a small fragmentation bomb blew the entire thunder-box into a thousand malodorous pieces.

The Germans were really giving us the lot, bombing and strafing at roof-top level until, from the jammed convoy in the road, someone managed to get a couple of Bofors guns (still mounted on their transporters) into action, and began banging away over open sights. It was a terrifying noise, but it was enough to trigger off our own official function. Cameras were hastily grabbed from boxes, but to our mortification, very few were loaded for a good run of film. I guess you can blame New Year's Eve for that, but the attack only lasted about 15 minutes, and a few of us got enough on the aftermath shambles.

One member of the section didn't hear a thing during the whole raid: my colleague Georgie Laws was spark out. George is not a great tippler, but the night before—and just for Auld Lang Syne—he had been encouraged to have a few. For a time, as glasses were passed around, he was enjoying himself until he removed his spectacles and began mopping his face, which in turn was changing from its normal healthy appearance to a sickly, greenish pallor. Then he quietly passed out. It was obvious this was no ordinary 'passing out' from too much to drink, and someone examined the contents of his glass. There was beer in it all right, until somebody risked a sip, 'Developer—the bloody stuff has been spiked with developer', and spat the small mouthful on the floor. It could have been a very nasty prank, but then, accident could not be ruled out as every container that would hold a drink had been pressed into service the previous night, and the tiny, boarded-up corner used to develop the occasional personal photo had a selection of glasses and beakers. Anyway, his horrible pallor had gone and he appeared to be breathing normally, but when he woke the next day, long after the raid, he mouthed a horrible 'Yeek!' then looked around at the debris and muttered, 'Boy, some party'. With that he went back to sleep and didn't return to the land of the living until next day.

*　　　*　　　*

Just prior to the thrust on Cleve and Goch, the worst tragedy to strike at the heart of AFPU was the death of Bill Gross, Vic Watkins and their driver. Very little information is available about the incident, but apparently they were proceeding quite confidently up the road towards Heinsberg—remember, they were veterans, but always willing to take a chance on a hunch. Perhaps the hunch began to ring the wrong sort of bells, for at some stage they stopped. The professional within them warned them of something wrong and they hastened to turn the Jeep around. But the ring of warning proved to be a German 88, and the Jeep was dead in his sights. As it turned, it became a better target and the pressure on the trigger-finger did the rest.

Bill and Vic died fast and clean—but what were they doing on a road up which no other British troops had dared to go? They were far more professional in warfare than a great number of the troops in the line were, and their instinct for danger had an assurance that no other 'paired cameramen' possessed. So why did they die on a cold morning of January 24 1945?

One of the nastiest operations was that of the Reichswald Forest and the seizure of the towns of Cleve and Goch. The forest itself was an ominous objective, with its trees huddled together in a permanent ground mist. It was nine miles by five in extent and there was a menacing lack of bird-life: the whole area exuded a stench of sudden death. The few tracks through the forest were narrow, rutted and often so muddy that their use for tanks and other heavy traffic was ruled out. The 51st and 54th Divisions had the job of clearing a passage through the forest. They only had one good road from Kranenburg to Cleve and the plan was that the 3rd Canadian Division would push in from the north, and with the 15th Scottish Division, complete the attack on Cleve. But at the last minute, the 51st was diverted to an all-out attack on Goch.

At 5 am on the morning of February 8 the attack began with a very heavy artillery barrage lasting for about five hours. It was an impressive array of field weapons: 4.5s, 5.5s, 17-pounders, 25-pounders, rockets and much more besides. It was estimated that 11,000 tons were fired from 1,200 guns. I was only present for the opening barrage when I received a message from Major Hugh Stewart to return to HQ—he had some other job for me. I cannot say I was disappointed, but I did feel sorry for Sergeants 'Slim' Hewitt and Harry Ames who were to film the battle under hellish conditions.

Ames went with the assault on Kranenberg, following closely on the heels of the 15th Scottish, mostly over marshy ground so soft he was often up to his knees in the oozy mess. Mines were another hazard, and to this day, Ames confesses that at times he thought he would never make it. 'Slim' Hewitt's long legs managed to get him through and he alternated between the 15th Scottish and 43rd Divisions, but heavy rain prevented him getting all the pictures he wanted. Often his only choice was to try and film with rain dripping from his lens, or take cover in a muddy ditch and dry out his equipment. But during the night of February 10/11 he arrived in Cleve with the 43rd Division, although in appearance it seemed as though he had been well and truly involved with a cement-mixer.

The big reason why I had been pulled out of the line was that Hugh Stewart had recently acquired a studio-type 35 mm camera—don't ask me from where—which had some dandy long-focus lenses. With it was a heavy-duty tripod which weighed about a hundredweight. He had also found access to a church tower used as an Observation Post, having an excellent view of what appeared to be a German defence line, which seemed to be in constant change. Stewart put these two components together and came up with a dilly of an idea. Why not film these Germans in close-up, going about their duties in normal fashion, and of course it was as safe as houses! (One of Stewart's standing witticisms.)

First I had a look at the narrow winding staircase going up to the bell-tower,

Left *The Reichswald Forest was one of those dark and ominous operations, and one I was glad to miss. But Sergeant Slim Hewitt, and colleagues, did a good job in hellish conditions. Hewitt is right of photo. But the camera on the left, with Sergeant Seaholme, is one of the reasons I missed the Reichswald. Major Stewart made me hump it up to a church tower and film the enemy on the other side of the river with that nice long lens. The second reason is, I went on local leave to Brussels afterwards.* **Right** *Sergeant Jerry Rennison using the new Vinten Normandy camera. I don't know what he's so happy about—I hated the darn thing!*

then a second glance at this hefty piece of camera equipment. I opened my mouth to say something, but Stewart had that look in his eyes which said, 'what the CO wants, the CO gets'. So, with the help of my driver and a few Dutch civilians we managed to heft it all up to the tower. I put the bits together and had a look through the long lens, and sure enough, those Germans suddenly became life-size. I observed with interest the trees they used to urinate against, and in some nearby bushes it was obvious that some of the Dutch girls were still generous with their talents. For the hell of it, I took a few feet of this 'for the boys back at Pinewood', then concentrated on other things. Close-ups of shoulder-flashes which would give some idea of what troops might be in the area. Types of weapons they carried and condition of their uniforms.

I was becoming quite interested, when a couple of low moans indicated the passing of German shells. Somebody had spotted me—which was not surprising with an enormous 12-inch lens stuck out of the tower and no doubt reflecting light. Then some damn fool on our side decided to make a reply, and a few 25-pounders popped off. That's it, I said to myself, get the hell out. I began to dismantle the camera with all speed, and my driver and myself—the Dutch having vanished at the first salvo—churned all that gear down the winding staircase with a speed that would put any studio 'grip' to shame. I got it all back to Hugh Stewart; said, 'Thank you very much, it was most instructive', and returned to the safety of Deurne.

About this time, AFPU introduced a new cine camera, the Vinten Normandy, and I was asked to try it out on the next assignment. Apart from having a carrying handle, it was heavy and bulky and after one trial, I very quickly retrieved my De Vry. Even though some cameramen swore by them—I just swore.

Chapter 18

The remainder of that winter was very unpleasant, and it became a daily chore to hack the snow from the front door. 30 Corps maintained numerous assaults designed to bring 2nd Army up to the River Rhine at Xanten and Wesel. Individually, AFPU members were sent out to cover these operations, but weather conditions, fog, snow and sleety rain prevented any good coverage. We all knew the next major assault was not far away—the crossing of the River Rhine.

Peter Norris and I made a journey up to the area opposite Wesel to watch the preparations. We had been working separate assignments, and I had no doubt that Peter was turning in some excellent material whilst fulfilling his personal forays. We pictured the Engineers placing their smoke-pots—hundreds of them—which would create the artifical fog, thus enabling our troops to move up to the banks of the river, together with the numerous Buffaloes and Weasels, unseen by the enemy. Naturally, this did not fool the enemy one bit—they knew an attack was being mounted and kept up a heavy fire of mortars and 88s. But they did not know *when*—our only ace card.

The night of March 23/24, Peter Norris and myself proceeded to make the initial crossing with No 1 Commando. We had been briefed as to which Buffaloes were taking Commandos and those carrying Weasels. There was one trick I wasn't too happy about; a company of Vickers machine-guns had been placed, line abreast, to fire lines of tracers, which were to be used as guidelines. To get into the river, the Buffaloes had to climb a steep embankment, then plop over the other side and into the water. It was at the top of this embankment that those tracers were only inches away, and if you strayed off course, you could come in for a nasty hair-singe.

Another neat trick, which I performed entirely by myself, was that, due to the noise, the dark and the artificial fog, I couldn't find the Buffalo to which I was allocated. So, figuring they wouldn't call off the attack until I sorted myself out, I made a dive for the nearest, shadowy Buffalo, only to find that it was carrying a Weasel. I shouted at the driver and he merely said 'make the best of it'. And the best I could do was to lie prone across the top of the Weasel with those glowing tracers cracking just above my head.

Some say the Rhine is about 1,500 feet across. I fool you not—it's at least two miles. One exhausted and positively petrified cameraman was eventually

Left *The build-up to the Rhine crossing. Sergeant Bert Hardy is seen taking pictures of the smoke-pots which created an artificial fog to hide the build-up.*

Right *For the Commandos' night-crossing of the Rhine, a Vickers machine-gun section fired lines of tracers, to point the right direction for our Buffaloes.*

Below right *3rd Division infantry prepare to cross the Rhine at dusk.*

deposited on the Eastern bank of the river. Fortunately there were enough ghostly figures in green berets to establish I was with friends, and all I had to do was follow the white tape-line towards Wesel. Many buildings were burning and I tried for some silhouette shots of Commandos going past, but they weren't hanging about, so it was not very successful. Eventually I met up with Peter at the Command HQ—and as it would be a few hours before the dawn necessary to start filming, we decided to kip down in a room next to the HQ.

The day of the 24th was to be a very busy one for us; we knew we had to get as much coverage as possible, then somehow get that film back across the Rhine. We decided to split up and go like the clappers. There was plenty to see for the town of Wesel was a wreck and many patrols of Commandos were soon mopping up what proved to be light resistance. The German Commander of Wesel presumably tried to make a get-away, but a well placed burst of machine-gun fire brought him down—dead. Our cameras rarely stopped, especially when the United States paratroops, and the British 6th Airborne, with cameramen Sergeants Bill Lawrie and Harry Oakes, went overhead at roof-top height. At one point I was approached by Lieutenant Colonel Mills-Roberts, Commander of the Commandos, who hastened me to where he had an enormous number of prisoners busily enlarging a vast shell-crater. This was to be a temporary POW cage, he explained, and pointed out he had several senior German officers digging like mad to enlarge the crater.

What he wanted me to do was take some film of this seqence, whilst he told the enemy in fluent German that copies of this film, plus close-ups of the dead German Commander of the area, Major General Deutch, would be dropped into their homeland, so that all could see how the mighty Wehrmacht were faring. When I tried to explain the technical problems in having copies made in time, he merely tipped me a wink and said, 'Don't even try—this is purely psychological'. I just nodded and went on filming, but I was thinking that our Mills-Roberts was

a bit of an extremist. Soon, it was decided we had enough material, and now faced the slight dilemma of returning the film to AFPU on the other side of the Rhine. We had noticed a number of Buffaloes being used to ferry wounded and prisoners, so we asked if we could have a lift. The answer was no, and for once the showing of SHAEF passes did not help. So, how to get back?

We looked at the broken bridge and its centre span in the river, and didn't like it at all. But there was no other way. We arrived at the span which rose out of the ground at right angles and looked up at this with just a shade of mistrust. The span ended high in the air with only the wreckage of the centre one hanging precariously into the river. From there the third span, with a perilous twist, carried on to dry land. A party of Royal Engineers were there, hastily constructing a Bailey bridge, and some were moving across the wrecked bridge with the agility of monkeys. They made it look too easy. When the RE Sergeant saw what we planned to do he suggested that a couple of his Sappers went ahead

Above *Sergeant Bill Lawrie who crossed the Rhine with the 6th Airborne.*

Left *Sergeant Harry Oakes accompanied Lawrie in the 6th Airborne crossing.*

Below *The German Commander of the Wesel area on the other side of the Rhine; Major-General Deutch was shot by a Commando whilst trying to escape.*

of us to show where the best footholds were. He then added a further ominous warning—some hidden Germans were still taking pot-shots. 'Lost a couple of my lads this morning, though it seems to have died out—but take care.'

We started to climb up the first span, and this was relatively easy, then we came to the swinging wreckage trailing into the river. Its movement was caused by the heavy river current, and just as the Sappers were pointing out the footholds, there was a metallic zing from one of the girders. 'That bloody sniper', I said. But the Sapper shook his head and cheerfully pointed out that some of the bolts holding the wrecked girder had been bent in the explosion and were now beginning to shear away! That was one piece of interesting information I could have done without, but the gesture from the Sapper indicated that we get on with it, so we started down this almost natural ladder. When we neared the surface of the river, the Sapper now pointed out that all we had to do was leap about three feet on to a concrete bastion and the next section would take us to dry land.

With that he left us, returning to the other side like some khaki-clad Tarzan. As it was, we made the rest of the climb with ease—although I didn't much care for that three feet jump across to the concrete bastion. Then, with the help of some Military Police, we made it back to HQ. Hugh Stewart welcomed us back and we had a good meal plus a few snorts of whisky, and I was heading for my bed when Stewart popped his head in the door. 'Get as much rest as you can—reveille for you and Norris will be 5 am. That Bailey bridge is almost complete and you are both going back into Wesel with the 11th Armoured Division. They move about 6.30.'

*   *   *

Once back with the 11th Armoured Division, both Peter and I felt much more at home. Everywhere, the German defences were crumbling and we were now romping over good roads into the heart of Germany. During this fast advance we passed thousands of German prisoners going the other way. Even AFPU were taking prisoners and Fred Palmer was no exception. Just prior to the outbreak of war, Fred had become a chartered accountant, which involved tax problems and often protracted arguments with Inspectors of Taxes. But now that we were 'swanning' across Germany, Fred got the opportunity of capturing his first honest-to-goodness prisoner.

He was with a section of tanks passing through a village when he saw what appeared to be a high-ranking German officer ducking back into the doorway of a very imposing house. Right, thought Fred, this is it—I'll get me a prisoner. Before proceeding up the drive-way he persuaded a Churchill tank commander to position his gun turret and give him some cover-fire if necessary. A good chartered accountant always thinks in terms of insurance. Revolver in hand, he entered the house to find the officer surrounded by his family. They were obviously stiff from fear and the officer did not hesitate when Fred ordered him outside. He then marched him down the drive and stood him by a wall, with the German's hands clasped above his head in approved manner.

Now it was Fred's turn to be uncertain about the next move, for neither could speak the other's language and by now the officer's wife and children were around him and plainly pleading for the man's life. But Fred was convinced he had a high-ranking officer, judging by the cut of the uniform with its gold braid and medals. He then shouted at the tank commander to find an interpreter, and eventually a Sergeant arrived saying he would escort the prisoner to be interrogated by Intelligence. Fred agreed to this, but insisted in going along. After all, it was his prisoner.

When they reached Intelligence, quite an exchange of German was bandied about, but after about half-an-hour the Intelligence Officer told Fred to return the German to his house, and he would accompany them to explain matters to the family. As they returned to the house, Fred tried to elicit an explanation from the Intelligence Officer, who turned away his queries with a twinkle in his eye. Back at the house, the whole party was soon surrounded by the family all chattering away in German, and by the tone, Fred had the feeling that the atmosphere had changed, and at last the Intelligence man decided to explain.

The high-ranking officer Fred had captured was a German Tax Inspector, and with the Germans' mania for uniforms, the man was entitled to wear one, but he had been told to return to his house, discard the uniform, and get into a suit of civilian clothes for his own safety. Although the joke was on Fred, he still proudly tells it, for he reckons that this may have been the first time on record that a chartered accountant had made a prisoner of an Inspector of Taxes! After all, he mildly protests, it could have been somebody really important.

*   *   *

Now, in the early part of April, the advance rolled on and, despite the 'No Fraternisation' signs stuck on every tree, when nightfall came and we sought a billet to spend the night the usual form was—find the best-looking house around and tell the German owners it was being requisitioned for the night, and if they didn't like it, then they could go sleep in the barn. Cooks and servants were retained, sometimes at gun-point and, after dinner, fraternisation was as good a way to spend the evening as any. My colleague, Peter Norris, had little to do with this—he had his own rounds of camera enthusiasts to make.

Each pair of cameramen as a functional team were now working very well indeed. George Laws went on with the now recovered Bill Leeson. Bob Jones and Fred Palmer were happy together. Blakeley and Cheetham were planning ahead towards the end of the war and the opportunities that would be available. Jock Gordon and Norman Johnston, who had excelled themselves on the Rhine crossing by artfully discovering that the second wave of 9th Cameronians near Xanten were making a dawn crossing, and so got the best actual crossing material together with a classic hand-held cine shot, using a six-inch lens, of the Airborne flying very low over the Rhine, and were lucky enough to get a pranged Dakota crashing behind a farmhouse.

Sergeant Pat Whittaker, however, had the good fortune of filming an armada of American Liberators flying low over Xanten and later, when he had made his own crossing, met up with the US paratroopers on the east bank of the river. When another flight of Liberators flew over at rooftop height dropping supplies, he got full coverage of this great demonstration of low flying, although he debated how much of the supplies fell to the enemy. But it was the team of Dickie Gee and Tubby Palmer who witnessed an incident that had a very strong effect on Dickie. They were with the Guards Armoured Division, and heard reports of isolated pockets up ahead being held by crack SS troops. On this occasion they were tagging a column of 'soft' vehicles with the tanks not too far ahead. Late on a spring afternoon they heard sounds of fighting amongst the lead tanks. Being with a soft column, it wasn't too difficult to pull out and race ahead.

Dickie Gee describes the scene that haunted him for a long time afterwards. A great, open German lorry was reared up a long, sloping bank on the side of the road, twisted and smoking after what had obviously been a near-direct hit. Bits of wreckage littered the road and two smaller vehicles could be seen tilted into the ditch some distance away. A small group of men, wearing Red Cross armbands of medical orderlies, were moving around the roadside near the lorry. As they drew nearer they saw three German soldiers—one of them a youth about 17— lying propped against the bank, in a grim row. All were still alive, but obviously dying. The youth seemed to be in a particularly bad way, his expression was one of incredible fear, and his eyes stared blankly from a pale green face. Their greatcoats lay open, arms hanging limply down their sides. Medical orderlies were tending these unfortunate men, but it was plain their lives were draining away as they watched.

With automatic reflexes, they filmed the sequence, but with little enthusiasm. All that Dickie could think of at that moment was the futility of it all—three men, dying on a spring evening. Countless numbers had already died, and many more would do so before this war ended—but this seemed so wretched and meaningless. Three determined and fanatical boys—and they were just boys— pitting their misplaced courage against a squadron of tanks. Sergeants Palmer and Gee returned to their Jeep and moved on up the line of advance. Two days later they had to pass that spot again on their way back to base. By the roadside were three new graves.

Chapter 19

Near the Dortmund-Ems Canal lay the town of Ibbenburen which fell to units of the HLI, and Sergeant Whittaker was with them when they encountered, initially, some stiff resistance from SS officer cadets. Maybe their training had just begun, for, when a fairly heavy 'stonk' was laid down, they hastily departed. Instead of setting up a line of defence, they took refuge in a nearby wood and went to sleep. Their dreams of becoming dashing SS officers soon disappeared when they were awakened by tough-looking MPs and very quickly gave themselves up.

Pat Whittaker took advantage of the situation, and filmed this SS 'brainwash' establishment where they had trained. All the stock-in-trade impedimenta were self-evident, the mandatory portrait of Hitler glared from the wall. Others depicting Goering and Doenitz lay about, and an SS uniform hung on a dummy. Posters displayed heroic Germans uttering slogans, 'Strength and Will to work— etc', and copies of *Mein Kampf* were laid out like Holy Scriptures. Somewhere, Pat felt, their training had gone wrong, and there was a growing feeling now that the war could end very soon—most of us had heard that many of Hitler's Generals had pleaded that he should cease this useless slaughter—but had only received a raving tirade that he was, 'surrounded by traitors', and a pointed, shaking finger indicated that the next officer making the suggestion shouldn't plan on long life and prosperity.

But the signs were there for all to see, which gave rise to two distinct schools of thought. One—let's blast like hell now for Berlin before the Russians make it first. Two—who wants to be the last man killed during hostilities? The last choice no doubt gave rise to the caution with which a ranking German officer carrying a white flag was eyed, as he walked through the 11th Armoured Division's lines and asked to see the Commanding Officer. Maybe the first choice was in other people's minds as they felt this might be an emissary seeking peace. True, the German officer was now asking 'Pip' Roberts for a cessation of hostilities, but only around an area known as Bergen-Belsen. It was painfully explained to a very sceptical 'Pip' Roberts, that in this area lay a huge political detention centre, and so many had contracted typhus that a show of arms by the 11th might cause some of those poor creatures to escape and spread their dreaded contamination amongst the British.

Well, this was no way to play gamesmanship with Roberts as he could smell the transparent stratagem a mile away. He bundled the officer back to his own lines, and just to satisfy any doubts, got his Military Police to prepare some 'Danger—Typhus' signs and stick them up ahead so that both sides could see them. He then proceeded to move his division forward to a comfortable hailing distance, got into his scout car with a couple of Shermans flanking him and bade Peter and me to follow him up to the gates of this detention centre. Here Roberts halted, and with two tough tooking tank men carrying Tommy guns, advanced on the gate. Peter and I were only yards away, but we were still unaware of what it was all about. Through the wire we could see groups of figures and, as we observed that Roberts was still waiting at the gate, we went over to the wire mesh and peered through. There was something odd about those figures and I rammed a telescopic view-finder on to my camera and stuck it through the wire. What now came into clearer focus made the hair on the back of my neck do the most frightening things.

If they were human, these groups were skeletons held together with rags. As if to prove they were alive, two of them pushed up into a standing position and began a slow shuffle in our direction. I pulled focus as they moved, and the gruesome sight of their emaciated faces made me pull away from the wire. At the same time I sensed some movement at the gates. They were open and 'Pip' Roberts was facing a man and a woman. The man was a real thick-ear type, face unshaven and head close-cropped; he wore a loose-fitting tunic and baggy trousers. By comparison, the girl's hair was blonde and long enough to hang loosely down the back of a sleeveless sweater, under which she wore a crisply clean, man's white shirt, buttoned to the neck with sleeves rolled up her forearms. Below that was a neat plaid skirt which fell over the high jack-boots on her feet. Their names were Irma Grese and Joseph Kramer.

Negotiations between them and 'Pip' Roberts were brief and he curtly ordered them to be manacled and placed in the guardroom. A section of the 11th, together

Exterior and general view of Belsen Concentration Camp.

Above *Commandant of Belsen Camp, Joseph Kramer, under heavy guard.* **Right** *A lone Belsen victim. Note the tatters of his prison clothing hanging round his boots. The blanket is probably his solitary belonging.* **Far right** *A British soldier has given one of the victims a tin of cigarettes. This one looks as though he may recover with medical assistance.* **Below** *The bodies of the dead were thrown into pits and covered with lime.*

with a large number of Red Cross were then allowed to enter the camp, but kept their distance from the prisoners. Peter and I went along and filmed as one horror after another was revealed. These inmates were scarcely alive and it was clear that little could be done to help them. But the sights and the smells soon became so odious that we retreated towards the gates, and it was also obvious that occupation of the camp by the 11th Armoured was not part of the plan and the grateful troops began to leave.

When, some weeks later, I met up with the AFPU group of unfortunates who had the job of recording for posterity on film the reality of Belsen, Carl Sutton told me how he felt on entering that awesome area. Before being allowed in the camp the team, consisting of Carl, Bert Hardy, Slim Hewitt and Captain Malandine, were inoculated against typhus and given a thorough dusting with anti-louse powder. Whilst this was being done the stench of decomposing corpses and the accompanying filth filled their nostrils so heavily that it became a taste rather than a smell. They were, in turn, and sometimes in unison, violently sick and the real job hadn't even been started.

Entering the compound Carl described as walking across a carpet of corpses, human excreta and tattered remnants of clothing in pieces too small to any longer give cover or warmth. Among this mess the few internees who were still able to walk shuffled aimlessly around. Naked, almost skeletal, men and women squatted like dogs to add their daily contributions to the stinking morass. There were no latrines or sanitary facilities for the camp internees. Carl said he was physically and mentally so deeply revolted that the long succession of battlefields they had photographed on the push from Normandy seemed almost clean by comparison. Here was the damning evidence of Hitler's determination to exterminate the Jews to be recorded for all the world to see and, he hoped, remember.

Swallowing his bile and trying to convince himself that this was just another photographic assignment, he entered the first of the huts which was carpeted just as gruesomely as the ground outside. Each hut was originally intended to house 60 people but up to 600 had been crammed in so that three or four inmates had to share one bunk in the three tier units. At least one of those in each bunk, where they huddled together for warmth, was already cold with death but the survivors were too weak to roll out the bodies. As Carl started to film one of the stacked up bunk units he saw, through the viewfinder, a woman reaching towards him, probably hoping her saviour had arrived. But, for her it was too late, as she slumped over the side of the bunk and dropped to the floor dead, joining several other corpses that had been left where they fell. She was just one of the 400 to 500 who died every day during those early weeks after our servicemen took on the tremendous task of trying to reverse the Nazi process of intentional death by starvation, disease and degradation.

When our troops first entered the camp, on April 15 1945, there were over 50,000 internees. The majority of these in addition to suffering from severe malnutrition, had typhus, typhoid, tuberculosis or dysentry. The camp inmates had been without food, water or electricity for seven days before the arrival of the British Army. Lying around the area, or inside the huts, or in open graves, there were at least 10,000 bodies, many of which were in advanced stages of decomposition. Most of the bodies were typhus infected. Some of the 'fresher' bodies bore signs of what little flesh had remained on them having been torn away, bearing mute witness that during the final stages of starvation some of the stronger survivors had been driven to that final, most frightening form of degradation—cannibalism. Eye witness accounts from healed internees confirmed this was happening through February, March and April and were by no means isolated cases.

Photographing the huge noisome open graves containing hundreds of bodies which should have been covered weeks ago, Carl almost fell into one as he backed off to try to get a mountain of boots 'in-frame'. These had been taken from bodies before cremation when the camp was working 'efficiently' in the hands of the SS and Wehrmacht. The pile was over 12 feet high and covered an area of about 650 square feet. A strange memorial to the hundreds of thousands who had taken their last walk in one of the pairs of boots in that pile.

Despite the fact that Belsen existed as a concentration camp throughout the war there seem to have been, among those released by us, no survivors from the hundreds of thousands of internees, who had been there longer than nine months. The majority could only date their arrival as about three to four months earlier. Certainly this isn't because any appreciable number were given their freedom by the Nazis. Of the very few who were given 'freedom' it appears more than probable that the majority were young girls destined for the officers' quarters. Unlike the dictated procedure at the infamous Auschwitz camp, where extermination of Jews was by the use of gas-chambers, that at Belsen was by use of starvation and untreated diseases.

The daily diet for Belsen internees was about eight ounces of black bread and three pints of swede soup. Prisoners' routine started at 0300 hours when they began the day by 'cleaning' out their huts. This entailed all who could still stand dragging out those who had died during the night. Death for the starving inmates was often speeded-up by being beaten or flogged by the SS men and women guards who derived a great deal of enjoyment from these all too regular sessions. Frequent indiscriminate shooting of prisoners was another popular pastime for the guards. For members of the camp's medical staff, who were more at home with a scalpel in their hands than a Schmeisser machine-pistol, but no less deadly, there was endless fun. An inexhaustible supply of human guinea pigs provided them with numerous opportunities for experimentation in areas which would never be permitted in a civilised community.

At the Nuremberg trial, massive documentation was produced as evidence to Hitler's 'Final Solution', regarding the Jewish community. It is a tale of horror of which the German medical profession cannot be proud, and revealed that scarcely a single member—many of whom were leading physicians of the Reich—ever uttered the slightest public protest. Not even Germany's most famous surgeon, Dr Ferdinand Sauerbruch, did, although he later became an anti-Nazi and conspired with the resistance.

Later, at the trial of SS Captain Josef Kramer—the 'Beast of Belsen'—who faced a host of charges (having been chief exterminator of Auschwitz, Mauthausen and Dachau, before Bergen-Belsen), he recounted several stories of his 'methods'.

'Whilst I was at Auschwitz, I met Professor Hirt of the Strasbourg Anatomical Institute, who gave me a bottle of cyanide salts, and instructed me on the correct dosage to use to poison a specific number of inmates. One day I received eighty prisoners who were to be killed with the gas Hirt had given me. That night I went to the gas chamber with about fifteen women, and I told them they had to go into the chamber to be disinfected. I did not tell them however, that they were to be gassed.'*

Kramer then continued to explain that, by a little trial and error, he soon perfected the technique, and how, with his staff, he was able to exterminate larger numbers. 'With the help of a few SS men', he continued, 'I stripped the women completely and shoved them into the gas chamber. When the door closed they began to scream. I introduced a certain amount of salt through the tube, and observed through a peep-hole what happened inside. The women breathed for about half a minute before they fell to the floor. After I had turned on the ventilation I opened the door, I found them to be quite lifeless and covered with excrement.'

Kramer was then asked what his feelings were at the time, and his answer reflects the complete domination of Hitler's fanatical 'Final Solution' decree. 'I

---

*Quotations from William Shirer's *The Rise and Fall of the Third Reich.*

had no feelings in carrying out these orders, because I had been told to kill the inmates in the way I already told you', then he added, 'that, by the way, was the way I was trained!'

But before continuing his advance, Roberts left a small section of tanks to await the arrival of Brigadier Hugh Glyn Hughes, Senior Medical Officer to the 2nd Army, who would soon be arriving with a huge team of medical workers. This was to be a fearsome task for the Brigadier, who would have to deal with 56,000 still living inmates, of whom 500 would die every day. We were very glad to leave this behind and continue with 'normal' warfare, although I later felt sorry for other colleagues like Sergeants Oakes, Hewitt, Lawrie, Lewis, Midgely, Hardy and Lieutenant Wilson, who had the unenviable taks of making a complete record of Belsen. There were many backward looks from the 11th Armoured's tank-men at the withered, emaciated figures clinging to the inside of their wired graveyard. As I considered my own feelings after seeing this exhibition of Nazi terrorism, I watched the faces of those others who had been there, and I knew that any future German who crossed their paths, be they man, woman or child, would have much to answer for. It was a frightening thought, but I knew it was inevitable.

The tougher line soon became apparent as we pushed our way through small German towns and villages. Orders had been relayed to the occupants of these places to display a white flag, sheet or any other white material from all their windows, as a token of their total surrender. It made good film material as the tank columns roared through, sometimes, deserted streets—although groups of silent Germans would gather at some points and, quite deliberately, turn their backs on us. But this silent demonstration, together with the rows of fluttering white, gave an added punch to our film. The tank-crews gave no sign of recognition at this obvious hostililty, but all turret guns were manned on their traverse and it was plain they would be used should anything occur to the contrary.

Then it happened. The scene looked the same—a single main street village with fluttering white sheets, but not a sign of any inhabitant. At a slight bend of the road, where the tanks bunched together and gears had been changed to a lower ratio, several petrol bombs were lobbed from an open window. Many tanks were soon ablaze and crews were getting out as fast as they could, but they were soon brought down by a hail of small-arms fire. Some radio man had hastily got off a message to Rear HQ, and within 30 minutes the remaining tanks withdrew from the village.

Fast decisions were made, and very soon a battery of 25-pounders and a couple of rocket launchers spent about an hour obliterating nearly every house in the village. After that, came the armoured bulldozer to clear the path for the tanks. In less than three hours from the time the first petrol bomb had been thrown, the tanks were now ploughing their way through the wreckage of what had been a perfectly whole village. Infantry were detailed to make a thorough search of the ruins and, paying special attention to houses only slightly damaged, found the source of the ambush and eliminated them. The bodies proclaimed they were Hitler Youth members, although many civilians were found with stores of arms and equipment, which literally made every civilian a potential enemy. During the search, two Hitler Youths tried to shoot it out with a section of our infantry. They died—not screaming for mercy, but with a series of 'Heil Hitlers'. An estimate of their ages put them at no more than 13 or 14 years.

Many Film Unit members came across such incidents which were duly filmed. To the best of my knowledge, these scenes were never shown on British cinema screens, for, stripped of their Hitler Youth arm-bands, they looked just what they were. Kids. The cinema-going public of England were still not discriminate enough to recognise the almost abrupt change in the style of warfare, now that their troops had moved from friendly countries into Hitler's fortress. Many of the English cinema-going public even disbelieved the scenes from Belsen and other atrocity camps. Another example of the new, tough measures taken by our troops in Germany was one that I myself witnessed. When filmed, it looked nothing at all—one would have required sound to show the realities of what was an almost macabre situation.

We were hell-bent for the River Elbe by now and on the outskirts of a small town we came under considerable sniper fire. A concentration of this fire was coming from a small granary on the outskirts of town, and the troop commander sent a few tanks to deal with the situation. They approached the granary and, through binoculars, one of the tank crew spotted the source of the sniper fire. It was coming from the top of a steel silo and gave good protection to the occupants. The tank commander weighed-up the situation and, realising that his own heavy tank guns would not elevate enough on their turrets to be of any use, decided to make use of a mechanical hoist some 30 yards away from the silo. The hoist was designed to take a railway truck containing grain, and haul it up high enough to tilt the whole affair and allow the grain to empty into a storage chamber. So he decided his Sherman was about to become airborne, and wedged it into the hoist—slightly bulging the uprights in doing so—but found it did not affect the upward movement of the mechanism.

The whole apparatus came to a halt a bare foot below the level of the silo 30 feet away. The tank commander traversed the turret and found he could elevate the gun and get it dead in his sights. All this time, a hail of Spandau fire had been coming his way, but only bouncing off the Sherman. But it did prove the enemy were not about to give up. Standing high in his turret, the tank commander, using a loud-hailer, shouted at the Germans to surrender. His only reply was a further burst of Spandau. His mind made up, the tank commander gave instructions to his gunner. 'One armour-piercing, then one explosive.' The gunner nodded, and the tank commander lifted up the loud-hailer, and from my ground level I could hear the tank commander's reply, 'OK Kraut—you asked for it. Now repeat after me, 'Our Father who art in heaven, hallowed be thy name', and right through the Lord's Prayer to the word 'amen'—when he added just one more word, 'Fire', and that silo just disappeared. I couldn't see the Sherman from my position, but I had a fairly good view of the silo—and I guessed what was coming—so I switched on the camera just a few words from the end of the Lord's Prayer. Through the view-finder I saw the silo just vanish and it didn't look very spectacular at all. But it disposed of the snipers. I realised by now, that my feelings towards the Germans had become indifferent to their own personal sufferings and Peter and I agreed that it was a case of 'to the victor go the spoils' and, if an all-out 'blitzkrieg' on the part of the Allies would get this war over and done with, then let's do it.

Another incident we observed with almost impassive disinterest occurred when we were riding our usual position near the head of the tank column. It was a thinly wooded area and one could see for some distance amongst the trees. Incredibly, we observed a thin-skinned, horse-drawn German column travelling the opposite direction about 100 yards away through the woods. Travelling in that direction could only mean they were retreating; attempting to surrender, or were lost. But with our Shermans clanking down the main road, why did they not approach us? We were plain enough to be seen and heard for miles. I am sure if a detachment of our infantry had intercepted them, then nothing would happen other than a straightforward surrender. But our troops were lazily sunning themselves in the early spring sunshine, lying across the backs of the tanks or in the open three-tonners. In any case, they had just had lunch. So, on an order passed down by radio, about every second tank traversed their guns and proceeded to rip the column to pieces. Several Germans made a hopeless attempt to conceal themselves behind the thin trees, but they too were soon blasted into eternity.

When the tanks finally ceased firing, we both went into the wood with a few curious infantrymen. Several of the lorries were on fire and others had spilled their contents for some distance around. There was very little left of the Germans, and my only sense of horror returned when I saw the pitiful remains of the horses. Some were still kicking in their death-throes and I was glad when some of the infantry finally despatched them. From the quantities of stores that were undamaged, the column had been carrying rations, clothing and small reserves of weapons. Whilst the infantry began sorting out some of the small arms for souvenirs, Peter waved me further down the column. An enclosed vehicle had burst open and its contents lay around in bundles. It was money! I began to shrug it off as I knew German money was worthless, until Peter shoved a bundle under my nose. It was all Danish kroner—and negotiable—but at that moment we knew not where. Certainly not large sums of this nature. It must have been a paymaster's truck. But Peter, who now had a nose for these matters, began stuffing bundles in his haversack and under his battle-dress blouse, so I proceeded to do likewise. Then we made our way back to our Jeep like pregnant ducks.

It was not until we reached Denmark—and I must point out, at that moment we had no idea we would ever see that country—that we found we had over £1,000 worth of Danish kroner between us! I know—I know, had we but known. For we must have left several thousands of good negotiable stuff back in that wood in Germany!

Chapter 20

The River Elbe was to be our last river crossing, and Peter and I went over with the Commandos at a point called Lauenberg. From our point of view, it was the biggest photographic flop of all time. The running had been fast and we had outdistanced our HQ by many miles. This is where the section officers should have been busy, but they too were burning up miles trying to do just that thing. It was partly our own fault too, Peter and I were anything but orthodox. Other cameramen obeyed the rules—'stick close to one's Divisional HQ or leave messages where you were going'. But we would shoot off at tangents, Peter might use the Jeep and with the 11th I could always borrow a scout car. We had also become friendly with our Division's Military Police, who were the best scroungers of overnight billets and we could always get them to return our exposed film to our own HQ by fast motorcycle. Sometimes we would remember to give them a signed chit for fresh film stock, but this was one occasion when our enthusiasm to be first across the Elbe let us down.

Through our complicated grapevine we got the message to transfer to the

Lining up the Buffaloes for the crossing of the River Elbe at Lauenberg. This was to be my last Commando operation.

Above *Gently as she goes! Those crazy Buffaloes are already starting to behave like their name-sakes!*
Below *A Commando surveys the River Elbe, and sees the reason why they had to cross in Buffaloes. This was my farewell to the Commandos; the same men with whom I had landed on D-Day. Complete with ack-ack, they stayed on.*

Commandos for the assault river-crossing. Mills-Roberts was going to make it in quick time, despite the thickly wooded slopes on the opposite side that could have hidden any number of the enemy. On the evening of April 28, Peter and I occupying a single Buffalo, slid into the river with a section carrying Bren carriers. There had been little build-up and it gave us the chance to nurse our diminishing film stock. We had hardly started when two Buffaloes collided and the Bren carriers punched themselves loose and gracefully slid to the bottom of the river. Precious film stock was exposed on this incident, and we prayed nothing

General view of a civilian POW Camp at Westertimke. These were mainly Merchant Navy prisoners, and the camp was called a Marlag.

more would happen until we got to the far bank, because, surprise—surprise, just as we slid into the river a Military Policeman had shouted that he had left fresh film stock with the driver of the Command Buffalo. We spotted the Command Buffalo by the pennant and we pleaded with our driver to stay close to it.

Two-thirds of the way over we felt home and dry, until we heard the sound of the aircraft. It didn't take long to spot them as three planes began their familiar steep dive, at the same time switching on their howling klaxons. They were Stukas, and probably only carried a couple of bombs apiece, but it was enough to create a slight chaos amongst the Buffaloes. Personally, I wondered where the hell had these Buffalo drivers come from. They must have been right off a training course—possibly replacements. First, that collision right at the start—and now they were trying to zig-zag a Buffalo! But what a scene it made and Peter and I began to make good use of it—but within a couple of minutes we were both out of film. At about the same time, the light bombs hit the river, so we just had to shrug and watch the show.

That was one time our anger at the Germans was overshadowed by what we felt about ourselves, and the drivers of the Buffaloes. Our own driver so lost his head, he also lost sight of the pennant on the Command vehicle, and when we hit the opposite bank it was a long squash to recover our fresh film. But the actual crossing was such a complete success that we caught the entire enemy contingent, about 300 all told, making themselves a meal in such leisurely fashion, it seemed a shame to break it up!

Nothing could stop the 2nd Army now and Norman Johnson and Jock Gordon got caught up in the sweep of the Guards Armoured Division. They entered Westertimke on April 28, overrunning a POW Camp—a Marlag version—for

Above *Myself and my partner, Peter Norris. Taken shortly before we made our run to Lubeck.* **Below right** *Whilst Peter and I are enjoying a comfortable run to Lubeck, the enemy are still very much in evidence in other sectors, and AFPU is kept busy with these 'last-ditch' fanatics.*

prisoners of the Merchant Navy. Six of those released had been sunk and captured on September 3 1939, just hours after the outbreak of war. On April 30 they entered Sandbostel Concentration Camp, where conditions were similar to that of Belsen. Then with a great surge the troops entered Hamburg on May 3, with some spectacular shots taken from the top of the main Elbe bridge.

George Laws and Bill Leeson were having the same experience on their own front. After Wesel, they crashed on through Dorsten, Haltern, Dulmen and Munster. It had been a pretty hectic drive for them and they were a bit gritty and tatty, when George decided to pop into Divisional HQ for some information. As he was pretty well known there, he wasn't at all aware of his appearance until he was faced with a new officer—obviously straight out from England—who elevated his nose a bit when George asked a straightforward question. 'I don't know about that, and to me you are a slightly scruffy Sergeant', was the officer's reply. George, the mildest of characters, merely told him, that where he had been there was no 'hot and cold' laid on and, as an afterthought, said 'Sir', swung a smart salute and departed.

But this was not the last he would see of him. George and Bill were right up front with a tank column which had been halted by a bit of opposition. A few minutes later, this officer comes up in his Jeep still looking like something right out of Sandhurst. George didn't speak to him as he watched the officer approach the nearest tank commander, and in a loud voice asked about the delay. The tank commander, obviously had experienced this one before, and told him in his strongest language, that 'There was one hell of a crossfire going on just around the corner, and what were you using for ears?' The warning was ignored and the officer got back into his Jeep and commanded his unfortunate driver to press on. He disappeared round the corner and above the other firing, they heard the steady thud of a Spandau. When the time came to move, they found the Jeep on its side with about 20 holes through it. The poor driver was very dead indeed, but there was not a sign of the officer. In fact, he was never seen again.

The 11th Armoured Division, Norris and myself, were now churning towards the Baltic city of Lubeck. This would bring the 2nd Army into a commanding position as, at this point, we would be eyeball-to-eyeball with the Russians. We were both looking forward to the capture of the city as, we reasoned, the end of the war must be very close indeed, and I detected a thoughtful twinkle in Peter's eyes as he considered what might lie ahead in a city untouched by bombing. It was late afternoon when the 11th Armoured halted about ten miles from Lubeck. A fast re-fuel was necessary, and as usual, given the slightest delay, those troops not engaged in the fuelling decided to have a brew-up.

We considered the light and time factor and guessed we had a good four or five hours filming time. If the column got off in about half an hour, and provided we

kept close to the head of it, we would have at least an hour and a half of useable light when we hit Lubeck. Driver Allingham wanted to brew some tea to wash down the dry corned beef doorsteps we had, but I'd seen a farmhouse less than 100 yards away and suggested they might have a few bottles of wine—we had found most farmhouses made their own and it was mostly quite palatable, and for once we weren't carrying a drop. Peter nodded and said he would walk up to the Command vehicle and get an ETA on Lubeck. Allingham got out the sandwiches and then checked his own petrol level.

It only took me a few minutes to reach the farmhouse, and then one disaster followed another. I rapped on the door with the butt of my gun, and when it opened an over-sized Alsatian dog flew at me. A fairly attractive woman stood there for about a minute with an amused smile on her face, until she said something in German and the dog backed off. I retrieved my .45 from the dust feeling very bloody-minded indeed and forced my way into the house. Then I let fly with all the German cuss-words I could think of, using the .45 to make my point.

To my surprise, she answered in perfect English and asked what the 'conqueror' was looking for? She used the word with a cynical smile on her face. This cooled me a little and I asked if she had any wine. 'That is all you want, Englishman?', and she moved her not unattractive body in a slightly provocative manner. 'Surely', she went on, 'the victor is entitled to take what he wants?' Given an extra couple of hours I wouldn't have hesitated, but I continued to ask only for a couple of bottles of wine. 'So', she continued, 'the Englishman does not find me attractive.' And then with some heat, 'But perhaps you do not care to sleep with a German?'

She was either a nympho, or her husband—I assumed—was on some Russian front. I replied that (a), no, she was not unattractive and (b), I was running out of time, and finally (c), the wine *now*, and hurry it. She pointed to a cellar and said it was all down there. I started to run down the first few steps when I suddenly

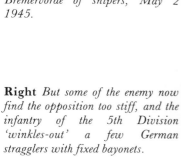

Left *With the surrender only a few short days away, our cameramen are now exposed to fighting of increased intensity. Men of the 5th Seaforth Highlanders clearing houses in Bremervorde of snipers, May 2 1945.*

Right *But some of the enemy now find the opposition too stiff, and the infantry of the 5th Division 'winkles-out' a few German stragglers with fixed bayonets.*

realised my bloody mistake, but not before I heard the cellar door shut and the catch go down. I pounded back up the steps and put my shoulder to the door—it didn't budge, and I could hear her laugh. A nympho, and probably a schizoid as well.

Then I remembered seeing an old detective film where they used a revolver to shoot the lock out of the door. Feeling just a bit silly, I shouted I was going to start shooting, then pointed the .45 at the lock and let fly with every chamber. I suppose one bullet would have done the trick, and the noise in the enclosed space just about took my head off, but when I pushed the door open, one very subdued woman was standing at the back of the room. But it was my turn to become subdued when Peter burst in—gaped a little at the scene—then proceeded to tear me off a large strip. The 11th Armoured Division had been on the move for more than 15 minutes now and it would take us ages to get to the head of the column.

By the time we got going in the Jeep, we were right at the end of the column amongst the soft vehicles, and although our driver did his best—weaving in and out and sometimes nearly hitting the ditch—we made Lubeck at dusk and the tail-end of the tanks. We had failed to film the fall of the city. But after we found billets for the night, I got myself an idea. I put it to Peter—who was mad as hell at me and impatient to get out and do a little 'shopping', but agreed—then departed with some haste. I spent some time looking for some of my best tank buddies and spoke to one tank commander whom I knew well, and put the idea to him. He wasn't over-enthusiastic, explaining that most of his lads were out on the town and wouldn't much care to run half-a-dozen tanks through the streets of Lubeck early the next day. But he finally agreed and we both went out and got grogged.

Next morning, we made three or four runs through different streets—not forgetting to get them to go past the Holstein Tower, then I raced both lots of film to the nearest RAF strip, where I convinced the pilot of a Dakota it was a life or death matter, to take the film on his first run to Northolt in England. I gave him Pinewood's number and assured him someone would pick it up. My luck held and it worked perfectly—in fact, nearly too perfectly when Stewart asked how I got the film back so soon. I warbled a bit about initiative, but I don't think he believed me. Anyway, Peter had apparently accomplished a reasonable amount of 'shopping' and was now speaking to me. But I don't think he ever forgave me.

Our link-up with the Russians was so inauspicious and so alien to whatever ideas I had conjured for this historical moment, that I began to doubt whether they were true Russians. We soon discovered this to be all too true. The motley, drunken mêlée proved to be Lithuanians, Poles, Czechs, Romanians and any other nationality, whose brains were away below their brawn. It was a reasonable cross-section of the Russian Army which used these men in tens of thousands; keeping them topped up with vodka and so providing very useful cannon fodder. We disentangled ourselves from this explosive mob and got back on our own lines. There we were joined by Lieutenant Peter Handford, who had been doing a great deal of sound-recording throughout the campaign, but joined Peter and myself for the final knockings. The signs were all too clear that any day now an armistice would be declared, so the three of us invented a little game.

By careful examination of maps, Intelligence reports and the general dispostion of our own troops, we planned to 'take' the surrender of one or two small towns lying on our advance line. For a short time this was quite a caper as we would drive into some obscure town, demand the presence of the Bürgermeister, and get him to inform the inhabitants that our two lonely Jeeps were the advance section of the British 2nd Army (logically correct, but without authority), and we required every inhabitant to surrender all firearms, cameras and binoculars. Naturally, we acquired quite a bit of booty in this manner—making Peter Norris' eyes light up like moonbeams. When we had loaded our two Jeeps, we bid them, 'Auf Wiedersehn', retired to the outskirts of the town and sorted out the junk, which we carefully deposited in a spot where it would soon be spotted by some curious inhabitant.

But we came a little unstuck in the town of Eutin, where we went through the same act—our driver always distributed cigarettes and chocolate at this time, no doubt making us appear very gracious conquerors indeed—and we had just spoken to the Bürgermeister, who trotted off in the accepted manner. This time we waited an anxious half-hour, and when he reappeared with an obviously high-ranking German officer, we began to feel rather uneasy. A faint rumble behind him indicated the presence of a number of tanks, and this officer just had to be the commander of an armoured group. The officer and the Bürgermeister approached Peter Handford, who was obviously the officer in charge. The German saluted Peter and there was a short exchange of perfect English which indicated that the German desired to surrender the remnants of his small Panzer Group!

Peter was petrified. This kind of booty would be hard to explain back at HQ, so Peter, with that disarming smile of his and as much composure as he could produce, explained that it would not be militarily correct for the German to surrender to an officer of his own rank, and he would retire and summon an

The German confusion becomes a collapsed balloon, and to the amazement of Peter and I in one Jeep, and Lieutenant Handford in another, we are offered *the surrender of the town of Eutin!*

officer of respective rank and command. With that, we retired as hastily and in as dignified a manner as we could, but that proved to be the end of our little game.

With the end so close, Stewart recalled all the outlying units back to base and a right good old natter we had. Arguments would arise between different campaigners, and many tall stories were forthcoming. As it was only a short time since the ignominious deaths of Mussolini and his mistress Claretta Petacci on April 28, those cameramen who had endured the Italian campaign, were able to enlighten us on the efforts of Sergeants French, Elvin, Gregory, Courtney, Barnes, Lambert and many others. Stories poured in regarding the harsh nature of the country, the almost unbearable winter and the grim tragedy of Monte Cassino.

The storming of Monte Cassino had many a frightening story to tell, not the least was that of Sergeant Bill McConville. In the rubble that lay about after the terrible bombardment of the Monastery, Bill was on the final approach to the very gates, and his shutter closed on a picture that was to become an award-winner. It shows the infantry with fixed bayonets forcing their final entry. Minutes later, he stepped on a mine, which blew his foot off. It was Blighty for Bill, but he later had the satisfaction of receiving a unique award, the Gold Medal of Buenos Aires Press Photographers' Association, for the best war action photograph of 1944. Formerly with the *Western Mail* of Cardiff, he now works as a cameraman for Visnews, a news-film distribution company, in London.

For the benefit of present-day TV viewers, Alan Whicker had proved to be a good officer and was well thought of, and a story was told of his strenuous efforts to lead a mule-train up the slopes of Cassino without batting an eyelid. We also learned that No 5 Unit was not alone in making a little extra money on the side. At Ferrara, where the campaign virtually petered out, a section of AFPU came

Above left *Within hours of the surrender, all cameramen are ordered back to base, where we meet friends we haven't seen since Pinewood. Sergeant McConville's stories of Monte Cassino are vivid in detail.* **Left** *McConville endured many days with the troops storming Cassino. Finally, he reached the gates, and took this award-winning photo as they pushed inside the monastery. But minutes later, as McConville followed the troops inside, disaster struck him down—he lost a foot on a German mine.* **Above** *During this general 'talk-in' amongst old friends, Peter Handford produced this photo of himself and the late Bill Gross and Vic Watkins. For sentimental reasons he had kept it—but Bill and Vic were everybody's friends.*

across an entire corral of horses purloined by the Germans. As the area around Ferrara was good farming country, AFPU very quickly turned in a quick profit by selling them at 500 lira a head.

One little mystery, too, was cleared up—whatever had happened to little Freddie Woods who had disappeared from our section at Pinewood? Apparently he and Bob Turner had gone to the Middle East—remained for some time, then Freddie was whisked off to the island of Leros, where he was taken prisoner during the first German Para drop on the island. He was later transferred to the Italian mainland, and became quite a personality in the POW camp as a photographer. Bob Turner remained in the Middle East after the surrender, but no one knew where he had taken root.

I expressed my disappointment at the lack of news regarding Bob Turner, for he had been a very 'positive' member of the small social group at Pinewood— which included Georgie Laws, Freddie Woods, Bill Leeson, Norman Clague and myself. We had held very closely together in those early days, with an impassioned feeling of solidarity—rousting about like children and often misquoting the line, 'One for all, and all for myself!' We had sworn never to be parted, but AFPU had thought otherwise—c'est la bloody guerre! No doubt that Hugh Stewart's little 'get together' had been a good idea, but it left me feeling depressed and, after a short 'natter' with Peter, we packed the Jeep and returned to where we felt was our natural habitat—up front where history was in the making.

Chapter 21

On May 4 1945 all hostilities ceased on Montgomery's front and the formal surrender terms were signed on Luneburg Heath. Several AFPU photographers and cameramen were present at the offical signing, but the Correspondents and many of the US Signal Corps tried to give them a hard time. Nevertheless, they got the necessary photographs although the American-backed PM journal noted, 'The indifferent coverage on the part of AFPU'. But our track record for the entire campaign had been very good indeed, and certainly the most productive of any campaign during World War 2.

The function of the 'battle cameramen' was now at an end in Europe, so several Sergeant-Cameramen were given commissions and, together with already established officers, sent out to No 9 AFPS in SEAC. Many of No 9, and those already working in the field, had gone direct from Pinewood. The departure of Derek Knight was a special loss to us all. Derek was now starting on his fourth campaign of the war!

For the forces left in Europe, we had one final liberation to make—that of Denmark. But the Danes took the firm stand that they only wanted a token force from the British, as they considered themselves quite capable of dealing with the small German force by themselves. The token force eventually sent to Denmark was about one-third Army Film Unit. We had come too far, seen too many battles, lost too many friends, and we had no intention of being left out of what promised to be a junket. And, more important, it placed Peter and myself in a very favourable position indeed: we still had all those Danish kroner we had picked up in Germany.

We still took plenty of film with us—we were certain there would be many scenes worth recording. So we began to run up Schleswig-Holstein and crossed the great bridge at Kiel. Eventually we reached the frontier at Flensburg and were greeted by the Danes. Their welcome was generous and sometimes spontaneous, but I use that last word with a slight reservation. The welcome was genuine enough, but I sensed a slight intolerance amongst the older members of the towns we passed through. Only amongst the younger ones—the teenagers and those in their early 20s—did the welcome appear truly wholesome. Everyone looked clean and well-fed—the countryside was abundant with crops—and nearly every country house appeared to have been recently painted white. Cleanliness and

Above *The surrender of all German forces to Field-Marshal Montgomery on Luneberg Heath, May 3 1945. Sergeant Dickie Leatherbarrow on the left, records the moment, with one of his colleagues making doubly sure! General Admiral Von Friedberg, representing Admiral Doenitz and Field Marshall Keitel, is in the foreground.* **Below** *With the surrender, comes that moment of wondering, 'where do we go from here?' and until official orders are given, our troops wait.*

Above *Having taken some German prisoners, there appears to be a slight confusion. And now that the war is over, these fellows are almost human!* **Below** *The Danes didn't want an armoured British force to liberate them. They agreed, however, to a 'token' force, which was two-thirds AFPU!*

whiteness were my main impressions, and the shops in those towns all the way up to Nyborg appeared to be plentifully stocked.

We made the steamer crossing to the mainland and decided to spend the night at a hotel in Nyborg. The dinner was delicious and the wine was splendid, but we were tired and soon went to bed. When the time came to depart the next morning—about half of the AFPU section had stayed at the same hotel—the concierge, or whatever you call them in Denmark—presented us with the bill! This in itself was unusual, but we had not time to waste—Copenhagen awaited us. Some of AFPU knew that Peter and I possessed some kroner (although, not how much), and in comic gesture passed the bill down the line for us to pay.

The nearer we got to Copenhagen, our reception grew in its warmth and we made the most of it. Never had I seen such pretty girls and their freshness rubbed off and gave us a kind of soothing consolation. They climbed all over the vehicles

Left *Lieutenant Peter Handford appears happy with the Danish welcome. Note the AFPU sign on the Jeep.* **Right** *The smile, the beauty, the warmth of our welcome to the capital.*

of the light armoured unit which formed the token force, and even forced their way on to the Army Film Unit Jeeps which soon became festooned with flowers. No protests were recorded. But the manner in which they were dressed impressed me most, and I thought of the rather drab clothing, carefully bought with precious coupons, which our wives and girlfriends were wearing in Britain. And this made me just a shade curious.

AFPU, in their fast moving Jeeps—our drivers had removed the governers a long time ago—were pretty far ahead of the rest of the bunch, and despite some Lieutenant Colonel screaming 'court martial' if we didn't keep convoy distance, we were soon within a few miles of Copenhagen. I was riding lead Jeep when a number of cars appeared from the city, the occupants giving us the big welcome sign. One car in particular caught my eye, a white painted job with huge lettering on the side in only two words: 'Movie Film'. I had the impression that most of the other vehicles were members of the Danish Press as well. But this white car kept lining up on our Jeep, and I could see two men and a blonde woman with hair streaming in the wind. When we pointed cameras at them, they did likewise and this little race was becoming interesting.

Their car was by far the faster and I got an unmistakable gesture to the effect that I join them. Well, it seemed to make sense and this I did. All spoke perfect English and the girl merely said, 'Kirsten Kobbeck, and the driver is my husband'. She mentioned the other chap's name but it wammed through one ear and out the other. You could say I was fascinated! Just for the hell of it I asked her if we could turn about and let me get a tracking shot of the British column. No sooner asked than done, and through my view-finder I got a good shot of the irate Lieutenant Colonel—his face several shades of purple. After that, we turned about and joined the head of the AFPU column now entering the city. It was quite a welcome and made good pictures as we drove to the main square.

Left *Copenhagen at its best. My blonde captor was called Kirsten, and she showed me how to blot out the horrors of the campaign for Europe.* **Right** *And next morning I woke up to see this photo on the front of the Danish newspapers, captioned 'The Spirit of Liberation'!*

The British contingent were soon lined up on three sides of the square and some official in uniform made a speech of welcome. Peter and I were busy, but I was very aware that my every step was followed by the occupants of 'Movie Film'. Eventually we all went back to the white car, and I was asked to pose, holding camera, and deep in conversation with the blonde Kirsten Kobbeck. It wasn't until next morning I found that picture plastered across the front page of their leading newspaper, and captioned, 'The Spirit of Liberation'! After that, invitations were flung about, and I accepted to come to dinner, although I indicated the clothes I stood in were all I had. But this was rejected with a reply that was in effect—it's you we have asked—so 'poof!' to the clothes. Peter and Jack were also receiving invitations and we parted with a grin. 'Have fun—we'll see you sometime', was their reply, and they slipped into the crowd. It was only then I found the real extent of Scandinavian hospitality when, after a delicious dinner, the husband announced that he would be busy with the newspaper all night, getting out the special editions—with my face plastered on the front! The Danish reputation of 'free love' became very real that evening!

Although we remained in Copenhagen for about ten days, there was plenty of work to do and we were glad we had brought enough film. The Danish King made formal appearances, and Field Marshal Bernard Law Montgomery received a very enthusiastic welcome. There were visits to the famous Tivoli Gardens, which the departing Germans attempted to destroy, and the now mandatory visit to the cages where the collaborators were being held by the Danish underground known locally as the 'Rhino'—don't ask me why. I also discovered why Denmark was so amply endowed by material things no longer seen in wartime England. The Germans had set Denmark up as being an example of German occupation—looting most of Europe to do so—with the Danish population quite happily accepting this condition of occupation.

A message from HQ put us back on the road to Germany. The order was to set up a temporary section HQ in Flensburg as Intelligence were getting whispers of certain high-ranking Nazis using the border town as an escape route. About six miles from Flensburg, we were stopped by a group of Danish troops who wished to point out that the last contingent of German troops about to leave Danish soil had decided to spend their final night in some woods close to the road. But, as the Danish officer pointed out, they were SS troops and still carried their weapons.

This was one of those peculiar decisions made by the Danes when they assured 2nd Army they could handle any German troops on Danish soil. They had come to terms with the enemy to retain their weapons, proceed to Flensburg and make their formal surrender to the British. Fortunately, it had all gone well up to now, but even this Danish officer was sceptical of SS troops, still fully armed, spending yet another night in Denmark. So, we were just two AFPU cameramen, a driver and a single Jeep. What, we enquired, did he expect us to do? Did he imagine that my Commando beret was going to scare the hell out of them? We finally agreed to take our cameras and have a look at them, providing he also came along with his small 'army' of three Danes. After all, it was still a news story.

The SS were sitting around having a meal, and I noted their weapons stayed close to them. At a rough estimation I put the number of the group about 50 strong. They looked dirty and tired, but still very tough looking, and when we began to use our cameras, there was a definite show of arrogance. A few stones were thrown in our direction and there was a general clicking of rifle bolts, fortunately on empty chambers. We weren't too happy with the look of it and

Left *But good things must end, and when I returned to Flensburg, the German-Danish frontier, I found some German SS troops being handled—not with kid gloves—by British and Danish troops.* **Right** *A British soldier removes pay-book and other documents from an SS soldier.*

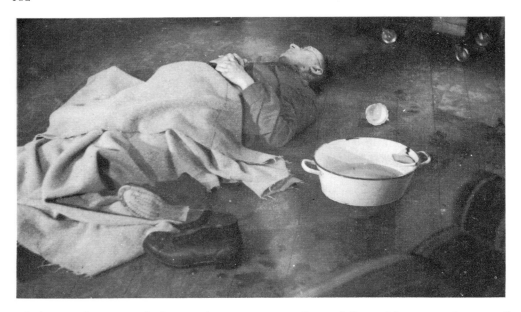

tried to make a nonchalant retirement to our Jeep, followed by many bursts of coarse, sneering laughter. At the Jeep, I lost my temper with the Danish officer, and in and outburst told him, 'You made the rules—it's still your country, and if there is any trouble, defend it'. I then indicated I would inform the frontier post at Flensburg to expect some very arrogant SS troops in the morning.

I did exactly that, and the British officer in charge thanked me with a look of anticipation on his face. 'Be here about 7 am,' he said, 'and I'll guarantee you some pictures.' Next morning we were there at the time he suggested and we did get some interesting pictures. The British officer had assembled a hard-looking bunch of troops and the SS group were just starting to pass the wire barriers. The book of rules had been thrown away for this diversion and the SS, in full marching order, were being run through the barrier with bullets from half-tracks kicking their heels. The German officers looked particularly uncomfortable as they ran, dressed in their heavy leather coats, and I saw a few well placed boots spur them on. The entire SS group got the complete treatment, their heavy packs being completely emptied as a thorough search was made and much personal property was confiscated. Their weapons were stacked to one side and, when the SS had been stripped down to their bare uniform, knife, fork and spoon and a razor, they were bundled into trucks and sent on their way to a POW camp.

By the time we established ourselves in Flensburg we found we were much too late to see anything of the fleeing Gestapo or SS. They had already taken the escape route through Flensburg shortly after the surrender at Luneburg Heath. Heinrich Himmler had remained in hiding for about two weeks then surrendered himself to the British—but he would never see the trials at Nuremberg, for he committed suicide on May 23, allowing Sergeants Carl Sutton and McCardle to get the first exclusive photos and film of this event. It was on the evening of May

Left *Sergeant Carl Sutton got one of the great scoops of the war's end. Whilst a POW, Heinrich Himmler committed suicide, and Carl dashed round the corner to get these exclusive pictures.*

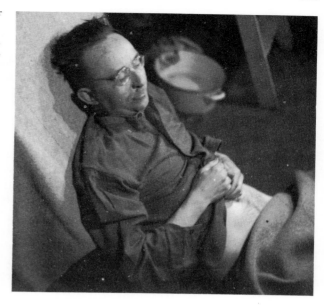

Right *Carl Sutton propped Himmler up on a box to get a better picture.*

23 1945, that three German prisoners were admitted to Kilkhagen Camp near the village of Barnstedt, south of Luneburg. Two of them were questioned—they were Grothmann and Macher—then placed in custody. The third, a small man wearing a cloth-patch over one eye, removed it and put on a pair of spectacles. The British officer present, Captain Thomas Selvester, immediately recognised that this was Heinrich Himmler. After informing 2nd Army HQ he was advised to transfer the prisoner to a house at 31A Uelzener Strasse, Luneburg.

Himmler had already been subjected to a body-search, but his mouth had been overlooked. Major Whittaker, who was in charge of this house, where high-ranking prisoners were interrogated, conferred with his colleague, Lieutenant Jack Ashworth, and they agreed to summon Army HQ's Medical Officer, Captain (Dr) C.J. Wells, who, when he arrived, decided to give Himmler a medical examination. He did this very thoroughly until he came to Himmler's mouth. He was asked to open it, and as he did so, gave his head a casual backward movement. The doctor examined his teeth, and saw a small object sticking to the inside of his left cheek. The doctor slipped a finger into the mouth, but Himmler, watching closely, suddenly clamped his mouth shut on the doctor's finger. There was a short struggle, and Himmler wrenched the doctor's hand from his mouth. For a moment he stood there, and then quite deliberately crushed the capsule between his teeth and took a deep inward breath. His face immediately became contorted with pain and his eyes glassed over. The doctor shouted, 'My God! It's in his mouth—he has done it on me'. There was a strong smell of cyanide, and Himmler was immediately upended with his mouth in a bowl of water. They tried to seize his tongue, and the doctor called for cardiac stimulants. They finally got his tongue fixed but, after a few more groans and twitches, Himmler died at 11.14 pm.

Just around the corner from Uelzemer Strasse, two Sergeants of AFPU were billeted. They had recently photographed the signing of the peace treaty on Luneburg Heath. Sergeants Carl Sutton and McCardle had made the long trek from Normandy to this now historic spot, which was about to erupt with an equally historic and exclusive story thrust into their hands. It was early on the morning of May 24 when a colleague burst in on Carl and breathlessly exclaimed to him, 'Holy Jeez, Carl, get round to 31A Uelzemer Strasse a bit schnell-like, some Sergeant-Major thinks they've got Himmler'. Carl didn't argue with a statement like that, he grabbed his Super Ikonta, a haversack of film, a couple of portable lamps and a flash gun and raced round the corner. The body, dressed only in an army shirt, lay peacefully beside the bowl of water used to wash out his mouth, and with a pair of steel-rimmed glasses on the now relaxed face, looked far from the monster of the SS. Rather incongruously, a pair of new British army boots—without laces—lay alongside him.

Carl immediately shot off a few pictures of the body, until he realised that the army shirt barely covered the lower part of the body. Also, the position was not a good one for ID purposes. Grabbing a couple of blankets and a box, he first covered the box with one blanket, then with McCardle's aid, they moved the body so that it now lay in a propped up position, covered the lower part of the body with another blanket, and proceeded to photograph from every angle. McCardle shot a roll of cine and, knowing that time was now the important factor, they began to retire, when two high-ranking Russian officers entered and suggested they too would like some pictures. 'Oh, hell', thought Carl, 'it's only film', and quickly shot off another roll and handed it to the beaming Russians whose only contribution were several delighted, 'da-das' and 'Dankes' and a sibilant, 'Zankew!' They now left in a hurry—speed was the basic for an exclusive—for the airport, and as they rushed towards their car, they almost knocked down the very large figure of Ken Gordon of Pathé News. Ken, in his well-known fashion, which was really just a front for a very clever and astute cameraman, snarled at him, 'You've beaten me to it, you basket—I'll not forget this'. With a cheerful wave, Sutton and McCardle got their car and raced for the airport. Yes, they had beaten Ken Gordon, and all other opposition, to the exclusive scoop of a lifetime. The COI in London went crazy, and in a few hours the exclusive pictures were on their way to every press media in the world.

*   *   *

One wet night I had gone to bed early and was roused by Peter to say the British had captured William Joyce, 'Lord Haw-Haw', but by the time we got to British Army HQ he had been spirited away, and no one was saying where. Apparently Joyce had been disguised and was just attempting to cross a bridge in Flensburg, when he was challenged by a British soldier. Joyce made no attempt to escape and the familiar, 'Jairmany calling' accent soon revealed his identity.

Admiral von Freideburg was also captured at Flensburg, but had been in his cell for less than an hour, when he too managed to commit suicide. Like Himmler he had concealed a cyanide pill in his anus. But this time, the press and the Army Film Unit were allowed to photograph his dead body. We were filtered in one at a time, due to the size of the cell, and after everyone had taken their pictures, were politely ushered out again. About an hour later all hell broke loose. Freideburg's diamond-studded Iron Cross had disappeared. We were all questioned, but by this time a number of the press were on their way back to Hamburg. So who stole the Freideburg Iron Cross? The guards claimed he was wearing the Cross when he was placed in his cell less than an hour before his death, but after a thorough search of the cell, no trace of it was ever discovered. After its mysterious disappearance, his widow tried to sue the British Government but to no avail.

The only good pictures Peter and myself got of Doenitz, Speer and Jodl was when they passed through Flensburg en route for Mondorf in Luxemburg. They were travelling by 'plane and we raced out to the airport where the trio were being allowed to stretch their legs on the landing strip whilst the 'plane was being refuelled. It was impressive to see Admiral Doenitz who, for such a short time after the death of Hitler, held what power Germany had left during those final days. Jodl, who walked step for step with him, had persuaded Doenitz to surrender and here they were, the last living symbols, outside of Goering, who had helped to bring Germany to its final shambles.

Peter and myself soon got all the orthodox pictures we wanted, and the US air crew were making signs that they wanted to go. The aircraft was a Dakota and probably carried only a single Elsan toilet, so Doentiz, Jodl and Speer decided to relieve themselves on the ground before boarding. As they did this quite openly, the US Signal Corps began dashing around taking pictures like crazy—but this was too much for myself or Peter, and we returned to our Jeep to watch the take-off. After that, we decided to return to Hamburg.

Chapter 23

Hamburg, July 1945, was a city wearing many different faces. Around the famous Alster, the fine, handsome houses still stood their ground, their untouched grandeur reflected in the waters of Hamburg's most famous lake. Many had been taken over by the British Allied Military Government, and soon the Control Commission—a piece of Whitehall right in the middle of Germany's second city. The other face was harshly different, entire districts were erased during the round-the-clock Allied bombing, but amongst the piles of rubble thousands of Germans lived in their god-forsaken ghettos. To pass that way, one recoiled from the stench of many dead still to be discovered. Black markets, from the lowest order, where haggard scarecrows offered their bodies for food, and of the number of these woman who died each day, many were still in their 20s. More astute were the men who had somehow forseen their future and had quietly looted stores and shops (probably during bombing raids) and were now trading with the British and their fellow-Germans alike.

We found the Army Film Unit Section in a large house in Heimhuderstrasse, a street relatively untouched considering it was close to the main railway station. There were many faces amongst the occupants we had only briefly seen during the campaign—Sergeant Bob Baker (who would, much later, produce the *Saint* and *Persuaders* series for television), Johnny Silverside, Blakeley and Chitham, and many others. Peter Norris left me at this point to go on an officer's course, when he would be shipped out to SEAC. As it happened, it never materialised, and I never saw Peter again until we were back in England.

With our front line job literally finished, there was no further need for pairing, so we made ourselves comfortable and took on the odd film job as it occurred. We now had detachments in Bremen, Berlin and HQ Vlotho, whilst a small number were sent to Nuremberg. Now we had to produce our own entertainment, which was not at all difficult to do as we were well stocked with food, wine and spirits, and the best black market butter of all, chocolate and cigarettes. Some astute photographer managed to create a story out of the Royal Navy—an all Petty-Officer wedding—and just by chance, the proud husband controlled most of the Naval stores, so our source of whisky never ran dry. Across the street, another Sergeant discovered that the original 'Lili Marlene' singer Lala Andersen was living, and with her assistance we gave a number of very successful and extremely alcoholic parties.

Left *En route for Hamburg, we find the celebrated cartoonist of the* Daily Express—Giles—*at work amongst the ruins.* **Right** *Lala Anderson, who created the original 'Lili Marlene', often invited us to her flat for a social evening. We provided the food and drink, as there was severe rationing. Bob Baker is seen with unknown friend.*

It was generally expected that we would now remain in Hamburg until we were all demobbed, so it was decided to look for a more luxurious billet. Johnny Silverside, who had an eye for the good things in life, was elected to be our surveyor. He soon found an ideal house in the exclusive Zeirichstrasse area, and approached the owners, who told him the house had once belonged to Herr Goebells, and was therefore much too good for the common British soldier. The owner had no doubt hoped to be approached by the Control Commission who, when they requisitioned German property, allowed the owner certain compensations and an authorised document to the effect that any damage incurred during their stay, would entitle the owner to a part cost of the damage.

But Johnny was not to be put off by such a small detail. He went straight to the Town Mayor of Hamburg, and by means known to himself, persuaded the Town Mayor to issue an order of occupation of behalf of AFPU. The lady of the house, who was the sister of Goebbels, was then told to get out at once. The woman protested that she would need to remove her valuables, but whatever terms of reference Johnny used to requisition the house, the good lady left with only a plate, a cup, and a knife, fork and spoon. AFPU moved in and the number of our parties increased. The neighbours dubbed the house 'Das Tollhouse'—the mad-house, and we enhanced its reputation to the extent that, after our departure, the

Our second home in Hamburg, reputed to be the property of a relative of Goebbels. I have been told there is now a plaque on the wall, to commemorate the AFPU ('Tollhouse'). For those interested, it is in Zeirichstrasse.

original owners erected a plaque to tell everyone that the Army Film Unit once lived there.

But it was not all sweet harmony. Two of our hired help had become a couple of 'Godfathers' to the black market community of Hamburg, and their share was carefully salted away in such a manner as to appear legitimate. One night they nearly came unstuck when they were returning from a successful deal, the car loaded with valuable goods and large amounts of cash. But this night they had been carefully watched by the German Police and some Military Police. At some point they knew they were being followed and they put their foot down on the accelerator of the powerful Mercedes they had acquired. As they shot on to the large bridge over the Elbe, they could see several sets of headlights on full beam approach from the other side. They were trapped. But they didn't intend to be captured. A few words passed between them and they sharply braked the Mercedes. A few steps took them to the edge of the bridge. In the dark they could see the river from the many lights fringing the shore, and it was a frightening distance away. There didn't appear to be any river traffic on their side, but they couldn't tell if anything was about to shoot out from the other approach. But the headlights were closing fast and with a small effort of will, they jumped. The drop seemed to go on forever and when they hit the cold water both the concussion and the temperature caused a temporary black-out, but they eventually found the firm ground of the river bank. When they reached the house in Zeirichstrasse they were just about all in and we let them swallow a few generous belts of whisky.

Their clothing was consigned to a dump outside and covered over, fresh clothing we had in stores—then we got them into the cellar. We had a small party going at the time and when the bucolic German police arrived—a couple who obviously eked out their meagre pay with a little side-graft—they presented no problem. A 100 pack of cigarettes, a few glasses of whisky and that was the last we saw of the local constabulary.

At most of our parties, the presence of Lala Andersen always attracted some good singers and musicians, plus a small selection of the Hamburg State Opera. One of our Sergeants had made it good with Lala and they plainly enjoyed each others' company. When we got word that we would soon have to close the house down and return to Vlotho, AFPU HQ prior to our demob, we were both saddened and cheered by the news. It was the end of a road, and it had been a long, heart-breaking, often tragic road, but somehow, the thoughts of returning to a rationed, and perhaps dull civilian life did not have the same attraction as it did, say, six months ago.

So, we decided to have one enormous blast of a party, one to remember for a long, long time. With the help of the decor department of the Hamburg State Opera, we completely refurbished the interior of that house. All the windows were blacked out, and when someone asked how long this party was expected to last, they were told, 'until the last couple drops'. The main room was cleared of all furniture except chairs, the dining-room contained nothing but tables where the cold buffet would lie, another room was fitted with low-key lighting and was devoid of all furniture except for thick rugs and scores of cushions. Three small groups were hired to play in shifts and the State Opera chucked in a baritone and a very attractive soprano. Half a dozen willing German waiters were taken on just to keep the empties filled, and the dirty crockery cleaned. They knew they could make a handsome killing by shifting much food and wine out to unseen, willing hands on the outside. We knew this too, so we had every exit door locked and barred, leaving only the front door for access.

The party lasted four days and nights and, considering the number of guests—about 60—there was very slight damage. I guess the only damage done was in the darkened room where couples would flop for a few hours, then rejoin the party. In those four days and nights, we consumed 200 bottles of champagne, about 100 bottles of whisky, gin, brandy and Steinhager—I do not know how many barrels of beer—and a great deal of it was provided with the compliments of the Royal Navy, whose Chief Petty Officer was a special guest. But even parties of that magnitude had to come to an end, and the final solo performance came from Lala Andersen who, under a single spot-light, sang chorus after chorus of *Lili Marlene*. Her Sergeant was a little heartbroken, but two days later we left for Vlotho.

Hugh Stewart made us welcome, with a few side comments of the happenings at Hamburg. But he paid us the supreme compliment that it was his consideration the No 5 AFPS had made the best contribution—and sacrifices—to visual propaganda of the war. But it was a hollow compliment. Through no fault of Hugh Stewart, the campaign film, *The True Glory,* directed by Carol Reed, gave a

Above *Lieutenant Peter Handford, who, apart from being a section officer, was also the sound recordist, and with colleague John Aldred, recorded the sound for the film* The True Glory. **Below** *The main line railway station in Hamburg, with British tanks in the forecourt.*

convincing demonstration of how the Americans conquered Europe. Nor was it an error on the part of Carol Reed, but his co-director, Garson Kanin, and a few plugs by Frank Capra, gave Kanin the opportunity to announce that, under his co-direction the General Eisenhower classic film report on the victory in Europe had won the Academy Award for the documentary of the year. Unintentional or not, it did not present a true picture of the involvement of the British, and we of AFPU wondered why so many of our cameramen had to die without recognition. It was hurtful to the living, and must have been equally painful to our staff at Pinewood who had dealt with hundreds of thousands of feet of film from cameramen who lived on the front line.

Apart from the cutting-room staff, one wonders if *The True Glory* would have been an effective film without, for example, its sound effects? Only once during the writing of this book have I mentioned the word 'sound', when I made a reference to Lieutenant Peter Handford, although some sound had to be produced artificially—and this is what I mean when I use the expression 'sound effects', as opposed to the real thing. The film, *The True Glory* was effective largely due to the *actual* sounds of warfare, recorded by a small group of dedicated men who lumbered a weighty Western Electric portable Q Channel which recorded directly on to Photo Film Nitrate. This small unit was commanded by Captain D.P. Field, who was responsible for organising Lieutenant Peter Handford, Sergeant George Croll and Sergeant John Aldred, as a field unit.

The unit then became the responsibility of Major Hugh Stewart, who then directed them to areas where they could operate with, he hoped, comparative safety and maximum mobility. A Ford Utility truck was put at their disposal, and driven with unique skill by Corporal Woodhouse of the RASC who, with that sang-froid which appeared to be prevalent amongst all our RASC drivers, made certain that his 'crazy' unit was on the receiving end of every imaginable 'battle noise' they required. Therefore, with a lot of guts and damned hard work, they produced the *real* sound of battle, and consequently added to the emphatic realism of the film, *The True Glory*. Their dramatic sound-tracks so impressed the BBC that, after the war, they purchased the copyright to every foot of 'track' held at Pinewood. As the BBC has a high regard for their own quality of sound-recording, this was indeed a salute to the Army Film and Photo Unit.

*　　　*　　　*

With the slow dying of the Army Film and Photo Unit, the 'last man in' claims will always be in doubt. The aforementioned John Aldred, who had done sterling work in the sound department, both in the field of the European Campaign and in the dubbing studios, claims to have been the very last man at Pinewood. But in the field, my dollar goes on Bob Turner, now of Visnews.

When I left AFPU and returned to my home, it was only a matter of a few weeks before I came back to London to join the newly-formed *This Modern Age*, the first documentary company under the Rank Organisation. Again, after only a few weeks, I became a member of a crew en route to the Sudan to make a documentary film. To do this, we had to pass through Cairo and, inevitably, the Egyptians found some fault with our shipment documents. This was to give us an enforced stay in Cairo, which I didn't mind a bit. My first thought was to try and find where AFPU had been based and, after much palaver—and if you have ever been to Cairo, you will know how much 'much palaver' can be!—I was directed to a large house on the outskirts of the city.

Once there, I knew my directions had been correct. Weatherbeaten boards with AFPU lettering pointed the way. I circled the house, which appeared empty, but eventually came across a lone figure seated in a deck-chair, drink in hand and facing the now setting sun. It was Bob Turner, and after much swapping of stories, we both sat silently, sipping our Stella beer. Strange, I thought, after all these years, to be here with Bob, as we had in the beginning, in that dreary old building in Marylebone Road, where we had endured the induction analysis to prove our qualifications for AFPU with me peeking at Bob's written answers over his thoughtfully exposed shoulder!

He must have read me, for he turned and smiled, reached another bottle and handed it to me. 'Water under the bridge now huh?'—and thoughtfully, looking at the desert—'or sand, miles and miles of the bloody stuff.' He gulped his beer and looked at the sky, its radiance declining with the setting sun. 'Poor old Norman . . .' quietly—almost to himself, ' . . . and all the other poor buggers—Harry—Robbo—Vic.' His body tightened in the chair, and he raised his voice a pitch, ' . . . and the others', he turned to me ' . . . the rest—how many Ian—twenty—thirty—?'

I nodded. 'Easy Bob, somebody had to catch it—it's over now.' But Bob was not to be conciliated. 'Why them—why—there were so many other bastards—why—and did the War Office give a monkey's?—no way, just as long as they got their bloody pictures.'

I looked at him. Bob was right out of character. This wasn't the same big, bouncy lad from the Pinewood days. But like he said, a lot of water under the bridge. That was the big one we had seen, and we all had our private hells to nurse. He caught my look, and I could see the moment blowing away. A memory returned and I thought I'd give it a whirl. 'Weight on, Bob—get your head in the sink.' He laughed. 'Uh-huh—those were the days—good old Pinewood.' The rancour had died—the old Bob Turner was home and dry. We talked a bit more. He told me he would be back in 'civvy street' very soon—back to Fleet Street, and be sure to look him up. I said yes, sure would, but it was time for me to get back to my hotel.

I stood up and slapped his back then, as the shadows lengthened across the desert, I left him, twiddling an empty glass, looking at the darkening sand-dunes, and maybe remembering the dark Crusaders and Valentines, and the thunder of massed artillery. This was where it had all begun—this was where those 'no ordinary Sergeants' were born—lived—and died.